S0-BSF-025

THE GRAND CANYON
AND THE AMERICAN
SOUTHWEST

Trekking in the Grand Canyon, Zion
and Bryce Canyon National Parks

CONSTANCE ROOS

Dr Constance Roos was killed after being struck by lightning in Corsica on 17 July 1999 shortly after the completion of this book. Constance Roos was 50. She was born in San Francisco, where she made her home and practised psychiatry. She received degrees from Stanford University and her MD from Case Western University. She was Assistant Clinical Professor of Psychiatry at the University of California, San Francisco. She had practised privately and was affiliated with Mount Zion, Pacific Presbyterian and Peninsula hospitals, was staff psychiatrist at the Community Crisis Center, San Francisco, and assisted with emergency room work at San Francisco General and John George (Highland) hospitals.

Constance was an avid traveller, hiker and climber. She had explored and climbed in Africa, New Zealand, Bolivia, Mexico, Europe and Alaska as well as the western states. Her climbs included Mount Hood in Oregon, the Grand Teton in Wyoming, Mount Rainier in Washington, Huayna Potosi in Bolivia, Kilimanjaro in Africa, Popocatepetl in Mexico and many others.

Constance was in Corsica researching the Cicerone guide to the challenging GR20 route, perhaps the hardest of Europe's mountain treks. She has also written Cicerone guides to Norway and New Zealand.

Although I knew her for only a short period, I mourn the loss of a friendship that was young. I hope you enjoy using Constance's Grand Canyon guide as much as we enjoyed publishing it, and that we have done her last book justice.

Jonathan Williams
Cicerone Press

Other Cicerone guides by Constance Roos
Classic Tramps in New Zealand
Walking in Norway

THE GRAND CANYON
AND THE AMERICAN
SOUTHWEST

Trekking in the Grand Canyon, Zion
and Bryce Canyon National Parks

by
Constance Roos

Updated by Siân Pritchard-Jones and Bob Gibbons

2 POLICE SQUARE, MILNTHORPE, CUMBRIA LA7 7PY
UNITED KINGDOM
www.cicerone.co.uk

Second edition 2008
ISBN-13: 978-1-85284-453-0

© Cicerone Press 2000, 2008

Photographs © Siân Pritchard-Jones and Bob Gibbons

First edition 2000
ISBN-10: 1-85284-300-4

A catalogue record for this book is available from the British Library.

Route profiles, charts, area maps and legend by the author/updaters

Trail maps by Carto Graphics, San Francisco

Acknowledgements for the first edition

This guide would not be complete without mention of all the friends who walked with me: Panos Antiochos, Dan Brooke and Cheryl Teuton, Jesse Brotz, Ute Dietrich, Bev Hedin, Terry Howard, Lynn Pelletier, Judy and Pete Sager, Tracy Shea, Betty Stanfield, and Mic Williams. Many thanks to the Grand Canyon Field Institute who shared with me their knowledge and expertise on several routes and trails described in this book.

A number of friends at home helped shape the book's final outcome. Trail maps were designed and produced by Kris Bergstrom and Shiela Semans of Carto Graphics, San Francisco. The United States Geological Survey provided the shaded relief used in the trail maps. Robert Shankland offered expert editorial guidance.

I am grateful to many thoughtful and friendly people, most of whose names I never knew, who went out of their way to make my visit in their home a pleasnt one. Memories of my travels remain special because of their kindness.

Acknowledgements for the second edition

Thanks to Christine and Phil Mitchell, Bob's sister and brother-in-law, in Calgary, Canada, for their hospitality before and after the trip, as well as their inspiring company on some of the walks. Thanks to all the patient rangers and backcountry staff of the national parks for their information. And last but not least, thanks to Jonathan at Cicerone for asking us to update this book at just the right time!

Front cover: View over the Grand Canyon

CONTENTS

GRAND CANYON NATIONAL PARK

BRYCE CANYON NATIONAL PARK

Legend

----------	Trail
- - - - - - - -	Route
....	Other trail
———⑨———	Highway
———————	Main road
———————	Secondary road
—[FR232]—	Unpaved road
▬ ▬ ▬ ▬	National Park boundary
▬ ▬ ▬ ▬	State boundary
🏠	Ranger Station
■	Building / Resthouse
▲	Campground
⯭	Picnic Area
Ⓟ	Parking / Trailhead
⌁	Spring / Perennial water

ABOUT THE UPDATERS

Siân Pritchard-Jones and Bob Gibbons met in 1983, on a trek from Kashmir to Ladakh. By then Bob had already driven an ancient Land-Rover from England to Kathmandu in 1974, led overland trips across Asia, Africa and South America, as well as driving decrepit old tourist buses around India. He also lived in Kathmandu as a trekking company manager. Siân worked in computer programming and systems analysis, but her heart was in the Himalayas, after a trip there on her way back from working in New Zealand.

Since meeting Bob and Siân have been leading and organising treks in the Alps, Nepal and the Sahara; they have hitched across Tibet, driven a bus with 'over fifties' clients to Nepal, and driven a less ancient Land-Rover across Africa to Gabon and Cape Town. Some of this was real work, but luckily that 'proper job' has not materialised. The latter journey provided the basis for the recently published fourth edition of the Bradt guide *Africa Overland*. In complete contrast they followed this by updating the Bradt guides to the Maldives and the Cape Verde islands.

However, they regularly return to their first love, Nepal, where they work with Pilgrims Publishing in Kathmandu. For Pilgrims they have produced a cultural guide to the valley – Kathmandu: Valley of the Green-Eyed Yellow Idol – as well as a new book on the monasteries of Ladakh, entitled Ladakh: Land of Magical Monasteries, and a detailed cultural and historical book about western Tibet and Guge, entitled Kailash & Guge: Land of the Tantric Mountain.

Their first guide for Cicerone was a trekking guide to the sacred mountain of Kailash in Tibet. Travelling to the USA to explore the canyonlands of Utah and Arizona was a new and completely unexpected opportunity.

Other Cicerone guides by Siân Pritchard-Jones and Bob Gibbons
The Mount Kailash Trek – a Trekker's and Visitor's Guide

PREFACE TO THE SECOND EDITION

The untimely death of Constance by lightning was a bitter blow, and following in her footsteps is not an easy task to accept. With the passage of some years, though, the updating of this guide has become necessary. It serves to keep her memory alive and to rekindle the fires of her tremendous enthusiasm for the great canyons of America's southwest.

The waters of the Colorado River flow like the passing of geological aeons, constantly reshaping the natural world. The few years since this book was first published are but a minuscule drop in the oceans of natural history, barely time for more than the odd trail to be affected. However, nature's work is relentless and a few changes have occurred. These trail changes have been incorporated into the text, but little else needed to be modified, such was the thoroughness with which Constance applied herself to the first edition.

The primary differences since 1999, when the first edition was published, are due to ever-improving technology. Communications through the internet make booking rooms or campsites, obtaining advance backcountry permits, and accessing information much quicker and simpler. Endeavouring to accommodate ever-increasing numbers of visitors takes some initiative, particularly with regard to ecological considerations. More than ever there is an imperative need to conserve, nurture and preserve the wonders of the world for the future.

Exploring the canyon regions of America is likely to be quite a revelation for overseas visitors. It's not always just the obviously famous places that remain imprinted in the memory. There are so many hidden gems to be discovered at every turn. The trails of the parks unfold like a kaleidoscope to infinity – constantly alluring, never disappointing and always magical.

The national parks of the Grand Canyon, Zion and Bryce canyons are justly famed for their inspirational vistas and exciting panoramas. But to explore nature's grandest artistry is a privilege one must temper with responsibility. Sublime beauty is partnered by dangers for the uninformed. And, yes, there is the unexpected and inexplicable controlled by chance.

The irony is that nature gives and nature takes. This updated book is rightly dedicated to the memory of Constance Roos.

Siân Pritchard-Jones and Bob Gibbons, 2007

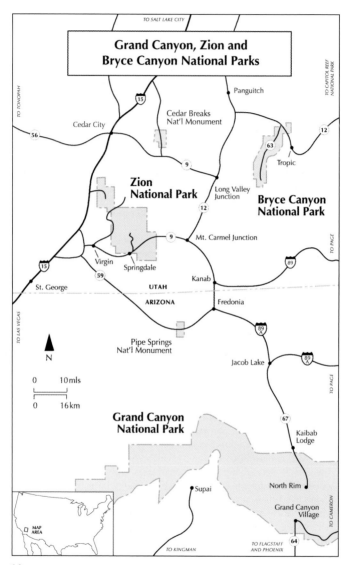

Grand Canyon, Zion and Bryce Canyon National Parks

TO SALT LAKE CITY

TO TONOPAH

TO CAPITOL REEF NATIONAL PARK

Panguitch

15

Cedar Breaks Nat'l Monument

Cedar City

56

9

12

63

Tropic

Zion National Park

Long Valley Junction

12

Bryce Canyon National Park

9 Mt. Carmel Junction

89

TO PAGE

15

Virgin

Springdale

59

Kanab

UTAH

St. George

ARIZONA

Fredonia

TO LAS VEGAS

TO PAGE

89

89
A

N

Pipe Springs Nat'l Monument

Jacob Lake

89
A

0   10 mls

0   16 km

67

Grand Canyon National Park

Kaibab Lodge

TO CAMERON

Supai

North Rim

Grand Canyon Village

MAP AREA

64

TO KINGMAN

TO FLAGSTAFF AND PHOENIX

INTRODUCTION

Introduction to the Second Edition

A vast swathe cut deep into the earth's crust, exposing a multitude of colours one can only begin to dream of... Layer upon layer of intense reds, golds and browns, rock and valley shapes defying the imagination with their indescribable twists and turns... Temperatures ranging from below freezing at the rim to the raging 30s or even 40s (centigrade!) at the bottom of the canyon... Thrilling paths plunging over the edge of the cliffs and steeply down into the unfathomable depths of the gorge cut by the Colorado River over millennia...

Such is the Grand Canyon. It is a very special place that the native people regard as the birthplace of the spirits, the *sipapu* of their ancestors.

Having been fortunate enough to have visited many exceptional parts of the world already, we wondered just how grand the Grand Canyon might be. Could it live up to its amazing reputation?

We were not disappointed. At first sight, the Grand Canyon is truly astonishing. Even after visiting many of the other beautiful canyons in the area, the Grand Canyon is not just majestic, it is monumentally magical. Its sheer supreme scale is almost incomprehensible – a vastness that one cannot really begin to understand.

Perhaps this is nature's grandeur at its grandest?

Siân Pritchard-Jones and Bob Gibbons, 2007

Introduction to the First Edition

*The price of wilderness still
includes eternal vigilance.*
Colin Fletcher

The southwestern corner of the United States, dotted with national parks and monuments, wilderness areas, state parks and recreational areas, boasts a seemingly endless variety of deep canyons, high and low desert, snow-capped mountains and raging rivers. Within this area Grand Canyon National Park, Zion National Park and Bryce Canyon National Park encompass some of the most extraordinary scenery in the United States. Though Grand Canyon National Park is well known worldwide, Zion and Bryce Canyon national parks are less so. Yet the parks offer such splendid scenery that each merits a visit of its own.

Come and view this magnificent corner of the United States. Join me in touring these parks on foot. Walk the high country of Zion and veer down into the valley from atop its towering red walls. Weave amidst the hoodoos of Bryce and descend into the hidden depths of the Grand Canyon. Walkers can easily steer clear of crowds and enjoy the backcountry in relative isolation.

I have tried to present material and information as accurately as possible. But how quickly things change! Paths can be re-routed; new buildings are built and others are removed; bridges are washed away. Changes in the landscape occur due to storms, flooding, rockfall and other natural causes. Be prepared for sudden changes in weather, wide fluctuations in temperature and unexpected obstacles blocking routes and trails.

Many of my trips to foreign countries have been inspired by guidebooks that I first studied from home. I hope this book will aid in planning a trip into this special area of the United States and, once you have arrived, help to make your visit a pleasant and meaningful one. I have presented travel and park information and trail descriptions in a style that I hope will be useful and practical, yet not overload you with too much detail.

Plan to arrive a day or two before your walk to get up-to-date information from the National Park Service. Without thoughtful planning many of these trips are dangerous or life threatening. Bring along your common sense and good judgement and you will enjoy the trip of a lifetime.

May you grow to love this section of the American southwest as I have. Have a great trip!

Constance Roos, 2000

CHAPTER 1

USING THIS BOOK

Every time I go anywhere out in the desert or mountains
I wonder why I should return.
Someday, I won't.

Edward Abbey

SUMMARY OF CONTENTS

Introductory chapters 1–3 discuss general guidelines on how to use this book. Chapter 2 outlines travel information and how to get around in the United States. Chapter 3 guides you on equipment necessary for overnight or day-walks.

The subsequent chapters provide trail descriptions and recommended long-distance walks for walkers and backpackers for all three parks. **Grand Canyon National Park**, covered in chapters 4–10, begins with an overview of the park, followed by information on walking in the Grand Canyon and permit procedures. Trails and routes from the South Rim, North Rim, Trans-canyon Rim and long-distance walks are then described in successive chapters. Associated fact panels, trail maps, charts and route profiles are provided. **Zion National Park**, in chapters 11–18, covers trails in Kolob Canyons, West Rim, East Rim and Zion Canyon. **Bryce Canyon National Park**, included in chapters 19–22, covers Bryce Canyon and rim walks as well.

All the walking trails in Zion National Park and Bryce Canyon National Park are described. In Grand Canyon National Park, all the maintained and non-maintained rim-to-river trails and rim trails are covered as well. All the walks described follow known trails or established routes along canyon bottoms or beside rivers.

The guide provides information on how to link together several trails in order to convert day-walks into long-distance walks. Choices of long-distance walks in all three parks are offered. Route profiles of the elevation gains and losses of the walks, and summary tables with walking-time estimates, are included. Appendices present succinct information on walking times of long-distance walks, local facilities, helpful addresses and phone numbers, and the author's favourite walks in each park.

FACT PANELS

Fact panels, preceding each trail description, list the distance of the trail in miles and kilometres, the starting and ending elevations, average time to walk the trail, the maps needed, the best time of year to walk the trail and other related information.

DISTANCES AND TIME ESTIMATES

The National Park Service (NPS) publishes trail distances. When these distances are unavailable, trail lengths have been estimated from the United States Geological Survey (USGS) 7.5 minute topographical maps. Distances are noted as one-way or a loop. A car shuttle may be necessary, but other transport options such as van, shuttle or taxi services sometimes exist.

Time estimates, which include rest stops, vary widely, especially in Grand Canyon National Park. Times depend on the direction travelled (ascent or descent), terrain, season, temperature, condition of the trail and strength of the party. Time estimates provided for the long-distance walks (chapters 10, 18 and 22) allow additional time for carrying a full backpack. Fact panels indicate whether the time estimates provided are for backpackers or day-walkers.

TRAIL RATING

An overview of each trail is presented in the fact panel, noting its difficulty, steepness and obstacles, such as creek crossings, snow, rocks or talus. Some trails or routes may be designated as one grading (e.g. 'easy'), even though

a few sections could lift the rating into a more demanding category (e.g. 'moderate'). 'Easy' therefore refers to the route as a whole and not to an atypical section. In addition, these ratings refer to the challenges of the route itself, exclusive of its length.

Sections are graded along the following guidelines.

Easy. You will encounter no major difficulties or obstacles on the trail. Level or gently undulating terrain predominates; elevation gains and losses are minimal. Beginners and visitors with children will find these walks suitable. This designation applies to rim walks in Grand Canyon National Park and Bryce Canyon National Park, and some of the Zion Canyon walks in Zion National Park.

Moderate. Gains and losses in elevation exceed those in the 'easy' category. The path may be rocky with some steep ascents or descents, although no scrambling is involved. In general, elevation gains and losses are more gradual and not as steep as in the 'strenuous' category. In spite of large changes in elevation, Corridor Trails in Grand Canyon National Park rate as moderate.

Strenuous. These trails, for experienced walkers in good physical condition, may present some rough and rocky terrain with exposure, scrambling, rocks, talus or scree. Parties with novices or small children should not attempt these trails. In Grand Canyon National Park, elevation gains and losses may be as great as 5000ft

(1524m). River walks in Zion National Park (e.g. the Narrows) involve exposure to very cold water, swift currents and flash-flood dangers.

Extremely Strenuous. Only experienced canyoneers and backpackers in excellent physical condition should attempt these unmaintained trails or routes. Talus-hopping and scrambling is necessary; exposure may be extreme. Water sources are scarce to non-existent. You need to be sure-footed, unafraid of heights, and able to use a map and compass.

Other unmarked options are sometimes described in national park literature as 'routes' rather than trails. These often follow dry riverbeds, and naturally extreme caution is needed in such places, especially concerning the possibility of flash floods.

MAPS

The most popular maps are those in the Trails Illustrated series, produced by National Geographic and priced at around $9.95. Contact National Geographic Maps, PO Box 4357, Evergreen, Colorado, 80437-4357; tel 800 962 1643, tel 303 670 3457; www.nationalgeographic.com/map.

The topographical maps produced by the United States Geological Survey (USGS 7.5 minute series) are increasingly difficult to find in park shops. You may be able to purchase some locally, but to be certain these need to be ordered by mail. Details can be obtained from the main office: USGS Info Services, PO Box 25286, Federal Center, Denver, CO 80225; tel 303 202 4700; http://store.usgs.gov.

Other maps may be available at the park visitor centres. Some of these are insufficient for true backcountry walking, but adequate for the average day-walker.

DIRECTION

Most of the trails in this book can be walked in either direction. If a particular direction is to be preferred, this is noted in the text.

In the **Grand Canyon**, the following directions are to be preferred:
- Trans-canyon, North Kaibab to South Kaibab or Bright Angel trails
- Kanab Canyon – Thunder River, counter-clockwise from Sowats Point to Indian Hollow
- Boucher to Hermit Loop, counter-clockwise descending the Boucher Trail and ascending the Hermit Trail
- South Bass to Hermit Trails, descending the South Bass, walking east on the Tonto Trail and ascending the Hermit Trail
- Escalante Route, travelling west from the Tanner Trail to the New Hance or Grandview trails.

In **Zion** the following directions are to be preferred:
- The Narrows, south from Chamberlain's Ranch to the Temple of Sinawava

- West Rim Trail, south from Lava Point to the Grotto picnic area
- East Rim Trail, East Entrance to Weeping Rock
- Across Zion, east from Lee Pass to the Grotto picnic area.

With respect to rivers, 'true left' and 'true right' apply to the sides of a river while looking downstream.

WATER

Know your water sources before you start out. It could save your life! Check with the Backcountry Information Centre (BIC) at Grand Canyon and visitor centres in Zion Canyon or Kolob Canyons and Bryce Canyon before you depart. Year-round sources are noted on the route profiles and fact panels. Seasonal water sources are mentioned in the text.

LONG-DISTANCE ROUTE RECOMMENDATIONS

Several multi-day long-distance routes are suggested. Route profiles, trail maps, fact panels, average walking times and an overview of the walks are included in the guide. You will find both the route profiles and book maps useful for planning your trip. However, neither should be relied on for walking – be sure to purchase topographical maps that cover your route.

ROUTE PROFILES

This book includes route profiles for most of the trails described and for each long-distance route. Route profiles indicate important trail markers, elevations, and year-round water sources or springs. Trail steepness can be gauged at a glance. The horizontal distance on the trail is represented on the horizontal axis and not by the length of the profile line. The steeper a segment on the profile line, the more this segment will exaggerate the true distance between the points. The limitation of the book's page area makes some segments of the trail drawn on the route profile appear steeper than they truly are. This vertical exaggeration becomes especially apparent for longer routes.

SUMMARY TABLES

Summary tables in Appendix A estimate how long it will take to walk from point to point along each long-distance route. Estimates assume you will be carrying a backpack of approximately 40 pounds (18kg).

CHAPTER 2

VISITING THE SOUTHWESTERN UNITED STATES

This land is your land, this land is my land
From California to the New York Islands
From the redwood forest to the Gulf Stream waters,
This land was made for you and me.

Woody Guthrie

TRAVELLING TO THE SOUTHWESTERN UNITED STATES

The airports at Las Vegas and Salt Lake City, in Nevada, and Phoenix in Arizona, are closest to the parks in this book. Currently non-stop flights from Great Britain are not available. You can reach Las Vegas, Salt Lake City or Phoenix easily on connecting flights from any major American city. Popular connecting cities are San Francisco, Los Angeles, Denver, Dallas/Fort Worth, Chicago, Washington DC and New York. Fares vary widely depending on class of service, level of airline competition and the time of year. Summer and the Christmas holidays are the most expensive times to fly.

PASSPORTS AND VISAS

British visitors staying less than 90 days need a full British passport. Currently British and most nationals of European countries do not require a visa to visit the USA. You might need to be able to show that you have sufficient funds for your stay, approximately $350/450 per week.

Following the 9/11 attacks, security for entry to the USA has been increased. Whether you enter by air or road, you will have a scan taken of your index fingers and a close-up facial photograph. A charge of $6 may be levied on land entrants (this is included in air tickets for those flying). The date stamped on your passport and your immigration form specifies the last date on which you should leave the United States. Don't overstay your visit. If you want to stay longer, get an extension from the United States Immigration and Naturalization Service (INS).

With likely changes in future to passports, identity checking and the security climate, you are advised to check the latest requirements before arranging a trip. See contact details on the following page.

Western United States

CANADA

Seattle

WASHINGTON

Portland

Helena

MONTANA

OREGON

• Billings

• Medford

Boise

IDAHO

WYOMING

Sacramento • Reno

NEVADA

Salt Lake City

Cheyenne

UTAH

Denver

CALIFORNIA

• Cedar City
St. George

COLORADO

San Francisco

Las Vegas

• Los Angeles

• Flagstaff

Santa Fe

N

• San Diego

ARIZONA

• Phoenix

NEW MEXICO

• Tucson

MAP AREA

MEXICO

TEXAS

| 0 | 200 mls |
| 0 | 320 km |

US EMBASSY IN THE UK

24 Grosvenor Square, London W1A 1AE; tel 020 7499 9000;
www.usembassy.org.uk.
Embassy operating hours are Monday–Friday 8:30am to 5:30pm, but some sections and agencies within the embassy may differ. All offices are closed on Saturday, Sunday, and US and British holidays. For Operator Assisted Visa Information, tel 09042 450100. Note that this is a premium rate number and costs £1.20 per min. It is available on weekdays from 8am until 8pm, and on Saturdays from 10am until 4pm.

CUSTOMS AND DUTIES

Customs allows 200 cigarettes and one litre of spirits to be brought into the United States free of charge. You may not bring any fresh food or freeze-dried meat. Your backpacking gear, especially boots and tents, should be free of soil.

WHEN TO GO

If you can choose the time and season of the year to visit, the spring and autumn win without contest. Although the weather can be fickle from mid-April to late May, temperatures are generally pleasant. Spring marks the revival of green leaves and trees, along with torrents of water and a colourful array of wildflowers. Be sure to carry some warm clothes in case a wave of cold weather arrives. Temperatures begin to warm up in Zion and the Grand Canyon by late April, but not until late May in Bryce Canyon.

Autumn, from September into late October, marks the very best time of year in canyon country. Gone are the summer crowds, the thunder showers and scorching temperatures – weather may remain stable for days on end. With crystal-clear blue skies and cool nights, this time of year sees the leaves turn to yellow and reds, accenting the canyon foliage.

In the summer, unbearable heat, often over 100°F (38°C), stifles the Grand Canyon and Zion Valley, although the rim areas of the Grand Canyon remain somewhat cooler, due to their elevation of over 7000ft (2133m). Bryce Canyon never reaches too great a temperature, because of its elevation.

The winter months are quieter, but the weather is likely to vary from cold to bitterly cold, with the possibility of snow on the rim. Lower down in the canyon, temperatures will be ameliorated by the lower altitude. The access roads to the North Rim are closed even in May.

Serious crowding in the United States national parks begins after the Memorial Day holiday, the last Monday in May, and extends to the Labor Day holiday weekend, the first

Monday in September. Even Easter can be crowded if the weather is fine. Another major holiday, Independence Day on 4 July, compounds summer congestion. Lodging or camping near any national park may be impossible during the summer. Limited access at viewpoints makes finding a parking spot a major accomplishment.

GETTING AROUND

With a dearth of public transport except between major centres, America is the land of car rental, and this is the only option for any comprehensive visit to the region. There is no public transport to any of the national parks except the Grand Canyon, and hiring a car from Las Vegas or Salt Lake City is easy. Rates vary and depend on what essentials and extras are added on, but a hire set-up that gives unlimited mileage and CDW (collision damage waiver) is highly recommended. It might in fact be easier to arrange the car hire in the UK in advance, as rates are often extremely competitive with, or even lower than, locally booked prices. Some homework will be required on the telephone and internet to secure a good deal, but it will probably be worth it.

A small economy car is perfectly fine in order to explore the major trails and sights in the parks, and with everything in America being so big, even a compact car can be quite huge! A mid-range car might be nec-

essary for those expecting to camp and bring a lot of equipment with them. If you intend to make use of some of the 4x4 routes to more remote areas of the main parks, then it might be better to look into more localised vehicle hire.

Another option is to check out the hire of a campervan or RV (recreational vehicle). This can be very expensive compared to car hire, but then again you do get provided with virtually all the equipment necessary to travel in comfort. There's no tent to worry about, no windy afternoons to battle with, and you have a vehicle relatively suited to most of the more accessible terrain. On the other hand they use more fuel, cost more on private camping plots, and their bulk can make them more difficult to handle in bigger towns. Various sizes of these vehicles are available for rent. The most common size equates to those seen throughout Europe, or perhaps marginally bigger (this is America, after all). One company that specialises in camper/RV hire is Cruise America, www.cruiseamerica.com.

Petrol prices vary according to octane rating, with about 10 cents' variation between regular, super and premium. Diesel is about the same, although few diesel cars seem to exist. Despite a lot of cursing in the local television media about sky-high prices for gasoline (gas), prices are still very cheap by European standards. A US gallon (3.75 litres) costs on average $2.90, although of course distances are considerable. Utah has one of the lower fuel rates (at the time of writing – $2.85), while in California, west of our region, a gallon rose to an average $3.45 (yes, damned expensive!).

USEFUL ROAD MAPS

- Western States/Provinces AAA, www.aaa.com
- Official Map of Utah, Department of Transport, available from tourist offices, fuel stations, hotels and information centres.

NATIONAL PARK ENTRANCE FEES/PERMITS

Each park charges an entry fee. This is normally $20–$25 per vehicle, depending on the season, and lasts for a given period – a week, two weeks or a month. Some parks have annual passes. However, by far the best deal is to buy the one-year national pass for a bargain $50. This entitles you to entry to any national park in America at no extra cost. Once you have purchased the $50 pass, for an extra $15 you could get a pass that covers all national monuments as well as national parks. (This adds up to the same as buying the Golden Eagle Passport, which entitles the holder to entrance into all US national parks and national monuments for one year for a fee of $65.) However, we found that our one-year $50 pass gave us free access to all the national monuments

we visited in the area anyway. A Golden Age Passport, for US visitors over 62 years of age, costs $10 for a one-time minimal lifetime fee. Golden Access cards are available for disabled visitors. Golden Age and Golden Access holders may receive discounts at campgrounds. Visitors arriving on foot or bicycle pay a reduced fee.

Backcountry Permits
For hikes in the backcountry, permits are required. These are given out in limited numbers to reduce the impact on fragile ecosystems. For further details see chapters 5, 12 and 20.

TIME ZONES

Apart from Alaska and Hawaii, the United States extends across four time zones. The Atlantic coastal zone, which extends inland to the Great Lakes and Appalachian Mountains, is on eastern time, 5hrs behind Greenwich mean time (GMT) and 6hrs behind UK summer time. The central zone extends from Chicago to Texas; this is 1hr behind the eastern zone and 6hrs behind GMT. The mountain zone includes the Rocky Mountains, the American southwest and the state of Utah; this is 7hrs behind GMT. The Pacific zone spans the Pacific coastal states and Nevada, and is 8hrs behind GMT. However, things are not so simple in summer.

The state of Utah – including Zion, Bryce Canyon, Capitol Reef, Arches and Canyonlands – operates on mountain standard time (MST). Daylight savings time (MDT or mountain daylight time), when the clocks are pushed ahead 1hr, comes into effect between early April and October. However, Arizona does not convert to summer time, so although in the same time zone as Utah, it is 1hr behind in summer. As Grand Canyon National Park lies entirely in Arizona, it is therefore 1hr behind Zion and Bryce canyons in summer.

Note that times in the USA are generally written using 'am' and 'pm' (e.g. 6am and 6pm), and not the 24hr clock system (e.g. 0600 and 1800).

CURRENCY

United States currency can be found in denominations of $1, $2, $5, $10, $20, $50, $100 and $500. One hundred cents (¢) make up a dollar and coins come as 50¢ (a half-dollar), 25¢ (a quarter), 10¢ (a dime), 5¢ (a nickel) and 1¢ (a penny). One-dollar coins (Susan B Anthony dollars) turn up in states that allow gambling (e.g. Nevada). Two-dollar and $500 bills are rare. The popular quarter operates telephones, laundry machines, parking meters and so on.

TRAVELLERS' CHEQUES AND CREDIT CARDS

Travellers' cheques in United States dollars provide the safest and most convenient way to carry money. Almost everyone accepts them if your passport proves your identity. Places of business and banks accept travellers' cheques at face value, although there may be a charge for converting them at exchange bureaux. You can also change your foreign currency at exchange bureaux in airports and, in larger cities, at American Express and Thomas Cook offices. Accepted everywhere, credit cards can be used to pay for goods and services or to withdraw cash from an automated teller machine (ATM). You cannot rent a car without one.

INSURANCE

The United States offers no national health insurance, so make sure you purchase travel insurance before your visit – a hospital stay could set you back thousands of dollars in expenses.

SALES TAX

A state sales tax, which is usually not included in the price shown/advertised, increases charges on purchases, rental cars, hotel and motel bills. The rate varies from state to state, but averages around 8%. (A few states do not charge sales tax.)

LODGING AND CAMPING

All three national parks offer hotels, motels and campgrounds within their borders or nearby communities.

Reservations are highly recommended for **lodging** in all three parks. Phantom Ranch (see chapter 4), at the bottom of the Bright Angel Trail close to the Colorado River, should be reserved at least one year in advance, especially if you wish to visit between spring and autumn. Winter reservations at Phantom Ranch can sometimes be obtained at short notice.

Camping is available all year round in all three parks. Reservations are essential from May to October for North Rim Campground, at Mather Campground on the South Rim and at Watchman Campground in Zion. Desert View Campground, open in summer, at the South Rim of the Grand Canyon, and campgrounds at Bryce Canyon and South Campground at Zion operate on a first-come first-served basis. Campgrounds fill early in the day in summer – see appendices B and C for information on making campground reservations.

With a general scarcity of accommodation within the parks and a never-ending demand for rooms and campsites, the range of **lodgings outside the parks** is extensive. Despite this, bookings are certainly advised for high seasons and even in shoulder periods.

This guidebook does not give accommodation prices, as they change frequently and vary with the seasons. Suffice to say that a few motel rooms can be found for $30, but they are generally $40–$75 and upwards. Bed and breakfasts (B&B) are often more expensive, and hotels will be more again, unless there is a special discount on offer. Rooms in the parks tend to be the most pricey.

Camping is sometimes free in National Forest areas. In the parks a site may cost from $10 to $18.

BUSINESS HOURS

Standard business hours run from 9am to 6pm. Hours are often extended into the evening near national parks during the busy summer season.

TELEPHONE

Public telephones can be difficult to find now that most people own mobile phones. If you are taking your own mobile phone from the UK, check with your operator whether it will work there. Even if it does, the roaming charges may be extortionate. It may be useful to carry a working phone in case of emergency, but be aware that many national parks and backcountry areas are not covered by mobile phone networks.

Public phones may still be found at bus and train stations, as well as on some street corners. Coins or phone cards (referred to as 'calling cards' in the US) may be used for local calls. For operator assistance, dial 0. If a call costs more than the amount

USEFUL PHONE NUMBERS

Local operator: 0
Local calls within your area code: the seven-digit phone number
Outside your area code: 1 + area code + phone number
International telephone operator: 00 (for assistance with international calls)
International calls: 011 + country code + city code + phone number
Emergencies: 911
Local directory information: 411
Long-distance directory information: 1 + area code + 555-1212
Directory information for toll-free numbers: 1-800-555-1212

deposited, the operator will ask for more. Calling from hotels and motels will be more expensive than from public or private phones. Lower rates apply between 6pm and 7am and all day on Sunday. Calling cards, available from local shops, save on charges.

Toll-free Numbers
Many agencies and private and public companies offer toll-free numbers within the United States. You call them at their expense by dialling the prefix 1-800 and then the number.

INTERNET

Surprisingly, in the birthplace of the internet, public access is very difficult to find. Most lodges provide a service, but there are only very limited public facilities. The community library at the Grand Canyon village has a service. At Bryce several cash-operated computers are available at Ruby's Inn.

POST

Post offices, located in small towns as well as large cities, usually open from 9am to 5pm on weekdays and 9am to 1pm on Saturdays (small towns are proud of their post offices). Blue, waist-high mailboxes stand in front of post offices and on selected street corners. Airmail to Europe takes about one week.

The last line of letters addressed to the United States should include the name of the city, the state abbreviation and the postal code. States are abbreviated with two capital letters (e.g. California is CA).

LAUNDRY

Laundrettes with coin-operated washing machines and dryers can be found in many small and medium-sized towns. They provide the most efficient and economical way to take care of this essential chore. Self-service laundries are available inside Bryce Canyon at the General Store; at the South Rim of the Grand Canyon next door to Mather Campground; and at the North Rim of the Grand Canyon next to the service station and campground. Visitors to Zion will find a laundrette in Springdale. A dry-cleaning service may be available at hotels or through independent dry-cleaners.

WEIGHTS, MEASURES AND TEMPERATURES

United States distance measurements are recorded in inches (in), feet (ft) and miles, weight in ounces (oz) and pounds (lb). Signs for walkers in the national parks give distances in miles and height in feet, although the metric system is occasionally used as well. Temperatures in the United States are most commonly described in degrees fahrenheit (°F), but – especially in the Grand Canyon – temperatures are also given in degrees centigrade (°C).

ELECTRICITY

The voltage is 110V AC. Electric plugs have two flat pins with a circular earth pin.

SMOKING

Smoking is a declining habit in the United States. In hotels and motels some rooms may be designated as non-smoking. Domestic aeroplane flights and some public buildings, outdoor stadiums and restaurants forbid smoking. Throwing a burning cigarette out of an automobile can result in a large fine in areas at risk from forest fires.

TIPPING

Tips are given to service providers, such as waiters/waitresses and taxi drivers, at the discretion of the customer, depending on your satisfaction with the service. Tips are usually given at 15% of the total charge. Baggage handlers often receive $2 per bag carried. (Many workers' livelihoods depend on tips.)

PARK AND CAMPING REGULATIONS

The following is a summary of park regulations from National Park Service literature.

1   Your permit is valid only for the date, time, leader and party size indicated on the front. To request changes in a permit you must return it to the backcountry-permit centre where it was issued (see chapters 5, 12 and 20).

2   You must use a backcountry stove – no fires are allowed.

3   In summer, carry 1 gallon (4 litres) of water per person per day. All water from water sources must be purified.

4   Keep food away from animals. Use food-storage tins where they are provided.

5   Take away all trash – 'Pack it in,

31

pack it out'. This includes used toilet paper, so bring plastic bags for this.

6 Use toilets where available. If toilets are not available, defecate at least 200ft (60m) from water.

7 Wash dishes or yourself at least 200ft (60m) from creeks and potholes. Scatter dishwater.

8 Stay on the main trails – do not cut switchbacks.

9 No pets are allowed in the backcountry or below the rim.

10 Do not alter campsites in any way. Choose previously used sites, and do not camp in drainage during the rain/flood season.

11 An Arizona state fishing licence is required for all fishing.

12 Do not feed wild animals.

For more about 'leaving no traces', see www.lnt.org.

Sunset at Grand Canyon

Bright Angel Trail to Plateau Point (Bright Angel Trail, Grand Canyon)

Indian Garden (Bright Angel Trail, Grand Canyon)

Near Skeleton Point (South Kaibab Trail, Grand Canyon)

Chapter 3

EQUIPMENT AND SPECIAL HAZARDS

I am glad I shall never be young without wild country to be young in.
Of what avail are forty freedoms without a blank spot on the map!

Aldo Leopold

EQUIPMENT

For your overnight trips in Zion, Bryce and the Grand Canyon you will need equipment considered essential for backpacking trips in other parts of the world. During summer and late spring, hot to scorching temperatures dominate your concerns in the Grand Canyon and in Zion. During winter, in all three parks you will need extra cold-weather gear. General gear requirements are outlined below.

Shelter

In summer, a lightweight tent should suffice, although some may prefer a groundsheet and tarpaulin. A tent guards against unexpected night-time visitors such as scorpions, ringtail cats, tarantulas, ants and mice. In spring, winter and autumn, a heavier tent offers more protection. Be prepared for sudden changes in weather at any time of year. Snow can fall from September to May. Summer thundershowers often deluge the southwest.

Sleeping Bag

A lightweight sleeping bag (or light blanket in summer only) offers more than enough warmth in the heat of summer. In spring, winter and autumn a warmer bag, adequate even for freezing weather, is to be preferred. A sleeping pad or Thermarest adds to comfort and warmth.

Stove and Fuel

You must carry a camping stove, as backcountry fires are prohibited. White gas (a liquid) and kerosene are available at most outdoor sporting goods stores and many fuel stations. Butane or propane cartridges can be difficult to locate. Do not count on finding your special brand.

It is a violation of federal law to carry any fuel (e.g. gas, kerosene or butane cartridges) on aeroplanes. Stoves with an attached receptacle for fuel or separate fuel bottles may be confiscated at United States airports and not returned. Fuel containers must be free of fuel and gas fumes.

Food

Grocery stores near all three parks stock dehydrated and lightweight foods. High-carbohydrate food provides invaluable energy. Electrolyte replacement drinks restore lost electrolytes in hot weather. As you will almost certainly be travelling by car, you might as well bring a reasonable supply with you, as park stores might have limited or no stocks of some items. Carry extra food in case you are delayed for any reason (e.g. bad weather, illness or poor road conditions). Always carry drinking water in your car; distances between settlements can be long.

Never leave food out unprotected, and be sure to guard your supply from uninvited visitors. Squirrels, mice or other rodents may eat through the outside pockets of backpacks. Established campsites in the Grand Canyon on the corridor trails and the Hermit Trail are especially vulnerable to these raids.

Hang your backpacks away from your tent, empty and with the zips and pockets open. Never store or sleep with food in your tent. Hanging food is the best way to store and protect it. Put food in any sealed container, e.g. a plastic or metal box, then either use the overhead wires provided by the park authorities for hanging food, or nylon cord – mice and squirrels have been known to chew at ropes used for hanging food so that the food bag falls to the ground. Outwitting these rodents challenges many a canyon hiker.

Clothing

Pack clothing that will keep you warm when wet. There are many new high-tech synthetic fibres designed for hiking. Layers of synthetic or wool clothing, waterproofs with full-length side zippers, a warm hat and gloves are necessary any time of year. Be prepared for fickle weather and varying temperatures, especially in spring and autumn.

In summer, carry a long-sleeved synthetic shirt, cotton shirt and shorts, and a fleece jacket. Loose-fitting, light-coloured cotton clothing shields from the sun and allows for air flow. During autumn and spring, when it can turn cold, wear synthetic long underwear under your shorts and carry another synthetic mid-weight long-sleeved shirt. In winter, pack another heavier synthetic shirt and trousers, overmitts, a balaclava, extra fuel and food, a heavier tent and a warmer sleeping bag and pad.

Boots

Medium to lightweight boots with a good sole will serve you well – note that trainers provide inadequate ankle support. Carry several changes of socks. Woollen socks are warmer than synthetic ones, but dry more slowly.

In winter and early spring in the Grand Canyon, instep crampons may be necessary to negotiate the icy upper sections of some trails as you descend off the rim. Gaiters protect your feet and socks from snow. Snow and ice may not be gone from the Grand Canyon South Rim trails until May, the North Rim until June, the

Zion high country until May and the Bryce Rim until June.

Miscellaneous

Do not forget your map and compass, signal mirror, extra food, water-purification tablets or pump, more water than you think you will need, pocket knife, nylon cord for hanging food or hauling packs, toilet items, camera and film. Medical kits should include general first aid supplies, an ankle wrap and blister care materials. Trekking poles help with balance on steep trails, although some find them too cumbersome. You will also need plastic bags for trash, some sort of pack cover or strong large plastic bags to line your pack, electrolyte replacement drinks, salty snacks, matches or lighter, trowel, whistle, flashlight and extra batteries.

SPECIAL HAZARDS

Lightning Storms

Stay in your car during lightning storms, and keep the windows closed. Seek cover if out hiking.

Water Requirements

Remember to drink as much water as you can before you leave camp in the morning. Make sure you know your water sources before you depart and plan ahead. Carry up to one gallon of water a day or more in high summer. On trails treat all water either with a filter or with tablets. Filters clog easily from dirty water. Electrolyte replacement drinks such as ERG® or Gatorade® help to prevent dehydration in hot weather. Urine colour should be pale yellow and output should be copious.

Heat and Sun

Pay close attention to sun protection. A hat with a wide brim shades your face and head, a bandanna shields your neck. You must have sunglasses that block UV light and strong sun block (SPF15 or higher) for your skin. White cotton shirts absorb less heat and long sleeves protect your arms and provide more sun protection.

Cold

Sudden changes in weather bring snow, rain and anything in between. Hypothermia, commonly known as the 'killer of the unprepared', strikes most commonly between 30°F and 50°F (0°C and 10°C). Snow can fall between September and May, and rain is possible at any time of year. You should always be prepared, with several layers of synthetic or wool clothing, shelter, full waterproofs, warm hat and gloves, and extra high-energy foods.

Rockfall

Humans cause much of the rockfall danger. Cutting corners and making new trails leads to erosion and increases the chance of kicking loose debris and rocks onto walkers below – watch where you place your hands and feet.

Flash Floods

Flash floods present a serious hazard in narrow canyons, especially in the Grand Canyon and Zion. In summer, large amounts of rain, often in thundershowers, fall in the higher elevations many miles from the park. The water rushes through tributary creeks, eventually overloading distant small run-off creeks. Stay out of side creeks during the high flash-flood season from July to early September – several deaths occur each year due to flash floods.

Animals

Wild animals pose a generally low risk in the parks. Snakes tend to lurk under rocks that invite the weary trekker, so check before sitting down. Coyotes will avoid humans and mountain lions tend to do the same. If a mountain lion approaches you, wave and shout, throw rocks or sticks, but do not run away, or you will appear to be prey and may be attacked. Do not hike alone in remote backcountry.

GRAND CANYON
NATIONAL PARK

CHAPTER 4

VISITING GRAND CANYON NATIONAL PARK

*It is unique. It stands alone...it is one of the few things
that man is utterly unable to imagine
until he comes in actual contact with it.*

George Wharton James, 1910

Over five million people from all over the world visit Grand Canyon National Park in a year. Known to the Indian Paiute tribe as Kaibab, or 'mountain lying down', no amount of pictures or reading will prepare you for what you will see. The park extends over one million acres of land. The Grand Canyon spans 18 miles across at its widest and 1.5 miles across at its narrowest. The canyon's 10 mile-wide central section measures 1 mile deep.

From the accessible South Rim Grand Canyon Village, walkers can choose from eight splendid rim-to-river trails, all direct and fast routes to the Colorado River. Far away from the crowds of the south, the cooler and higher North Rim Village receives only 10% of the number of visitors that go to the South Rim Village. The North Rim's magnificent viewpoints indent the canyon walls in finger-like projections that boast sweeping views of the upper Inner Canyon. Superlative day-hiking on the rim awaits walkers at the North Rim Village, although only the North Kaibab Trail provides access into the Inner Canyon.

GETTING THERE

Located entirely within the state of Arizona, the Grand Canyon Village at the South Rim is easily reached from Phoenix, Las Vegas or Salt Lake City. Located 59 miles north of Williams, Arizona on Hwy 64, and 78 miles north of Flagstaff, Arizona via Hwy 180, Grand Canyon National Park is 310 miles from Bryce Canyon National Park, 272 miles from Zion National Park and 215 miles from the North Rim of the Grand Canyon. In addition it is 440 miles from Death Valley, California, 649 miles from Los Angeles, California, and 334 miles from Tucson, Arizona.

There is a limited air service to the Grand Canyon Airport (South Rim) from Las Vegas. Scenic flights over the canyon, in helicopters and fixed-wing aircraft, also operate from the airport, which is just south of Tusayan. For a list of operators, contact: Grand Canyon Chamber of

Commerce, PO Box 3007, Grand Canyon, AZ 86023. Note that poor weather can ground these small sightseeing planes.

There is a year-round shuttle service between the airport and the South Rim, for a nominal fee.

A 24hr taxi service also provides a link between Grand Canyon Village and the airport, as well as trailheads and other destinations. Tel (928) 638 2822 or (928) 638 2631 ext 6563.

'Open Road Tours' runs two daily buses from Flagstaff to Grand Canyon Village on the South Rim. They also have a connection to Phoenix. For schedules and costs, tel (928) 226 8060 or (800) 766 7117.

The Greyhound bus line has services from Flagstaff and Williams to other major US cities.

The Grand Canyon Railway has a vintage train service from Williams to Grand Canyon Village. It is possible to ride on the train one way and take a bus back. Tel (800)-THE TRAIN (800 843 8724) for information and reservations.

The best way to reach the North Rim of the Grand Canyon is by car – no public transportation serves this remote location. The closest major airports are Salt Lake City, Nevada, 379 miles away, or Las Vegas, Nevada, 276 miles away. Small commuter airlines and car-rental agencies serve Page, Arizona, 119 miles away.

From mid-May to October, a daily shuttle bus service between the South and North rims is operated by Transcanyon Shuttle, tel (928) 638 2820. There is one bus each way per day. The drive from the South Rim via Jacob Lake, a tiny crossroads settlement in the forest, to the North Rim is 215 miles and takes 4–5hrs.

ENTRANCE FEES

Winter fees are $20 per vehicle, and from 1 May charges rise to $25 per vehicle. The Golden Eagle Passport and all other annual passes are valid here.

GETTING AROUND – SHUTTLE SERVICES

Note that new roads and a new shuttle system are currently under construction at Grand Canyon Village, so the following information may change.

Parking is limited at all viewpoints and near the hotels. Trailheads for rim-to-river trails are found at Hermits' Rest (Hermit and Boucher trails), near Bright Angel Lodge, and Kolb Studio (Bright Angel Trail), Yaki Point (South Kaibab Trail), Grandview Point (Grandview Trail), Moran Point (New Hance Trail) and Lipan Point (Tanner Trail). Private cars are not permitted to use the West Rim road and the approach road to the South Kaibab trailhead from spring to late October.

Parking, traffic and smog present serious problems, particularly in the summer months. On the South Rim, national park shuttle buses serve the

West Rim road to Hermits' Rest, East Rim Drive to Yaki Point and the Village Loop. The Village Loop shuttle stops at all major facilities within Grand Canyon Village. The National Park Service operates alternative-fuel shuttle bus services.

The West Rim, Hermits' Rest, shuttle buses take 75mins in driving time for the round trip. There are eight stops westbound, but only two (Mohave and Hopi Point) on the return leg. Heading east to the South Kaibab trailhead and Yaki Point, the travelling time is 30mins, with three stops. Buses run every 15mins during the day. Shuttles also run every 30mins from 4.30am to 7.30am or 9.30am, depending on the season, and from sunset to one hour after sunset. The village shuttle bus takes 1hr in travelling time and runs from 4.30am to 10pm, with buses every 15mins for most of the day. A direct shuttle also operates from the Bright Angel trailhead and the Backcountry Information Centre to the South Kaibab trailhead three times in the early mornings. For exact times check beforehand, as they vary each month.

WEATHER AND SEASONS

The main seasons at the Grand Canyon are only loosely defined. The South Rim, at 7000ft, remains open all year and receives 15in of precipitation per year. Roads may be closed by snow from October to April, due to treacherous icy sections. It can get very cold on the rim in winter, although mild temperatures predominate in the canyon. The least amount of precipitation falls during May and June. Weather patterns are fickle – snow may come and go, or it may stay on the ground all winter. Temperatures on the rims are very pleasant in the late spring and autumn; inner canyon temperatures begin to soar by late spring.

The North Rim, located at over 8000ft (2438m), is only open from mid-May until late October, even if there is no snow in late spring. Mid-July to late-August thunderstorms mark the rainiest season – flash-flood dangers reach their peak during this time of year. The North Rim receives over 25in of precipitation in the average year, and during winter over 10ft of snow may accumulate. You will need warm clothes in the evening any time in the summer.

When the hotel and concession services close in mid-October, day-visitors are allowed until snow blocks the access road. At the Colorado River, at 2400ft (732m), only 8in of rain reaches the canyon bottom each year – raindrops often evaporate before they reach the ground. Unbearable temperatures reign in the Inner Canyon in summer and late spring; early spring and autumn mark the most pleasant walking seasons. Winter can be pleasant and not too cold, although the days are short and many trees lack their leaves.

Average South Rim Temperatures (°C/°F) and Rainfall (cm/in)

Month	Av. High	Av. Low	Av. Rainfall
Jan	4 (41)	-8 (18)	3.3 (1.3)
Feb	7 (45)	-7 (21)	4.1 (1.6)
Mar	10 (51)	-4 (25)	3.6 (1.4)
Apr	16 (60)	0 (32)	2.3 (0.9)
May	21 (70)	4 (39)	1.1 (0.7)
Jun	27 (81)	9 (47)	1.0 (0.4)
Jul	29 (84)	12 (54)	4.6 (1.8)
Aug	28 (82)	11 (53)	5.6 (2.2)
Sep	25 (76)	9 (47)	4.1 (1.6)
Oct	18 (65)	2 (36)	2.8 (1.1)
Nov	11 (52)	-2 (27)	2.3 (0.9)
Dec	7 (43)	-7 (20)	4.1 (1.6)

Average North Rim Temperatures (°C/°F) and Rainfall (cm/in)

Month	Av. High	Av. Low	Av. Rainfall
Jan	2 (37)	-9 (16)	8.1 (3.2)
Feb	3 (39)	-8 (18)	8.1 (3.2)
Mar	7 (44)	-6 (21)	6.6 (2.6)
Apr	11 (53)	-2 (29)	4.3 (1.7)
May	17 (62)	1 (34)	3.1 (1.2)
Jun	23 (73)	4 (40)	2.3 (0.9)
Jul	26 (77)	8 (46)	4.8 (1.9)
Aug	24 (75)	7 (45)	7.1 (2.8)
Sep	20 (69)	3 (39)	5.1 (2.0)
Oct	16 (59)	-1 (31	3.6 (1.4)
Nov	8 (46)	-4 (24)	3.8 (1.5)
Dec	4 (40)	-7 (20)	7.1 (2.8)

Average Colorado River Gorge Temperatures (°C/°F) and Rainfall (cm/in)

Month	Av. High	Av. Low	Av. Rainfall
Jan	13 (56)	2 (36)	1.8 (0.7)
Feb	17 (62)	5 (42)	1.9 (0.75)
Mar	21 (70)	9 (48)	2.0 (0.8)
Apr	28 (83)	13 (56)	1.2 (0.5)
May	32 (92)	18 (64)	1.0 (0.4)
Jun	39 (101)	22 (72)	0.8 (0.3)
Jul	42 (106)	27 (79)	2.4 (0.85)

Average Colorado River Gorge Temperatures (°C/°F) and Rainfall (cm/in), cont.

Month	Av. High	Av. Low	Av. Rainfall
Aug	40 (103)	25 (75)	3.6 (1.4)
Sep	36 (97)	20 (69)	2.5 (1.0)
Oct	28 (83)	15 (58)	1.7 (0.65)
Nov	20 (69)	8 (46)	1.0 (0.40)
Dec	15 (58)	2 (37)	2.3 (0.9)

LODGING

Reservations for camping or lodging on either the North or South rims should be made months in advance – don't expect to find lodging if you arrive without reservations. Especially during the spring, summer and autumn, the Grand Canyon (particularly the South Rim) is overcrowded with people. Lodging and camping sites are very limited on the North Rim, and it's a long drive to alternative accommodation.

For all major lodgings within Grand Canyon National Park, contact Xanterra Parks and Resorts, 14001 East Iliff, Ste 600, Aurora, CO 80014, tel (928) 638 2631 same day or (888) 297 2757 for advance reservations.

On the **South Rim** you can choose between six different lodges in Grand Canyon Village: El Tovar Hotel, Bright Angel Lodge, Kachina Lodge, Maswik Lodge, Thunderbird Lodge and Yavapai Lodge. The upgraded El Tovar Hotel, the canyon's masterpiece of architecture, sits majestically near the beginning of the Bright Angel Trail in the centre of Grand Canyon Village. Bright Angel Lodge and Maswik Lodge offer separate rustic cabins as well as lodge rooms.

Other accommodation can be found 5–6 miles south of the Grand Canyon in Tusayan. You may choose between the Grand Hotel, Grand Canyon Squire Inn, Holiday Inn Express, Quality Inn and Red Feather Lodge. There are no other towns very close by. Flagstaff, a major hub, is 83 miles southeast, while Williams is 59 miles south, and 55 miles to the east is Cameron.

On the **North Rim** is stately Grand Canyon Lodge. Designed by the architect Gilbert Stanley Underwood in 1928, this magnificent structure near the rim offers panoramic canyon views with luxury accommodation. Reservations should be made at least one year in advance. Eighteen miles north of the North Rim is Kaibab Lodge. Jacob Lake, 44 miles to the north, offers limited accommodation. Jacob Lake Inn is one of the options, while further north are Fredonia and Kanab, two pleasant places with a good selection of motels.

Lodging in the Canyon at Phantom Ranch

Phantom Ranch, located near the Colorado River at the junction of the South Kaibab, North Kaibab and Bright Angel trails, can be reached by mule or on foot. Offering the only accommodation inside the canyon, reservations for cabins and same-sex dormitories should be made up to one year in advance through Xanterra Parks and Resorts. Space is extremely limited. Phantom Ranch provides meals, towels, bedding and pillows, soap and shower facilities. Meals must be booked in advance. You do not need a backcountry permit if you are staying at Phantom Ranch.

Children are welcome at Phantom Ranch, but are discouraged during summer and winter because of the extreme temperatures and remote location. Families with children up to five years of age are limited to cabin use only.

Snacks, beverages and very limited supplies are sold at the Phantom Ranch canteen (Phantom Ranch is thought to sell the best lemonade in the canyon). Summer high temperatures average 103°F (40°C), but can reach 120°F (48°C). Mail sent from Phantom Ranch is postmarked 'Mailed by mule from the bottom of the Canyon'. For a fee, mules will transport your luggage out of the canyon between Phantom Ranch and the South Rim Village. Reservations for baggage transport can be made at the Bright Angel Lodge on the South Rim or at Phantom Ranch.

Camping

On the **South Rim** the largest site is Mather Campground in Grand Canyon Village, and it remains open all year. At the time of writing (2007) campsites are $18 a night. Reservations are advised for Mather Campground from April to October, although visitors in early May should find spaces easily. Trailer Village, with hook-ups, is close to Mather and is $24 per night for two people. In summer after mid-May, a first-come first-served campground operates at Desert View 25 miles east of Grand Canyon Village. This charges $12 per night for a site.

Outside the park entrance in Tusayan is the Camper Village, with hook-ups and showers. South of Tusayan, operated by the Kaibab National Forest, is the Ten-X Campground. At $10 per site, it is basic, without showers or hook-ups.

On the **North Rim** is North Rim campground, 3 miles north of Grand Canyon Lodge, near the General Store, and open from mid-May to mid-October. This pleasant, shaded campground offers a good alternative to a fully booked hotel. Trans-canyon walkers are allowed to stay at North Rim campground without a reservation. For all other people, reservations are absolutely essential at North Rim campground all summer.

Outside the park on the North Rim is the Kaibab Camper Village with hook-ups, just south of Jacob Lake. Others are De Motte campground 16 miles north of the north rim, and Jacob Lake campground, a forestry service site. In additional camping is allowed in some areas of the national forest.

See appendices for contact addresses and further information on camping reservations for all campgrounds shown above.

FOOD

On the South Rim there is a general store in the centre of the village, open daily from March onwards, from 8am till 7pm or 8pm. Check out the restaurants for sustaining nourishment. There is snack food at Hermits' Rest and at Desert View Marketplace. The Desert View Trading Post also has a snack bar. On the North Rim, basic groceries can be found near North Rim campground and 18 miles north of the rim at the County Store. Meals are provided at the hotels mentioned above.

VISITOR SERVICES – SOUTH RIM

The Canyon View Information Plaza, which houses the visitor centre, bookshop and toilets, is located near Mather Point. Currently you can park at the Mather Point/Canyon View parking area and it is 5mins walk to the visitor centre. A long-planned update to the transport system has yet to be built, but it is set to link into the Canyon View Plaza. The visitor centre is open daily from 8am to 5pm.

The Yavapai Museum/Observation Station, an historic building at Yavapai Point, chronicles a geological history of the Grand Canyon. It has recently been refurbished and remodelled. The Tusayan Museum, 3 miles east of Desert View, presents insights into 800 years of Native Indian cultures in relation to the archaeological history of the Grand Canyon. Some remnants of their ancient buildings can be viewed from a trail adjacent to the museum. In the historic area of Bright Angel trailhead is the restored studio of the Kolb brothers, early pioneering photographers of the area.

For advance information, contact Grand Canyon National Park, PO Box 129, Grand Canyon, AZ 86023; tel 928 638 7888; www.nps.gov/grca.

INTERPRETATIVE PROGRAMMES

The National Park Service offers several daily talks by rangers, and also junior programmes. The *Guide*, the national park newspaper, available when entering the park, lists specific hours and location of programmes.

GRAND CANYON ASSOCIATION

The Grand Canyon Association, a non-profit organisation, aids research, interpretation and education at Grand

Canyon National Park. Membership entitles you to their quarterly newsletter, discounts on purchases at all national park visitor centres and on Grand Canyon Field Institute classes. Since its inception it has raised over $23 million. The association operates many of the bookstores in the park. (Some of the books available are listed in the bibliography).

GRAND CANYON FIELD INSTITUTE

The Grand Canyon Field Institute, a non-profit organisation sponsored by the Grand Canyon Association and Grand Canyon National Park, presents educational programmes in the park. The institute offers courses on geology, ecology, photography, human history and wilderness studies, as well as women's classes. There are many classes for backpackers, although some courses use mules or llamas to transport gear. Expert instructors, some known the world over for their knowledge of the Grand Canyon, lead trips.

OTHER FACILITIES

The Grand Canyon Village on the South Rim has a fully stocked general store, including camping equipment purchase or rental, a post office, banking and ATM, dog kennels, lost and found office, community library with internet and the Backcountry Information Centre (BIC). Summer automotive services include a petrol station, a car mechanic and towing services. A petrol station at Desert View opens in summer only. Nearby Tusayan has year-round petrol stations and automobile repair shops. For additional services see Appendix B.

MEDICAL CARE

24hr emergency care, tel 911 (or 9-911 from a hotel room).

The North County Grand Canyon Clinic is open from March onwards, from 8am to 6pm, tel (928) 638 2551.

Dentist, tel (928) 638 2395 between 8am and 4pm.

VISITOR SERVICES – NORTH RIM

On the North Rim, you will find a small general store, a post office, laundrette and showers (near the campground), a post office in Grand Canyon Lodge, a petrol station, and a Backcountry Information Centre (BIC). On the North Rim, the National Park Service Visitor Information Centre office and a bookstore run by the Grand Canyon Association operate next to Grand Canyon Lodge. Other services include fuel and minor car repairs at 18 miles and 44 miles.

HAVASUPAI INDIAN RESERVATION

Not quite within the park, but along a southern tributary of the Colorado River, is the Havasupai Indian

Reservation. The main village of Supai is an 8 mile hike. Visitors can contact the reservation tourist office by telephoning (928) 448 2141.

TIME ZONES

Grand Canyon National Park, entirely in the state of Arizona, remains on mountain standard time (MST) all year.

GRAND CANYON SKYWALK

The Grand Canyon Skywalk is a looped glass bridge protruding 70ft out over the depths of the Grand Canyon. Its construction started in March 2004, and it first opened to the public three years later, on 28 March 2007. Buzz Aldrin, the second man to set foot on the moon, was one of the first men to tread on its almost invisible surface.

Situated in Grand Canyon West on the Hualapai Indian Reservation, and owned by the Hualapai Indians, the bridge is certainly impressive and an engineering first. However, while some members of the tribe are pleased that it is attracting visitors to an area of high unemployment, others are unhappy that it is desecrating sacred ground.

According to official statistics, when tested the bridge was found to exceed engineering requirements by 400%, so visitors should feel quite safe when looking down the uninterrupted 4000ft to the dizzying depths of the Colorado river racing below. Made of more than one million pounds of steel, it was built to withstand the force of 71 fully loaded Boeing 747 jumbo jets. It can survive winds of over 100 miles per hour from eight different directions, as well as an 8.0 magnitude earthquake within 50 miles.

At the time of writing, a lookout building containing shops and restaurants was still being built, but it should be completed some time in 2008.

The cost of walking on the structure is $25, but to that you must add the cost of a tour including an optional walk on the Skywalk. This is in the region of $50, and with a total cost of $75 each, it is not a cheap option. These prices will no doubt change in the future, and may vary at different times of year, so do check before you go!

CHAPTER 5

WALKING IN GRAND CANYON NATIONAL PARK

Leave it as it is. You cannot improve on it.
The ages have been at work on it, and man can only mar it.

Theodore Roosevelt

One of the world's greatest scenic wonders, there is no other place on earth like the Grand Canyon. The national park's 1.2 million acres protect the canyon's 277 mile length. Most people simply enjoy Grand Canyon National Park from its viewpoints. However, only walkers can truly experience and appreciate this great area.

Gone are the days when we could walk freely in many of the wilderness areas of the United States, and the National Park Service strictly regulates backcountry visits. Though the rules in Grand Canyon National Park may seem excessive, this system allows miles of the canyon to remain as wilderness. Today's solitude in the backcountry exists because of these regulations.

Overnight Grand Canyon trips require careful planning. You must carefully consider the amount of water and food needed, altitude gain and loss, as well as the water sources available. For many, canyon-walking will be a new experience, different from anything else they have enjoyed in other parts of the world, and, caught under the canyon's spell, they will return again and again.

OVERNIGHT BACKCOUNTRY PERMITS AND PROCEDURES

In order to stop congestion and overuse of certain areas in Grand Canyon National Park, a permit system has been established to regulate overnight hiking below the rim, and obtaining a permit requires considerable advance planning. (A permit is not required for day-hikes.)

Nearly 40,000 people per year camp in the backcountry overnight. The National Park Service issues approximately 13,000 permits for backpacking parties each year, and requests for permits exceed the number issued. A backcountry permit is required for all overnight stays in the canyon below the rims, except for those pre-booked into rooms and accommodation at Phantom Ranch. Permits must be carried at all times, and are only valid for the date specified, the number of hikers in the party, and the given itinerary and route.

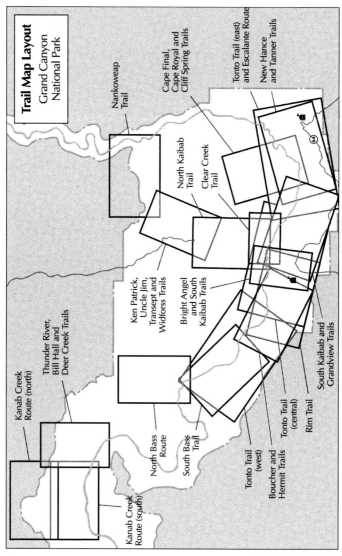

Trail Map Layout
Grand Canyon
National Park

Nankoweap
Trail

Cape Final,
Cape Royal and
Cliff Spring Trails

Tonto Trail (east)
and Escalante Route

New Hance
and Tanner Trails

North Kaibab
Trail

Clear Creek
Trail

Ken Patrick,
Uncle Jim,
Transept and
Widforss Trails

Bright Angel
and South
Kaibab Trails

South Kaibab and
Grandview Trails

Thunder River,
Bill Hall and
Deer Creek Trails

Kanab Creek
Route (north)

North Bass
Route

South Bass
Trail

Tonto Trail
(west)

Boucher and
Hermit Trails

Tonto Trail
(central)

Rim Trail

Kanab Creek
Route (south)

To obtain up-to-date information on how to obtain a permit, and help in filing an application, write to or e-mail the Backcountry Information Centre (BIC) for the Backcountry Trip Planner (see below). Because changes in these procedures are made from time to time, only a general outline of how to obtain a permit is included here. There is a sample application in Appendix G.

At the time of writing, requests for backcountry permits are considered no earlier than the first day of the month, four months before the proposed starting date of your walk, so apply on the first day of the correct month to ensure the maximum opportunity of obtaining the permit you wish (e.g. for April permits, write on 1 December). To increase your chances of obtaining a permit, offer alternative starting dates and routes.

To apply you have three options, as follows.
• In person at the Backcountry Information Centre.
• Use the internet to obtain a form and instructions for application – go to www.nps.gov/grca.
• Fax the Backcountry Information Centre on (928) 638 2125 to obtain forms and to return your application.

(You can also write to the Backcountry Information Centre, but this is slower and not recommended.)

Having filled in an application form, post it to the Backcountry Information Centre, Grand Canyon National Park, PO Box 129, Grand Canyon, AZ 86023 (or fax as above). Post early to allow for delivery times.

A limited number of last-minute corridor permits may be available from the Backcountry Information Centre. They are available on a first-come first-served basis to anyone waiting in line at 8am at the office. However, the wait for a corridor permit can be several days, with no guarantee as to the location of the overnight stop.

Remember that your backcountry permit is valid only for the date, time, leader and party size indicated on the front. To request changes in the permit you must return it to the Backcountry Information Centre.

Fees
In 1997 the National Park Service instituted a backcountry-use fee system for overnight camping below the rim. An initial charge for your permit and a small fee per person per night must be paid when you apply for your permit. Fees are currently $10 for the permit application and $5 per person for each participant per night below the rim. Frequent visitors can pay $25 for a one-year membership, which negates the need to pay the $10 permit fee each time. Hikers passing through the Havasupai Reservation (South Bass Trail and Pasture Wash Trail) need to pay an additional fee.

The fee system covers the cost of administration, additional patrols on corridor trails, improved search-and-rescue services and also educational displays.

Groups
Individual permits are issued for 1–6 people and large group permits for 7–11 people. Large groups are allotted fewer campsites than smaller groups. Groups also have to pay an additional $5 per group camping above the rim outside regular sites.

Backcountry Management Zones – 'Use Areas'
The National Park Service has developed a system of backcountry 'zones' to classify areas of the park by accessibility and usage. These are shown in the Backcountry Trip Planners issued to visitors. Each 'use area' allows for a defined number of overnight campers, depending on its size, topography, number of available camps and ecological sensitivity. You will need to designate 'use areas' when you apply for your permit.

There are some rules regarding the length of stays. Camping within the 'use areas' in designated overnight camps is limited to two nights. Trips are limited to seven nights per 'use area.' Beyond these use areas, camping is not limited to specific spots. The National Park Service describes the zones as follows.

Corridor zone   Recommended for first-time hikers. Maintained trails. Purified water. Paved roads to trailheads. Toilets, signs, and emergency stations.

Threshold zone   For experienced Grand Canyon hikers. Non-maintained trails. Dirt roads to trailheads. Water needs purification. Pit toilets.

Primitive zones   For highly experienced Grand Canyon hikers. Non-maintained roads and routes, 4x4 roads to trailheads. Occasional developments.

Wild zones   Only for very fit and highly experienced Grand Canyon hikers. Indistinct to non-existent routes require route-finding ability. Water may be non-existent. No development.

Primitive and wild zones are not recommended for use during the summer, because of high temperatures and lack of reliable water sources.

DAY-HIKING

Day-hiking does not require a permit. For day-walking, try the Hermit Trail to Dripping Springs or Santa Maria Spring, the Grandview Trail to Horseshoe Mesa and the South Kaibab Trail to Cedar Ridge or Skeleton Point.

The scenic South Kaibab Trail, much less crowded than the neighbouring Bright Angel Trail, offers superb views from its ridge line. For day-walkers in good condition, a superb 6–7hr, 13.4 mile day-walk descends the South Kaibab to the Tipoff, turns west on the Tonto Trail past Pipe Spring, and continues west for 4. 2 miles to Indian Garden. From here you can ascend to the South Rim on the Bright Angel Trail.

Limited day-hiking above the South Rim is confined to the 9 mile Rim Trail and a shorter, but splendid, walk to Shoshone Point.

From the main North Rim Village, only the North Kaibab Trail, following a creek bed with limited views, drops below the rim. Several North Rim day-walks, such as the Widforss or Cape Final trails, provide a cooler alternative to the North Kaibab Trail. Do not miss the short walks to the spectacular viewpoints of Cape Royal and Bright Angel Point. (See Chapter 9 for the Grand Canyon Rim Walks.)

TRIP PLANNING

Although summer is the most *popular* time to visit the Grand Canyon, it is not the optimal season for a visit. American families and Europeans on holiday peak at this time. And in addition to the unbearable heat, the trails, hotels, parking and access roads are horribly overcrowded. Spring and autumn bring fewer visitors and cooler temperatures. Winter trips are less popular, because although inner canyon temperatures are reasonable, heavy rain or snow can make canyon access difficult or dangerous. Corridor trails offer the safest routes into the inner canyon during the winter.

MAPS

The most widely available maps at present are the waterproof and tear-proof 'Trails Illustrated' Grand Canyon National Park (TI) (1:73530), by National Geographic (map number 207). The waterproof 1:40,000 Grand Canyon National Park map, by cartographer Ken Schulte, is one such useful publication, produced by Sky Terrain, PO Box 808, Boulder, CO 80306, www.skyterrain.com. Other maps are available from Earthwalk Press: Grand Canyon National Park (EP) (1:48000), and Bright Angel Trail Hiking Map and Guide (EP) (1:24000). The above maps are carried by the Grand Canyon Association, the North Rim and South Rim visitor centres, and many local stores, although they tend not to stock USGS maps – see below.

Formerly, United States Geological Survey (USGS) maps were more commonly used, but they are harder to locate now. The larger scale USGS 7.5 minute maps are useful for off-trail hiking. Some USGS maps may be available in Grand Canyon Village in high season, but they were not available in the spring. Outdoor shops in Flagstaff and Page, Arizona, and Willow Bank Bookstore and Bureau of Land Management (BLM) in Kanab, Utah, might stock them. United States Geological Survey (USGS) maps can be purchased from their office in Denver, Colorado: United States Geological Survey (USGS), Box 25286, Denver, Colorado 80225, tel 303 202 4700, http://store.usgs.gov.

The Kaibab National Forest, North Kaibab Ranger District map, published by the United States Forest Service (USFS), is essential for reaching Sowats Point and Indian Hollow Campground (Kanab Canyon to Thunder River trailheads), Saddle Mountain (Nankoweap trailhead), and Swamp Point (North Bass trailhead). Use the Kaibab National Forest, Tusayan District (USFS) map to reach the South Bass trailhead. The Kaibab National Forest Service map (USFS) should be available at neighbouring outdoor shops and petrol stations, at the North Kaibab ranger station in Fredonia, Arizona, or at the Tusayan ranger station in Tusayan, Arizona.

GETTING TO THE TRAILHEAD

On the South Rim, distant East Rim trailheads such as Grandview Point (Grandview Trail), Moran Point (New Hance Trail) and Lipan Point (Tanner Trail) can be reached by private car, taxi or tour bus. Shuttle buses serve Yaki Point (South Kaibab Trail). From spring through to autumn, you must take the West Rim Drive shuttle bus service to Hermits' Rest. During the rest of the year you can reach Hermits' Rest by private car, bus tours and taxi. From the Grand Canyon Lodge at the North Rim, a hikers' shuttle serves the North Kaibab car park.

CORRIDOR TRAILS

The three corridor trails – the North and South Kaibab and Bright Angel – make up the only maintained and patrolled trails in the canyon. They are linked by the Black Bridge and the Silver Suspension Bridge, which span the Colorado River near the Bright Angel campground and Phantom Ranch.

Wild camping is not allowed along the corridor trails. If you are planning to stay at Bright Angel campground (next to Phantom Ranch), Indian Garden or Cottonwood campground, you must have a backcountry permit. These heavily used corridor campsites, with water, toilets, telephones, buildings, and rangers in residence, detract from the wilderness experience of walking in the Grand Canyon.

FIRST-TIMERS ON CROSS-CANYON TRIPS

The National Park Service recommends that first-time walkers in the Grand Canyon use the corridor trails (North and South Kaibab and Bright Angel). One of the most popular walks from the South Rim descends the South Kaibab Trail to Bright Angel campground and Phantom Ranch and ascends back to the South Rim via Indian Garden on the Bright Angel Trail (South Kaibab to Bright Angel Trail). The South Kaibab is recommended for descending to Phantom Ranch because of its quick access and splendid ridge views. The longer but more gradual Bright Angel Trail eases your ascent back to Grand Canyon Village. There is no water on the South Kaibab Trail, but the Bright Angel Trail has year-round water sources. (See Chapter 6 for descriptions of South Rim rim-to-river trails.)

Popular trips from the North Rim descend the North Kaibab Trail to Phantom Ranch and Bright Angel campground, cross the Colorado River on one of the suspension bridges, and ascend on the Bright Angel Trail to Grand Canyon Village on the South Rim (North Kaibab to Bright Angel Trail). This cross-canyon venture is only possible from May to October, when the North Rim is open. May, September and October are the best months for this trip, as summer can be unbearably hot. Ironically, this overcrowded cross-canyon trip uses two of the canyon's least scenic and busiest trails.

Other overnight trips into the canyon from the North Rim Village descend to Cottonwood campground. A recommended layover day can include a trip to Ribbon Falls or, for the hardy, a walk all the way to the Colorado River. On the third day ascend back to the North Rim.

Although the National Park Service recommends that first-time walkers use the corridor trails, experienced walkers should be able to handle some non-maintained trails in the Grand Canyon. Try the Hermit to Bright Angel Loop, or the Grandview

to South Kaibab trails (see Chapter 10, Grand Canyon National Park, Long-distance Trails). A day-walk on any of the corridor trails tests your ability to handle one of these more difficult alternatives.

TRAIL CATEGORIES

Trails vary from the maintained corridor trails to rocky, slippery and steep non-maintained trails. In the early days, these trails were used by Indians to transport metal from mines; later, the white man guided tourists along them from the canyon rim to the river. Years ago the trails were used so little that they were faint and difficult to find; today, with more walkers in the remote areas of the Grand Canyon, these same trails are now maintained by the walkers who use them.

Each trail is classified according to the following criteria.

Rim Trail These easy, well signed and busy trails are on either the North or South Rim. There is little to no elevation change. These high-use trails may be paved or have wheelchair access.

Corridor Trail The corridor trails (Bright Angel, North and South Kaibab) are maintained, busy and patrolled backcountry trails, which make up the main cross-canyon trail system. Paths are wide, well signposted, and often have emergency telephones, water (North

Kaibab and Bright Angel trails only) and rangers in residence. These trails are recommended for walkers without previous Grand Canyon experience.

Wilderness Trail These unmaintained trails are not patrolled, and require route-finding, map and compass and scrambling skills. There is moderate exposure on wilderness trails and previous Grand Canyon-hiking experience is recommended.

Route These off-trail routes are indistinct, difficult to follow, require scrambling and may be obscured by brush. Extremely rugged terrain predominates. Ropes or other aids may be necessary and water may not be available. A high level of fitness, extensive Grand Canyon-walking experience and careful pre-trip planning is required.

WAYMARKING

Waymarking is excellent on the maintained corridor trails. On unmaintained trails in the primitive and threshold zones, signposts may be lacking and trails faded or non-existent.

WATER SOURCES

Except along corridor trails, water can be scarce to non-existent. In hot weather, carry a minimum of one gallon (four litres) or more of water per person per day. Primitive and wild zones are not recommended

54

during the summer, because of high temperatures and lack of reliable water sources.

On corridor trails, purified drinking water is available at Phantom Ranch, Bright Angel campground and Indian Garden all year. Seasonal water can be found from May to October at Cottonwood campground and Roaring Springs on the North Kaibab Trail, and at Mile-and-a-Half Resthouse and Three Mile Resthouse on the Bright Angel Trail. All other water, including that obtained from the Colorado River and Bright Angel Creek, must be purified.

Always ask the Backcountry Information Centre about available water sources. Usually reliable water sources can be dry, so pay attention to their advice. See table page 56.

SEARCH AND RESCUE

The corridor trails are the Grand Canyon's only patrolled trails. Most of the 400 rescues per year involve first-time canyon walkers on corridor trails. Over 1000 visitors each year are treated for heat-related illness, and many more incidents go unreported. Take a close look at the temperature charts towards the beginning of Chapter 4 before departing on your walk. Avoid the heat between 10am and 4pm and take advantage of shade. Carry one gallon (four litres) of water per day – more in the summer months. **Remember it takes twice as long to hike out of the canyon as it does to**

HOUSE RULES

1 Keep your feet off the furniture – archaeological sites are fragile.
2 Don't eat in the living room – no picnicking at or near archaeological sites.
3 No slumber parties – camping in ruins or sites is forbidden.
4 Don't touch the paintings – human oils damage pictographs.
5 Don't pee in the parlour – or any other site.
6 Don't go in if you're not invited – many sites are closed to visitors.
7 Don't rearrange the furniture or mess with the knick-knacks – leave everything as you found it.
8 Tell mum if you see anything wrong – contact a ranger if you see any violation of these rules.

hike into the canyon. Do not plan on being rescued, and travel prepared. If you *are* rescued, expect a large bill.

VISITING ARCHAEOLOGICAL SITES

As you explore the Grand Canyon, you may come across archaeological sites that are invaluable to the understanding of long-ago inhabitants of the Grand Canyon. **Vandalism or theft of park cultural or archaeological resources is a violation of federal law.** The house rules above are taken from national park literature.

TOUR AIRCRAFT

Intrusions into the quiet of the Grand Canyon occur mainly from tour aircraft, although flights below the rim were banned some years ago. The national park is working to try to limit tour flights and restore some of the canyon's natural peace.

RIVER-RUNNERS

You may share a beach with river-runners – private rafters have waited several years and paid high fees for the privilege of running the canyon. Commercial rafts vary from the huge, motor-powered 'banana boats' to quieter and smaller oar-powered boats. Many clients on these commercial trips are enjoying their first wilderness experience, and river-runners often share beer and food with hungry backpackers, and can sometimes provide emergency assistance. It is fun to stop and chat with these visitors – remember, you are all here for the same reason.

MULES

Mule trains will pass you on corridor trails, and large steps are built into these trails to minimise erosion from the hooves of the animals. Trails used by mules are dusty in summer, muddy in winter, and smelly all year

Year Round Water Sources
Grand Canyon National Park

Boucher Creek
Bright Angel Creek
Buck Farm Creek
Clear Creek
Colorado Creek
Crystal Creek
Dripping Springs
Garden Creek
Grapevine Creek
Hance Creek
Haunted Creek
Havasu Creek
Hermit Creek
Little Colorado River

Kanab Creek
Miner's (Page) Spring
Monument Creek
Nankoweap Creek
Olo Creek
Pipe Creek
Phantom Creek
Royal Arch Creek
Santa Maria Spring
Shinumo Creek
Tapeats Creek
Thunder River
Vasey's Paradise

long. When you see mules approaching, stand quietly on the uphill side of the trail, give them right of way, and obey the instructions of the lead rider.

INSECTS, BIRDS, REPTILES AND MAMMALS

Eagles and birds of prey frequent the canyon. Several species of rattlesnake call the Grand Canyon home – the rose colour of the pink rattlesnake, endemic to the Grand Canyon, may have been developed to help them blend in with the red canyon walls. Rattlesnakes rest in the shade under bushes or rocks to escape the midday heat, so do not place your hands or feet in places you cannot see, and be careful when stepping over boulders or trees.

Scorpions can enter your boots, clothes or sleeping bag, so shake out these items before using them. Be sure to wear shoes in camp and do not leave your boots outside your tent at night. Stinging red ants follow crumbs of food and irritating bites are common. Camp away from anthills and avoid leaving scraps of food around.

Rodents such as squirrels and mice may bite into packs. Protect packs by hanging them on overhead wires with their pockets open, or by using the metal boxes provided at corridor campgrounds. Over recent years these troublesome rodents have become increasingly bold, sometimes chewing through ropes from which

sacks of food are hanging. Never store, or sleep with, food inside your tent.

HEAT

Grand Canyon temperatures at the river in July average over 106°F (41°C), and at times temperatures peak as high as 120°F (48°C). Heat will increase as you descend, and generally it is 20°F or 30°F (11°C) warmer by the river than at the rim. There can be little to no shade, so in hot weather try walking early in the morning and in the early evening; rest in the shade during the hottest part of the day. Better yet, do not visit in summer. Spring and autumn bring fewer visitors and moderate temperatures.

OTHER GRAND CANYON DANGERS

You can be stabbed accidentally by the spines of yucca and cactus plants, and this can be painful.

There is a danger of flash floods in the canyon, especially in the late summer months when thunderclouds unleash intense storms miles away, leading to torrents of water rushing down side-canyons. Canyon bottoms should not be used as campsites during the flash-flood season from July to early September, but flash floods are known to occur at other times of year as well. Areas included in this book that are prone to flash-flood dangers are: Jumpup Canyon, Kanab Creek, the side-canyons to Bright Angel such as Phantom Canyon, and the creek beds along the Escalante route. (In September 1997 two people were killed in Phantom Creek near Phantom Ranch, and Bright Angel campground was evacuated due to concern about rising waters.)

USEFUL WEBSITES

www.nps.gov/grca
www.thecanyon.com
www.grand.canyon.national-park.com
www.kaibab.org
www.grandcanyon.com
www.americansouthwest.net/arizona/grand_canyon
www.grandcanyon.org
www.thegrandcanyon.com
www.airgrandcanyon.com
www.grandcanyon.org/fieldinstitute
www.grand.canyon.national-park.com

www.gcnpf.org
www.grand-canyon.com
www.arizonaguide.com

WARNING

The Grand Canyon has one of the harshest, most unforgiving environments in the world, and every year hikers die in its depths. Temperatures soar to extremes, water is scarce to non-existent, and even for experienced hikers the slippery, steep trails provide treacherous footing. Be careful when planning your trip, heed all warnings in this book, obey National Park Service rules and regulations, and use common sense. Always carry a map and compass and know how to use them, and do not expect the park service to rescue you. Be responsible for your own safety and you will enjoy the trip of a lifetime.

CHAPTER 6

GRAND CANYON NATIONAL PARK: SOUTH RIM, RIM-TO-RIVER TRAILS

The Grand Canyon seems a gigantic statement for even nature to make.

John Muir

Two maintained rim-to-river trails – the South Kaibab and Bright Angel trails – and six other unmaintained rim-to-river trails provide the major access from the South Rim into the Grand Canyon. These are described here from east to west, from the South Bass Trail to the Tanner Trail. The Grandview, not a true rim-to-river trail, provides poor access to the Colorado River, but Horseshoe Mesa, at the end of the Grandview Trail, makes a splendid destination for an overnight hike.

In order of increasing difficulty, the trails are: Bright Angel, Grandview, South Kaibab, Hermit, South Bass, Tanner, Boucher, and New Hance. The trails described are accessible and reasonable to walk all year *only if there are available water sources on the way.*

SOUTH RIM, RIM-TO-RIVER TRAILS				
Trail	Distance (miles) one way	Distance (km) one way	Rating	Difficulty
South Bass Trail	8.0	12.8	Wilderness	Strenuous
Boucher Trail	10.5	16.5	Wilderness	Ex. strenuous
Hermit Trail	8.9	14.2	Wilderness	Moderate
Bright Angel Trail	8.9	14.2	Corridor	Moderate
South Kaibab Trail	6.3	10.1	Corridor	Moderate
Grandview Trail	3.0	4.8	Wilderness	Moderate
New Hance Trail	8.0	12.8	Wilderness	Ex. Strenuous
Tanner Trail	9.0	14.4	Wilderness	Ex. Strenuous

The Hermit and Bright Angel trails, with perennial water sources, are described as 'all year' trails. If there is no water available along the way, summer trips on, for example, the South Kaibab Trail are not recommended. Time estimates vary widely depending on the direction travelled (ascent or descent), terrain, season, temperature, condition of the trail and the strength of the party.

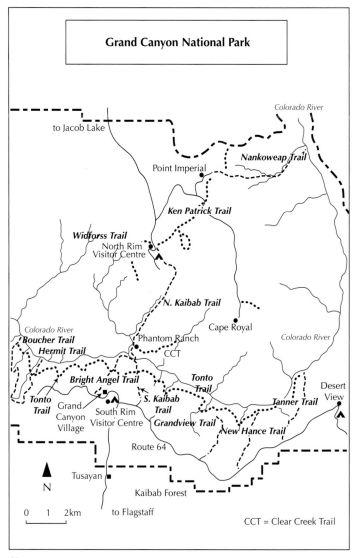

Grand Canyon National Park

Colorado River

to Jacob Lake

Nankoweap Trail

Point Imperial

Ken Patrick Trail

Widforss Trail

North Rim
Visitor Centre

N. Kaibab Trail

Cape Royal

Colorado River

Boucher Trail

Hermit Trail

Phantom Ranch
CCT

Colorado River

Bright Angel Trail

Tonto
Trail

Tonto
Trail

S. Kaibab
Trail

Grand
Canyon
Village

South Rim
Visitor Centre

Grandview Trail

New Hance Trail

Tanner Trail

Desert
View

Route 64

N

Tusayan

0   1   2km

Kaibab Forest

to Flagstaff

CCT = Clear Creek Trail

South Bass Trail

Start	South Bass trailhead at Bass Camp (6650ft/2027m)
End	Bass Rapids (2250ft/686m)
Distance, one way	8 miles (12.8km)
Times, one way	4–5hrs down, 5–7hrs up
Maps	Havasupai Point (United States Geological Survey 7.5'); Grand Canyon National Park (TI); Kaibab National Forest: Tusayan, Williams, and Chanlender Ranger Districts (United States Forest Service)
Season	Spring and autumn
Water	Colorado River
Rating	Strenuous

William Bass, best known for his tireless trail building in the 1880s, prospected the area around the South Bass Trail. Bass improved an original Indian trail and extended it to the river, in order to take tourists across the river to the north side.

The South Bass Trail starts at Bass Camp, 29 miles west of Grand Canyon Village on Rowe Well Road and 4 miles north of Pasture Wash Ranger Station on Forest Service Road FR328. The drive takes about 2–3hrs from Grand Canyon Village. You will find the Kaibab National Forest map indispensable. This unmaintained, rutted road can flood at any time of year – high clearance 4x4 vehicles are mandatory.

From West Rim Drive proceed 0.1 miles south of Bright Angel Lodge and turn left on to Rowe Well Road. If West Rim Drive is closed, drive from Bright Angel Lodge to Maswik Lodge and then to the Kennels. Take several right 90° turns to reach Rowe Well Road heading south. Or, from Tusayan, just south of Moqui Lodge, turn west on to FR328 and go west to Rowe Well Road.

Back on Rowe Well Road, the surface soon ends as you enter Kaibab National Forest. Follow this road across several railroad tracks. In 1 mile meet FR328 and turn right to Pasture Wash. Drive almost 16 miles from the FR328 intersection, enter the Indian Reservation and proceed for 1.8 miles. Turn right onto a poor dirt road to Pasture Wash. Exit the Indian Reservation and re-enter

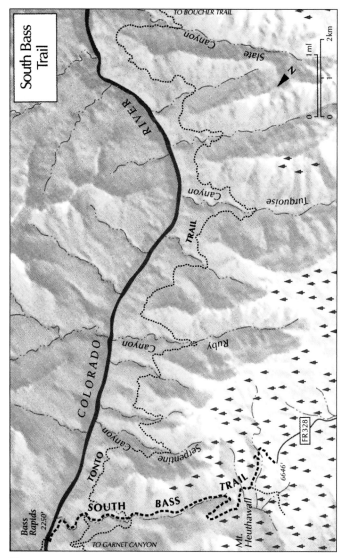

South Bass Trail

TO BOUCHER TRAIL

Slate Canyon

N

0 1 2km
0 1 1ml

Turquoise Canyon

TRAIL

COLORADO RIVER

Ruby Canyon

Serpentine Canyon

TONTO Canyon

SOUTH BASS TRAIL

Bass Rapids 2250'

Mt. Heuthawall 6646'

FR328

TO GARNET CANYON

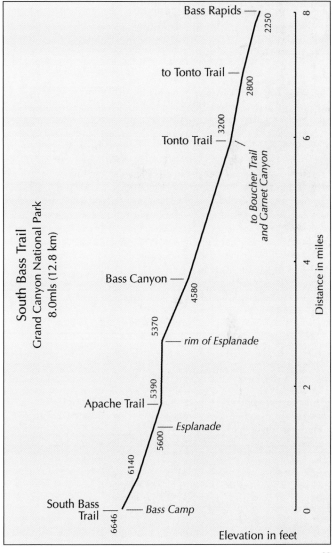

South Bass Trail
Grand Canyon National Park
8.0mls (12.8 km)

Bass Rapids — 2250

to Tonto Trail — 2800

Tonto Trail — 3200

to Boucher Trail
and Garnet Canyon

Bass Canyon — 4580

5370

rim of Esplanade

5390

Apache Trail — 5600

Esplanade

6140

South Bass
Trail — 6646

Bass Camp

Distance in miles

Elevation in feet

63

Kaibab National Forest and, as the road deteriorates even more, pass by the unstaffed Pasture Wash ranger station. The road continues 3.5 miles further to the South Bass trailhead. You can camp at the roadhead if you have obtained a backcountry permit for this use area.

Directions

From Bass Camp, head east through the Kaibab and Toroweap formation to reach an eastern drainage. Descend steeply through the Coconino Sandstone to the terraced Esplanade. The Apache Trail joins from the west, 1.5 miles from the start. Following the cairns, continue 1 mile north across the flat Esplanade to the east of Mt Huethawli. Turn south and descend steeply off the Esplanade through the Supai to the head of Bass Canyon. Next, double back through the Redwall.

Criss-crossing a wash, remain east of the Bass Canyon drainage and follow the bushy trail to the Tonto Trail junction. Drop down to a creek bed just before the Tonto Trail turn-offs. First the Tonto Trail branches west, and shortly another turn-off veers east. Another mile down the creek you cross another connecting trail that turns west to join the Tonto Trail. Continue down the creek bed to lower Bass Canyon. Pools of water can be found here in the spring. Nearer the river your route turns west from the drainage and reaches a cairn that marks your descent to a beach above Bass Rapids. The map shows a route that heads further west for 0.5 mile to a beach at the head of Shinumo Rapids. Both beaches are popular with river-runners.

Boucher Trail

Start	Hermit trailhead at Hermits' Rest (6640ft/2023m)
End	Boucher Rapids (2320ft/707m)
Distance, one way	Hermits' Rest to Boucher Rapids, 10.5 miles (16.9km)
Times, one way	6–8hrs down, 8–10hrs up
Maps	Grand Canyon (United States Geological Survey 7.5'); Grand Canyon National Park (TI); Grand Canyon National Park (EP)
Season	Autumn, winter and spring
Water	Dripping Springs, Boucher Creek and Boucher Rapids
Rating	Extremely strenuous

Colorado River canyon (Bright Angel Trail, Grand Canyon)

South Kaibab Trail, Grand Canyon

Ooh Ah Point on South Kaibab Trail (Grand Canyon)

View from Skeleton Point (South Kaibab Trail, Grand Canyon)

The Boucher Trail was originally named the Silver Bell Trail by its founder, Louis Boucher, who lived near the river along Boucher Creek. He built a cabin at Dripping Springs and prospected granite in the 1890s.

The Hermit Trail, which connects to the Boucher Trail, starts at the far west end of the Hermits' Rest car park, 9 miles along West Rim Road from Grand Canyon Village. Except in winter, shuttle buses go to Hermits' Rest, and the road is closed to private vehicles.

The Boucher Trail, one the canyon's steepest and grandest, starts 2.5 miles from Hermits' Rest along the Hermit Trail. The Boucher Trail itself measures 8 miles from its start near Dripping Springs to the Colorado River. If you start walking from Hermits' Rest and plan to go all the way to the Colorado River, you've got a long, 10.5 mile day ahead of you. The popularity of canyon-walking has changed a faint route into an obvious trail, but only experienced, sure-footed and fit walkers should attempt this trail.

Directions

To reach the Boucher trailhead, descend the Hermit Trail into the Hermit Basin, down the rocky steps for 1 mile until the Waldron Trail branches south. Continue straight ahead or west on the Hermit Trail and descend 0.5 miles more to reach the Dripping Springs Trail junction. Here the Hermit Trail bends north. Turn west on the Dripping Springs Trail and continue for 1 mile to the junction of the Boucher and Dripping Springs trails. This part of the trail passes high above Hermit Creek on a long and lovely traverse. An excellent 6 mile round-trip day-hike from Hermits' Rest goes to Dripping Springs.

The Boucher Trail officially starts from the Dripping Springs Trail junction. Dripping Springs, 300 vertical feet and 0.5 miles from this trail junction, is the only water source near the trail. Since the round trip to Dripping Springs will take you 45mins, you may wish to carry all the water you will need from the start.

From the start of the Boucher Trail, follow the Supai formation 2.5 miles to Yuma Point. Not for the acrophobic, this spectacular section merits special care in winter, due to ice. There is no true exposure, although some steep cliffs grace the eastern edges of the trail. You will find a fine, dry camping spot on Yuma Point, just where the trail circles around the point and turns southwest.

For the next mile, cross west around Yuma Point before you descend steeply on a very rocky trail through the Supai. Some short sections before Travertine Canyon require scrambling. The trail continues to the west of Travertine Canyon and ascends to Whites Butte, a fine but dry camping spot.

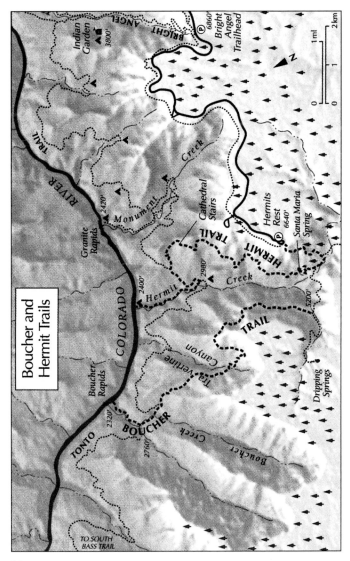

Boucher and Hermit Trails

BRIGHT ANGEL

Indian Garden

3800'

Bright Angel Trailhead

6860'

N

1 ml

1

0

2 km

0

RIVER TRAIL

2420'

Monument

Creek

Cathedral Stairs

Granite Rapids

HERMIT TRAIL

Hermits Rest

6640'

Santa Maria Spring

COLORADO

2400'

2980'

Creek

Hermit

5200'

TRAIL

BOUCHER

Boucher Rapids

Travertine Canyon

Dripping Springs

2320'

2760'

Boucher Creek

TONTO

TO SOUTH BASS TRAIL

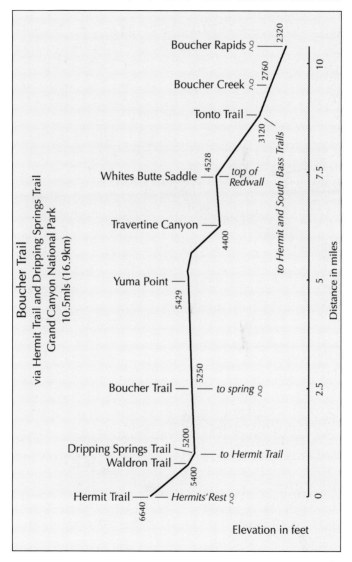

Boucher Trail
via Hermit Trail and Dripping Springs Trail
Grand Canyon National Park
10.5mls (16.9km)

Boucher Rapids ⚲ — 2320
Boucher Creek ⚲ — 2760
Tonto Trail —
3120
to Hermit and South Bass Trails
Whites Butte Saddle — 4528 *top of Redwall*
Travertine Canyon — 4400
Yuma Point — 5429
Boucher Trail — 5250 *to spring* ⚲
Dripping Springs Trail — 5200
Waldron Trail — *to Hermit Trail*
5400
Hermit Trail — *Hermits' Rest* ⚲
6640

Distance in miles

Elevation in feet

Pass west of Whites Butte and northwest of the saddle, and descend steeply through the loose Redwall scree for your last jarring descent to meet the Tonto Trail. From this junction, turn west and continue 0.3 miles to the camping area at Boucher Creek. Continue 1.5 miles further down rocky Boucher Creek to reach Boucher Rapids at the Colorado River.

Hermit Trail

Start	Hermit trailhead at Hermits' Rest, 6640ft (2023m)
End	Hermit Rapids, 2400ft (732m)
Distance, one way	8.9 miles (14.2km)
Times, one way	5–6hrs down, 6–7hrs up
Maps	Grand Canyon (United States Geological Survey 7.5'); Grand Canyon National Park (TI); Grand Canyon National Park (EP)
Season	All year
Water	Santa Maria Spring; Hermit Creek, Colorado River
Rating	Moderate

The Hermit Trail was originally constructed in 1896 and improved with cobblestone inlay in the early 1900s. It was extended in 1913 to bypass the tolls charged by Ralph Cameron on the Bright Angel Trail. The Santa Fe railroad built an overnight station at Hermit Camp. You will find remains of the camp, in spite of the National Park Service's plan to remove the partially torn down stone corrals and cabins.

Walkers with some canyon-walking under their boots on the Bright Angel or Kaibab trails often graduate to the Hermit Trail. The well-graded, wide and rocky, but heavily travelled Hermit Trail resembles a maintained trail, although rock slides on the path require scrambling in several sections. The Hermit, Tonto and Bright Angel trails connect into a popular overnight trip. Experienced walkers will enjoy the more remote Boucher to Hermit Loop.

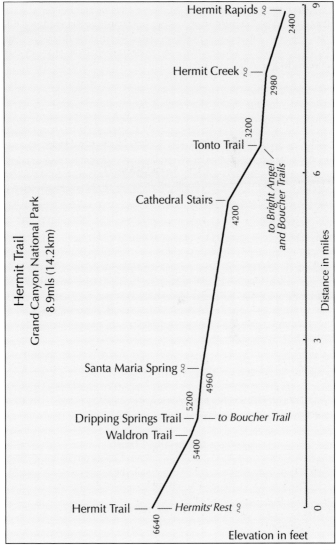

Hermit Rapids ⚲ —
2400

Hermit Creek ⚲ —
2980

3200
Tonto Trail —
to Bright Angel
and Boucher Trails

Cathedral Stairs —
4200

Hermit Trail
Grand Canyon National Park
8.9mls (14.2km)

Santa Maria Spring ⚲ —
4960
5200
Dripping Springs Trail — — to Boucher Trail
Waldron Trail —
5400

Hermit Trail — — Hermits' Rest ⚲
6640

Distance in miles
9
6
3
0

Elevation in feet

Directions

The Hermit Trail starts from Hermits' Rest, 9 miles west of Grand Canyon Village along the West Rim Road. Shuttle buses serve Hermits' Rest during the summer.

From the directional sign at the west end of the Hermits' Rest car park the trail switchbacks west down a rocky staircase to the Hermit Basin. Here the trail, constructed in cobblestone switchbacks known as White Zigzags, passes through the Coconino Sandstone. In a little over 1 mile, and a 1300ft drop, the Waldron Trail branches south. The Hermit Trail continues west and in 0.3 miles you reach the Dripping Springs and Hermit Trail junction at the head of the Hermit drainage.

Proceeding northeast from the junction, descend through the Supai over several long traverses to Santa Maria Spring, 2.5 miles from Hermits' Rest. This rewarding day-walk presents you with tremendous views down the Hermit drainage.

The 1913 shelter provides welcome shade and water during the summer. In autumn, check with the BIC regarding water at Santa Maria Spring – late in the year the amount of water available may be just a trickle. The Redwall Narrows of Hermit Creek are visible 1000ft below the spring. To the west you can see Yuma Point, Dripping Springs and the general route of the Boucher Trail.

Continue to descend further through the Supai to the top of Cathedral Stairs. Many boulders and rock slides block the trail in this section and you will have to scramble through piles of rocks. The trail remains easy to follow.

Next criss-cross through the Redwall on the switchbacks to Cathedral Stairs to below Cope Butte. The descent lessens as you reach the Tonto Trail junction. Turn west and go 1 mile to the designated campsites at Hermit Creek. South of the campsites, Hermit Creek merits exploration, with its pools, waterfalls and spring wildflowers.

Back on the Tonto Trail, a sign just before Hermit Creek campground directs you to a shortcut to Hermit Rapids. If you are lucky enough to have a reservation for Hermit Rapids, follow the creek bed north from Hermit Creek campground or from the Tonto Trail sign, around 1.5 miles to the Colorado River. The high waves of Hermit Rapids provide one of the canyon's best rides.

Bright Angel Trail

Start	Bright Angel trailhead at Kolb Studio (6860ft/2091m)
End	Silver Suspension Bridge at the Colorado River (2440ft/744m)

Distance, one way	8.9 miles (14.2km)
Times, one way	4–5hrs down, 5–7hrs up
Maps	Phantom Ranch, Grand Canyon (United States Geological Survey 7.5'); Grand Canyon National Park (TI); Grand Canyon National Park (EP)
Season	All year
Water	Indian Garden, Colorado River, Bright Angel camp ground (year round). Mile-and-a-Half Resthouse and Three Mile Resthouse (May to September only)
Rating	Moderate

Following the Bright Angel Fault, the Bright Angel Trail was originally used by Indians to reach the springs at Indian Garden. Indian pictographs can be seen on a rock face just above Two Mile Corner. Prospectors improved the original trail in the 1890s. It was previously known as the Cameron Trail, after its owner, Ralph Cameron. In 1903, when he started charging each visitor for usage, trails were built in other parts of the canyon to avoid the toll. In 1928 ownership of the trail passed to the National Park Service and it was renamed the Bright Angel Trail in 1937.

Well waymarked for its entire length, this popular trail provides the easiest access to the river from any point on the rim. Warning signs recommend the appropriate clothing and water requirements. Overcrowded with 10,000 people per year, the trail supports one of the main mule routes into the canyon. If you dislike crowds, look elsewhere either for a day-walk or overnight trip.

In the summer, with Inner Gorge temperatures hovering around 100°F (38°C), to walk the round trip from rim to river in one day is not recommended. When the temperatures are more moderate during other seasons of the year, an experienced and fit walker can complete the round trip. In this case your best route descends the South Kaibab Trail and ascends the Bright Angel Trail.

The majority of the 400 canyon rescues per year are for heat-related illnesses suffered on the Bright Angel Trail. Though it is the 'easiest' of rim-to-river trails, you still must be fit. Visitors who have underestimated the difficulty of climbing out of the canyon in scorching heat are prone to exhaustion and dehydration. On

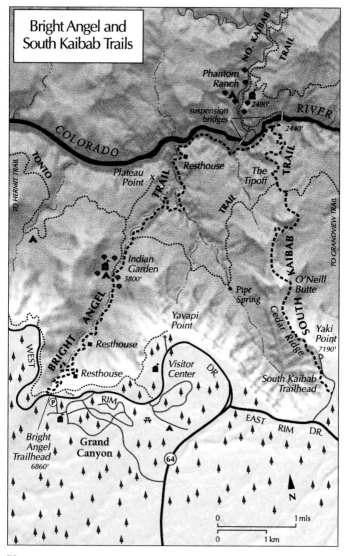

Bright Angel and
South Kaibab Trails

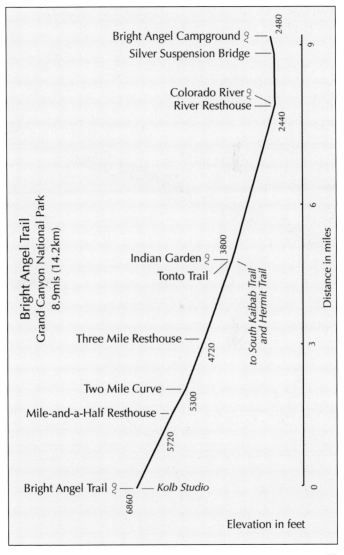

Bright Angel Trail
Grand Canyon National Park
8.9mls (14.2km)

2480

Bright Angel Campground ⚲ —
Silver Suspension Bridge —

9

Colorado River ⚲
River Resthouse —

2440

6

3800

Indian Garden ⚲
Tonto Trail

to South Kaibab Trail
and Hermit Trail

Three Mile Resthouse —

4720

3

Two Mile Curve —
Mile-and-a-Half Resthouse —

5300

5720

Bright Angel Trail ⚲ — — Kolb Studio

6860

0

Distance in miles

Elevation in feet

a day-walk in winter, be sure to carry warm clothing and adequate food and water.

Directions

From the trailhead west of the Kolb Studio and Bright Angel Lodge in Grand Canyon Village, the Bright Angel Trail begins its descent into the canyon with steep switchbacks. Dropping 3000ft for the first 3.1 miles, the trail follows Garden Creek until it meets Pipe Creek just past Indian Garden. From the start, you can't miss Indian Garden, with its lush green campsites shaded with cottonwood trees.

You pass shelters, One-and-a-Half Mile Resthouse and Three Mile Resthouse, built in the 1930s by the Civilian Conservation Corps, offering water from May to September, shade, and emergency telephones. Just after Three Mile Resthouse, the trail levels off until it reaches Indian Garden (camping, water, corrals, toilets, shade). An overnight stop at Indian Garden, 4.6 miles from the start, offers far from a wilderness experience. A 1.4 mile side-trail goes north from Indian Garden to Plateau Point, a fine day-hike from the rim, offering splendid views of the Inner Gorge.

If you are planning to take the Tonto Trail west towards Monument Creek, camp your first night at Horn Creek. If you plan to turn east on the Tonto Trail towards the Grandview Trail and Horseshoe Mesa, the South Kaibab Trail presents a more scenic and direct descent into the canyon.

From Indian Garden, the Bright Angel Trail descends north through the Tapeats Narrows until it reaches the Devil's Corkscrew. Here the trail switchbacks through the Vishnu Schist to reach the River Resthouse at Pipe Creek. Turn east on the River Trail for 1.5 miles to reach the Silver Suspension Bridge. Cross here for the fastest way to Bright Angel campground and Phantom Ranch. Continuing east on the River Trail, still south of the Colorado River, in 1 mile you meet the South Kaibab Trail at the Kaibab Suspension Bridge.

South Kaibab Trail

Start	South Kaibab trailhead near Yaki Point (7190ft/2192m)
End	Kaibab Suspension Bridge at the Colorado River (2440ft/744m)
Distance, one way	6.3 miles (10.1km)

Times, one way	3–5hrs down, 5–7hrs up
Maps	Phantom Ranch (United States Geological Survey 7.5'); Grand Canyon National Park (TI); Grand Canyon National Park (EP)
Season	Autumn, winter and spring
Water	Colorado River
Rating	Strenuous

Built by the National Park Service in 1924, the South Kaibab Trail soon became an alternative to the Bright Angel Trail. At that time a toll was charged on the neighbouring Bright Angel Trail, or Cameron Trail. To build the Kaibab Suspension Bridge that crosses the Colorado River at the bottom of the South Kaibab Trail, workers carried the gigantic steel cables from the rim to the river. In 1928 the National Park Service completed the cross-canyon system of trails known today as the corridor trails.

Since the South Kaibab Trail follows a ridge, rather than a depression between two ridges, it provides some of the finest Grand Canyon views. This wide, mule-travelled trail, easy to follow all the way to the Colorado River, makes a fine outing for either day-walkers or backpackers. Many day-walkers descend the short distance to Cedar Ridge. A more rewarding outing continues to Skeleton Point before the uphill return trip. You will meet mule trains ascending the South Kaibab Trail. Mules have the right of way – stand quietly on the uphill side of the trail and allow them to pass.

If you are walking cross-canyon from the North Kaibab Trail during the summer, consider ascending the Bright Angel rather than the South Kaibab trail. The Bright Angel Trail, though longer, ascends more gradually than the South Kaibab Trail and provides year round water sources not available on the South Kaibab Trail. During the cooler months of the year, you may wish to consider ascending the more scenic and less crowded South Kaibab rather than the Bright Angel Trail. If you do decide to ascend the South Kaibab Trail, leave before dawn and carry at least one gallon (four litres) of water per person.

Directions
After turning on to Yaki Point Road, 1.2 miles east of the junction of Hwy 64 and East Rim Drive, turn left into the trailhead car park. During the summer, shuttle

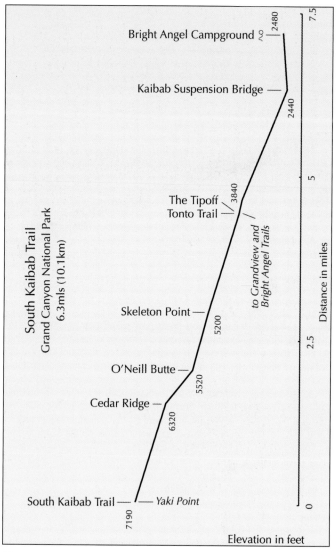

South Kaibab Trail
Grand Canyon National Park
6.3mls (10.1km)

Bright Angel Campground — 2480

Kaibab Suspension Bridge — 2440

The Tipoff
Tonto Trail — 3840

*to Grandview and
Bright Angel Trails*

Skeleton Point — 5200

O'Neill Butte — 5520

Cedar Ridge — 6320

South Kaibab Trail — *Yaki Point* 7190

Distance in miles

7.5

5

2.5

0

Elevation in feet

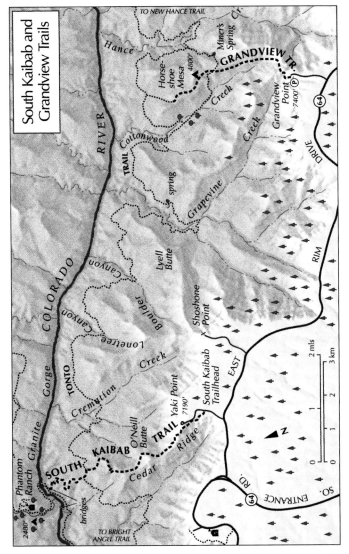

South Kaibab and Grandview Trails

TO NEW HANCE TRAIL

Hance

Miner's Spring Cr.

GRANDVIEW TR.

Horse-shoe Mesa 4600'

Creek

Grandview Point 7400' (P)

64

Cottonwood

spring

Grapevine

Creek

RIM

TRAIL

RIVER

COLORADO

Lyell Butte

Canyon

Boulder

Shoshone Point

Canyon

Loneetree

South Kaibab Trailhead

Creek

EAST

Cremation

Gorge

Granite

TONTO

O'Neill Butte

Yaki Point 7190'

KAIBAB

TRAIL

Ridge

N

SOUTH

Cedar

Phantom Ranch

2400'

bridges

TO BRIGHT ANGEL TRAIL

64

SO. ENTRANCE RD.

2 mls

3 km

buses from Grand Canyon Village serve the South Kaibab trailhead and Yaki Point. When the shuttle bus is not operating, a bus service links Bright Angel Lodge with Yaki Point. There is no private car access to the South Kaibab trailhead and Yaki Point.

From the South Kaibab trailhead, switchback down the wide trail 1.5 miles and 800 vertical feet through the Kaibab limestone, the Toroweap and the Coconino to reach the Hermit shale of Cedar Ridge. From Cedar Ridge you get fine views west towards Plateau Point, Pipe and Burro Spring on the Tonto Trail leading into Indian Garden from the east.

Descending east off Cedar Ridge through the Supai, you proceed along a lengthy 1 mile traverse with fantastic views east. You can see the Tonto Trail as it meanders east across the Tonto Platform, past Newton Butte and across Cremation Canyon. From here the Tonto Trail leads to Horseshoe Mesa and the Grandview Trail. Reaching Skeleton Point, you get fine views both towards the east and west Tonto platforms. You will also get your first fairly close-up view of the green oasis of Phantom Ranch and the Bright Angel campsite on the banks of the Colorado River below.

Next you begin a steep descent on switchbacks through the Redwall, and in 1 mile past Skeleton Point you arrive at the Tipoff. If you turn west from the Tipoff, you will pass Pipe Spring, a perennial water source, and in 4.6 miles reach Indian Garden. If you turn east along the Tonto Trail, a 2-day, 23 mile trip brings you to the Grandview Trail and Horseshoe Mesa.

From the Tipoff, the South Kaibab meanders north. After 10mins the descent angles steeply down into the Inner Gorge and you are rewarded with fine views of the river's suspension bridges. Bright Angel Creek and Phantom Ranch are soon obvious, along with the wide Colorado River below. After zigzagging through the Tapeats, you reach the Kaibab Suspension Bridge 2 miles from the Tipoff. Cross the Colorado River on the bridge and continue ahead to Phantom Ranch and Bright Angel campground.

Grandview Trail

Start	Grandview trailhead at Grandview Point (7400ft/2256m)
End	Horseshoe Mesa (4800ft/1463m)
Distance, one way	3 miles (4.8 km)
Times, one way	2hrs down, 3hrs up

Maps	Grandview Point, Cape Royal (United States Geological Survey 7.5'); Grand Canyon National Park (TI); Grand Canyon National Park (EP)
Season	Autumn, winter and spring
Water	None (Miner's/Page Spring off-route)
Rating	Moderate

In 1895 the Grandview Hotel offered horse trips into the canyon to visit the mines on Horseshoe Mesa. However, when the El Tovar Hotel was constructed across from the railroad station in 1902 in Grand Canyon Village, and easier access into the canyon became available, the Grandview Hotel quickly lost its attraction.

The copper mines of the Grandview area, especially the Last Chance Mine, were worked from the late 1800s until 1910. Burros were used to bring the ore to the rim. Relics of this historic area, such as wheelbarrows, nails and pots, still dot the canyon near the mines. The mines are considered unsafe to enter, due to danger of collapse and high levels of radon.

If this is your first overnight trip into the Grand Canyon, Horseshoe Mesa provides a spectacular introduction to canyon-walking. Superior views of the canyon greet you and side-canyon walls do not constrict your views. The Mesa offers expansive canyon views. Not a true rim-to-river trail, the Grandview is impractical if you wish to reach the Colorado River.

Horseshoe Mesa also makes a fine base camp trip, although you will probably have to make the 500ft descent east to Miner's (Page) Spring for water. A fine day-walk from Horseshoe Mesa descends east to Miner's Spring, joins the Tonto Trail, where it heads north and then west, traverses the north side of the mesa, and then returns to the mesa directly southwest on a 'route' (note – not a trail) up the front of the west wing of the mesa and past the Cave of the Domes. A longer outing passes Cottonwood Creek and dry O'Neill Spring and ends with a steep, crumbly ascent 500ft back up to your camp.

Directions
The Grandview Point road turns north from East Rim Drive, 9 miles east of the junction of East Rim Drive with Hwy 64. The Grandview Trail descends into the canyon from the north end of the car park.

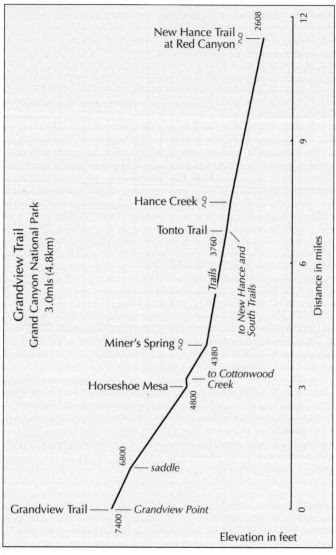

Grandview Trail
Grand Canyon National Park
3.0mls (4.8km)

New Hance Trail at Red Canyon — 2608

Hance Creek

Tonto Trail

Trails 3760

to New Hance and South Trails

Miner's Spring — 4380

to Cottonwood Creek

Horseshoe Mesa — 4800

6800 — saddle

Grandview Trail — Grandview Point

7400

Distance in miles

Elevation in feet

Several sections of steep wooden-braced steps and pavement characterise the top rocky steep section of the Grandview Trail. This first section is continually being improved. Unrestricted views of Horseshoe Mesa and across the Colorado River present themselves from this upper section. After 1 mile the trail crosses a saddle between Grapevine and Hance Canyon. Heading east for a short section, the trail flattens out but soon drops north, switchbacking at an even steeper angle. The descent becomes more gradual as the Supai is traversed all the way to the southern section of Horseshoe Mesa. The trail to Miner's (Page) Spring veers off to the east. If you are spending the night, continue north across the mesa for 5mins to the designated campsites near the abandoned building.

New Hance Trail

Start	New Hance Trailhead near Moran Point (7040ft/2133m)
End	Hance Rapids at Red Canyon (2608ft/795m)
Distance, one way	8 miles (12.8 km)
Times, one way	6–7hrs down, 8–9hrs up
Maps	Grandview Point, Cape Royal (United States Geological Survey 7.5′); Grand Canyon National Park (TI)
Water	Colorado River
Season	Autumn, winter and spring
Rating	Extremely strenuous

The Hance Trail has long been considered one of the Canyon's most difficult trails. The original Hance Trail, following an old Indian route, was built by John Hance around 1900 to accommodate the growing number of tourists wanting to reach the bottom of the canyon. Steep, slippery, rocky and torn with boulders, in the 1880s tourists were originally lowered down some sections on ropes. Today little remains of the original Hance Trail. After it washed away, the New Hance Trail was relocated to the east of the original trail, to its current location in Red Canyon. The New Hance Trail also has the reputation of being the most difficult of the South Rim rim-to-river trails.

Parking for the New Hance Trail is at Moran Point, 14.9 miles east of the junction of Hwy 64 and East Rim Drive. Walk 1 mile west from Moran Point along the rim

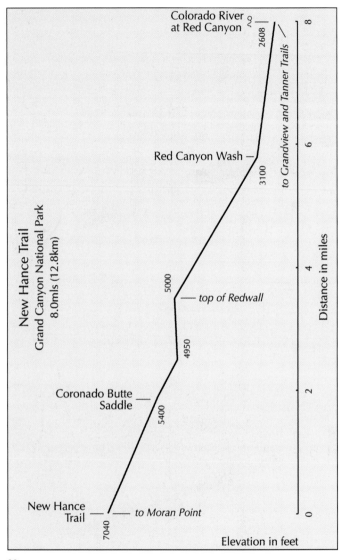

Colorado River
at Red Canyon

2608

to Grandview and Tanner Trails

Red Canyon Wash —

3100

New Hance Trail
Grand Canyon National Park
8.0mls (12.8km)

5000

— *top of Redwall*

4950

Coronado Butte
Saddle

5400

New Hance
Trail

— *to Moran Point*

7040

Distance in miles

Elevation in feet

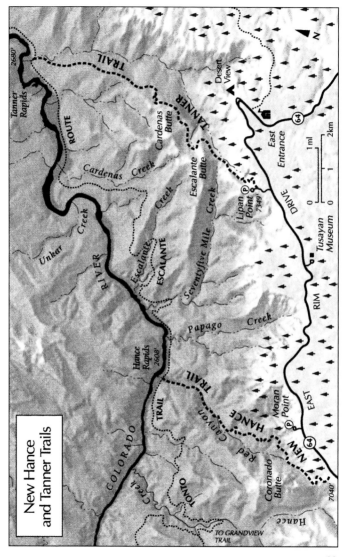

New Hance and Tanner Trails

to the trail sign for the New Hance Trail. If you are planning to link the New Hance Trail with other rim-to-river trails, it is always easier to descend rather than ascend the New Hance Trail.

Directions

From the trailhead immediately descend very steeply, switchbacking down the drainage east of Coronado Butte. Follow the trail as best you can through rocks and washouts. Coronado Butte rises on the west. This upper section may be covered by snow and ice during the winter. Once reaching Coronado Butte Saddle, the trail turns northeast and traverses the Hermit Shale, Sandstone and Supai, continuing up and down through several rocky draws. Be careful in this section, and visually locate the top of the Redwall and its large cairn.

Descend through the rocky and loose Redwall above two drainages and cross the Tonto Platform. Enter the eastern drainage, which flows southeast below Moran Point, and follow the creek all the way to Hance Rapids at the Colorado River.

Tanner Trail

Start	Tanner Trailhead at Lipan Point (7349ft/2240m)
End	Tanner Rapids (2680ft/819m)
Distance, one way	9 miles (14.4 km)
Times, one way	6–7hrs down, 8–9hrs up
Maps	Desert View (United States Geological Survey 7.5'); Grand Canyon National Park (TI)
Season	Autumn, winter and spring
Water	Colorado River
Rating	Extremely strenuous

The Tanner Trail, initially used by the early Indians in the 16th century, was maintained by the Spanish looking for gold. In the late 19th century, the Mormons improved the trail in order to mine copper along the Colorado River. In later years, horses stolen in Utah were herded down the northern slopes of the Colorado River on the Nankoweap Trail and forded across the river. After the brands had been changed, they were driven up the Tanner Trail and resold. The Tanner Trail became known as the Horsethief Trail.

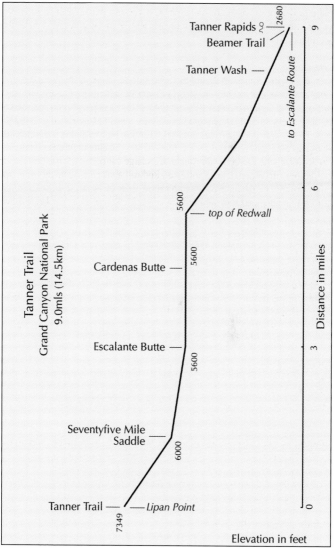

Tanner Rapids

Beamer Trail

Tanner Wash —

to Escalante Route

2680

5600 — top of Redwall

5600

Cardenas Butte —

Escalante Butte —

5600

Seventyfive Mile
Saddle

6000

Tanner Trail —— Lipan Point

7349

Tanner Trail
Grand Canyon National Park
9.0mls (14.5km)

Distance in miles

9

6

3

0

Elevation in feet

85

The Lipan Point car park can be found 20 miles east of the junction of Hwy 64 and East Rim Drive. The Tanner Trail begins 100yds east of the car park, near the information sign.

Directions

From the Tanner trailhead, follow the west side of Tanner Canyon for the entire route to the river. Descend very steeply down the initial series of switchbacks in and out of the trees to the base of Seventy-Five Mile Saddle, your first good camping spot. From the saddle, contour through the Supai Sandstone around the base of both Escalante and Cardenas Buttes for 3 miles. Fine camping spots exist here along the flat contour line.

Next the trail descends steeply again through the Redwall formation towards the bottom of Tanner Canyon. After 45mins of jarring descent, the trail veers northward for 1hr, remaining high along a low ridge on the west side of the creek. You are rewarded with fine views of the Unkar Delta and the Colorado River. The descent on the east side of the ridge continues for another hour through the Dox formation and becomes more gradual as you approach the canyon bottom. Continue through the Tanner Wash for 10mins to the river at the Tanner Rapids. Camping is prohibited in the high sand dunes at the river on either side of Tanner Wash.

If you have time for a day-hike, the Beamer Trail heads east up the river, contouring in and out of many drainages for 9.5 miles to meet the Little Colorado River and Marble Canyon.

CHAPTER 7

GRAND CANYON NATIONAL PARK: NORTH RIM, RIM-TO-RIVER TRAILS

*Some element of fear probably lies at the root
of every substantial challenge.*

Colin Fletcher, *The Man Who Walked Through Time*

North Rim Village, located 45 miles north of Jacob Lake, Arizona, on Hwy 67, hosts only 10% of the number of visitors to Grand Canyon Village on the South Rim. Several cool alternatives to unbearably hot Inner Canyon temperatures in summer are available for walkers. Paths wind through conifer forests, leading to views of faraway deserts and the Inner Canyon. Several viewpoints display the finest of Grand Canyon vistas.

While the South Rim trailheads into the Inner Canyon centre around Grand Canyon Village, North Rim trailheads, except for the North Kaibab, are accessed from remote entry points at the end of miles of dirt roads. These remote trailheads require lengthy drives over secondary or unpaved roads. In spite of the extra planning needed to reach these distant trailheads, these North Rim trails are well worth the effort. Advance planning, previous experience on South Rim unmaintained trails, knowledge of map and compass use and thoughtful judgement are absolute requirements before you attempt these trails.

As the North Rim is over 1000ft higher than the South Rim, the elevation gain and loss to the Colorado River are greater and the ascents and descents more severe than on the Canyon's south side. North rim-to-river trails, in order of increasing difficulty, are: North Kaibab, Thunder River, Bill Hall, Nankoweap and North Bass. Easily reached from the North Rim Road, north of the visitor centre,

NORTH RIM, RIM-TO-RIVER TRAILS				
Trail	Distance (miles) one way	Distance (km) one way	Rating	Difficulty
Thunder River Trail	16.0	25.6	Wilderness	Ex. Strenuous
Bill Hall Trail	12.0	19.2	Wilderness	Ex. Strenuous
North Bass Trail	13.5	21.6	Route	Ex. Strenuous
North Kaibab Trail	14.2	22.9	Corridor	Moderate
Nankoweap Trail	14.5	23.2	Wilderness	Ex. Strenuous

the North Kaibab Trail provides the North Rim's only maintained or corridor trail into the Inner Canyon.

Thunder River and Bill Hall trails, with Deer Creek Extension

Start	Thunder River trailhead at Indian Hollow (6380ft/1945m) or Bill Hall trailhead at Monument Point (7050ft/2148m)
End	Lower Tapeats at the Colorado River, 1980ft (603m)
Distance, one way	Thunder River Trail, 16 miles (25.6 km); Bill Hall Trail, 12 miles (19.2km)
Times, one way	8–10hrs down, 13–15hrs up
Maps	Tapeats Amphitheatre, Fishtail Mesa, Powell Plateau (United States Geological Survey 7.5'); Grand Canyon National Park (TI), Kaibab National Forest, North Kaibab Ranger District (United States Forest Service)
Season	Spring and autumn
Water	Thunder River, Tapeats Creek, Colorado River, Deer Creek, Deer Spring
Difficulty	Extremely strenuous

The upper portions of the Thunder River Trail were built by gold miners in 1876 and the final sections into Tapeats Creek were completed in 1926. The Bill Hall Trail was named after a ranger who was killed in an automobile accident while on the way to assist in another accident. Thunder River, one of the world's shortest rivers at only 0.5 miles long, and the world's only river to flow into a creek, terminates when it flows into Tapeats Creek.

To reach Indian Hollow campground from Jacob Lake, Arizona, take Hwy 67 for 26 miles to Forest Road FR422. Drive 18 miles west towards Dry Park to Forest Road FR425, turn west and drive 8 miles south to Forest Road FR232. Turn west and drive 5 miles to the end of the road to Indian Hollow. Forest Roads FR422 and FR425 are all-weather gravel roads. You may be able to negotiate Forest Road FR232 in a car, although high clearance 4x4 vehicles will almost certainly be necessary in spring.

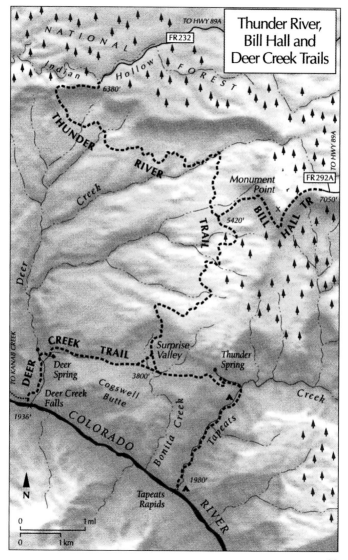

Thunder River, Bill Hall and Deer Creek Trails

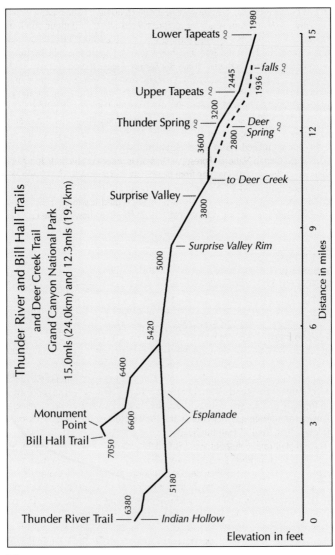

Thunder River and Bill Hall Trails
and Deer Creek Trail
Grand Canyon National Park
15.0mls (24.0km) and 12.3mls (19.7km)

Lower Tapeats ♀ — 1980

– falls ♀
1936

Upper Tapeats ♀ — 2445

Thunder Spring ♀ — 3200
3600

Deer Spring ♀
2800

to Deer Creek

Surprise Valley —
3800

Surprise Valley Rim
5000

5420

6400

Monument Point
6600

Bill Hall Trail
7050

Esplanade

5180

Thunder River Trail — Indian Hollow
6380

Distance in miles

Elevation in feet

Forest Road FR422 can also be accessed from Fredonia, Arizona. Drive 1 mile east on Hwy 89A and turn south on to Forest Road FR422. Continue south on Forest Road FR422 past Big Springs, turning west on Forest Road FR425 and west on Forest Road FR232. You'll find Indian Hollow campground 5 miles south of Fredonia and 17 miles southwest of the Big Springs ranger station.

To reach the Bill Hall trailhead, take Forest Road FR425 for 10 miles from Forest Road FR422 to FR292 at Crazy Jug Point. Continue west along the rim on Forest Road FR292A to the Bill Hall trailhead. Crazy Jug Point is accessible to passenger vehicles. Follow signs to Crazy Jug Point by turning right after 0.25 miles. At the four-way junction, 1.5 miles from Forest Road FR425, take the middle fork on to 292A and proceed 1.5 miles to the trailhead.

The North Kaibab National Forest (USFS) map is indispensable in helping you reach these trailheads. Driving time from Jacob Lake or Fredonia is approximately 1.5hrs. Check with the North Kaibab Ranger District in Jacob Lake or Fredonia to see if the roads are open. Alternative roads may be used if winter snows block Forest Road FR422. Roads close for the winter after the first snows in late October or November.

Directions

From the car park at Indian Hollow, the Thunder River Trail heads west for 0.5 miles on a long sweeping traverse along the rim to Little Saddle. The trail then descends abruptly through the Toroweap, Hermit and Coconino formations to reach the rolling Esplanade. You will see occasional signs for Forest Service (FS) Trail 23. Once the Esplanade is reached, the trail fades as it turns east. First you are in shrub but, as you continue east, the trail winds through red rock terraces, along the northern fingers of Deer Creek. Terraces just north of the trail provide rain protection if you are caught in a storm.

Approximately 4 miles from Indian Hollow, you reach the junction with the Bill Hall Trail as it descends from Monument Point. Collect water here for your return trip. Longer than the Bill Hall Trail, the Thunder River Trail descends into the canyon on a more gradual course and Indian Hollow trailhead lies almost 700ft lower than the Bill Hall trailhead.

The Bill Hall Trail, Forest Service (FS) Trail 95, drops 12 miles from Monument Point to the Colorado River. From the Monument Point car park, the trail ascends southwest to Millet Point and then descends to Monument Point. Heading directly south, it drops steeply through the Kaibab and Toroweap to a break in the ridge between Monument Point and Bridger's Knoll. Scrambling may be required on the initial exposed section. Turning west, the trail undulates for 0.5 miles below Monument Point, as fantastic canyon views open up. Then it turns and heads straight downhill for 0.75 miles through the Hermit to meet the Thunder River Trail.

From the junction with the Bill Hall Trail, the Thunder River Trail heads east across the Esplanade. Cairns mark your route to the rim of the Esplanade, where there are sweeping views of Surprise Valley and the South Rim. Next you descend through a break in the Redwall to Surprise Valley. Thunder River Trail heads east as it crosses through Surprise Valley to a viewpoint above Thunder River.

Now the trail descends via switchbacks to the east side of Thunder River, a dramatic sight as the powerful torrent drops steeply into the creek (spray provides a cold shower for anyone who wishes one). Camping is not allowed from the rim of Surprise Valley down the Thunder River drainage to Tapeats Creek.

Continue descending via several switchbacks to Upper Tapeats campground, just below the junction of Tapeats Creek and Thunder River. A 2 mile trail descends on the eastern side – or true left – of the creek to Lower Tapeats; the trail crosses the creek twice. Though it is possible to descend on the western side, a deep gorge blocks your passage and numerous scrambles and detours are necessary. Crossing Tapeats Creek may be impossible in the spring.

Back in Surprise Valley, another trail veers west to Deer Creek Valley. Dropping off the Surprise Valley Rim, the trail switchbacks down into Deer Valley, soon passing Deer Spring. At the valley bottom the trail descends, following the true left of the creek, passing several campsites before entering the narrows. A few cottonwood trees offer welcome shade. This exquisite location, an oasis in this desert environment, makes a superb spot for a layover day. Layovers can be spent visiting the narrows, swimming, exploring the springs, traversing over to above Bonita Creek or visiting the Colorado River and the waterfall at Deer Creek.

Entering the narrows, you traverse high above the gorge past some white Indian handprints and then descend a trail to meet the Colorado River at Deer Creek Falls. One of the most photographed spots in the canyon, the pool at the base of the waterfall invites swimming from boaters and backpackers alike.

After your drop off the rim, Deer Spring and Thunder River offer your first perennial water. Though this descent is often made in one long day, plan on collecting water for your climb out or carry extra water on the two-day ascent.

North Bass Trail

Start	North Bass trailhead at Swamp Point (7500ft/2236m)
End	Colorado River (2200 ft/670m)
Distance, one way	14 miles (22.5km)

Times, one way	9–11hrs down, 15–18hrs up
Maps	King Arthur Castle, Havasupai Point (United States Geological Survey 7.5'); Grand Canyon National Park (TI); Kaibab National Forest, North Kaibab Ranger District (United States Forest Service)
Season	Late spring and autumn
Water	Muav Saddle, Colorado River
Difficulty	Extremely strenuous

The North Bass Trail, or Shinumo Trail, built by Wallace Bass, helped assist with transporting tourists across the river via a cable from his South Bass Trail, and up to the North Rim. Today, walkers wanting to complete the strenuous cross-canyon trip have the difficult chore of hitching a ride across the river. Problems include making transportation arrangements to two very remote roadheads, not to mention descending or ascending the obscure and extremely difficult North Bass Trail. **Do not consider attempting this route unless at least one member of your party has walked the route previously.** All walkers should have extensive experience in the Grand Canyon.

The North Bass, one of the canyon's most strenuous descents, is really a route. Due to its indistinct nature, hiking this trail requires extensive Grand Canyon hiking experience to follow its challenging, brushy course. Only small segments of the original trail exist. If you choose to try, you'll be route-finding, talus and boulder-hopping, and needling your way through brush for the entire time. If you plan to do a round trip, stop to look uphill and visualise your route out.

High-clearance vehicles are recommended for the trip to the North Bass (Swamp Point) roadhead. From Jacob Lake, take Hwy 67 for 26.5 miles to Forest Road FR22 toward Dry Park. In 2 miles, at Forest Road FR270, turn west on Forest Road FR223. Proceed 7 miles and turn left on Forest Road FR268 towards Swamp Point and left on Forest Road FR268B. Continue 1.4 miles to the park boundary to road W4. From the park boundary on the deteriorating road, proceed 0.3 miles and bear west, passing a campground 8 miles from the boundary. In 0.1 miles you reach the Swamp Point trailhead, 16.5 miles from Hwy 67. Snow or fallen trees may block this road even in June.

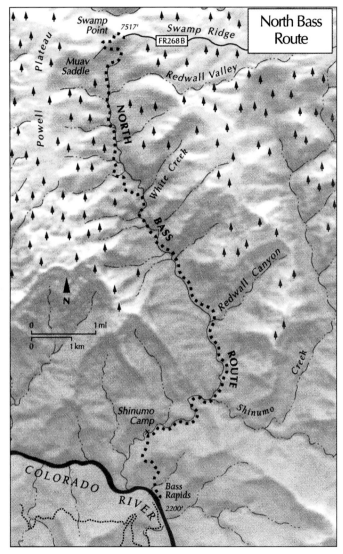

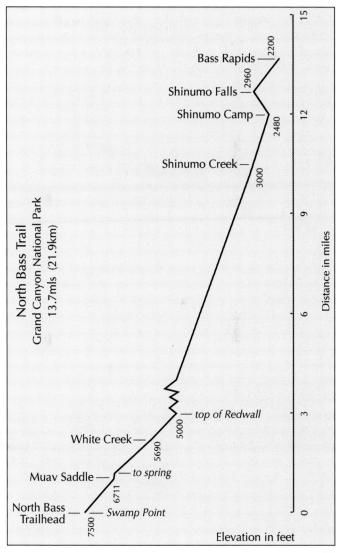

North Bass Trail
Grand Canyon National Park
13.7mls (21.9km)

Bass Rapids — 2200
Shinumo Falls — 2960
Shinumo Camp — 2480
Shinumo Creek — 3000
top of Redwall 5000
White Creek — 5690
Muav Saddle — to spring 6711
North Bass Trailhead — Swamp Point 7500

Distance in miles

Elevation in feet

Directions

From the Swamp Point trailhead, descend west on switchbacks to a trail junction on Muav Saddle. From the Muav Saddle to the river, you'll follow White and Shinumo creeks. At the first junction, take the left branch southeast through thickets and brush along the Coconino Sandstone. The right branches to the Muav Saddle cabin; the middle to Powell Plateau. You'll find a spring and another abandoned cabin 1.4 miles from the roadhead at White Creek, on the eastern side trail before the trail turns south.

Heading south at a cairn, descend extremely steeply on rocky sandstone through the Coconino and Hermit past your first pour-off. Switchback through the Esplanade. The route next descends the talus into the dry White Creek as you boulder-hop or bushwhack through the Supai. Continuing your creek descent, follow the wash as best you can over rocks and boulders and around obstacles, until around 2 miles from Muav Saddle you reach the top of the Redwall. Before you proceed further, locate the huge cairn marking the Redwall descent.

The trail now climbs east out of the drainage, descends briefly into another drainage, rises up again and drops into a second and finally a third drainage. Switchbacks drop through the Redwall to reach White Creek. Water flows intermittently now all the way to the Tapeats Narrows. Views spread out to the south into Muav Canyon and Shinumo Amphitheatre.

The route continues on the west side of the creek through the Muav sandstone. At the bench marker BM 4001 on the King Arthur Quadrangle you cross the east side of the creek and descend through the shale to bench marker BM 3480 and a cairned junction.

From here most walkers choose to descend the wash in and out of drainage through the Tapeats Narrows to below the junction of White and Shinumo creeks. You will encounter several pour-offs and down climbs. Reaching Shinumo Creek, you find several campsites.

Continuing downstream, you'll cross Shinumo Creek many times, pass by Bass's old cabin and camp and then join the well-trodden trail. From Shinumo Camp, the trail actually ascends Shinumo Creek to a wide saddle, where there are views of the Colorado River and Bass Rapids. At bench marker BM 2917 the now obvious trail descends to the river above Bass Rapids, a popular camping spot for river-runners and walkers. You'll want to rest for at least a day before returning to the rim, a task usually spread out over two days.

Grand Canyon in evening light

Sunset on Grand Canyon

Grand Canyon views

Grand View Trail (Grand Canyon)

On the Grand View Trail (Grand Canyon)

North Kaibab Trail

Start	North Kaibab trailhead (8241ft/2515m)
End	Bright Angel campground (2480ft/747m)
Distance, one way	14.2 miles (22.9km)
Times, one way	8–9hrs down, 7–9hrs up
Maps	Bright Angel Point, Phantom Ranch (United States Geological Survey 7.5'); Grand Canyon National Park (TI); Grand Canyon National Park (EP); Bright Angel Trail (EP)
Season	Summer through to autumn
Water	Supai Tunnel, Roaring Springs, Cottonwood Camp, Phantom Ranch, Bright Angel Campground, Colorado River
Difficulty	Moderate

Francois Matthes, a surveyor who pioneered the North Kaibab Route in 1902, one year later constructed a tourist camp at the mouth of Bright Angel Creek. His original route descended the shorter north arm of Bright Angel Creek. Today the North Kaibab Trail drops through Roaring Springs Canyon. The entire cross-canyon trail system, consisting of the North and South Kaibab trails and the Bright Angel Trail, was completed in 1928.

The North Kaibab Trail begins at the east end of the North Kaibab car park, 2 miles north of Grand Canyon Village and 11 miles south of the North Rim entrance station.

Directions
The well-maintained North Kaibab Trail descends from the North Rim, dropping all the way to the Colorado River. Mules share the hot, dusty and crowded trail for the first 4.7 miles to Roaring Springs. Following a creek bed rather than a ridge line, canyon walls and trees limit your views. The trail first switchbacks through the Toroweap and Coconino Sandstone, passing through the upper reaches of Roaring Springs Canyon. You reach the Coconino Overlook after 0.5 miles. Looking west you can make out the intersection of Bright Angel and Roaring Springs Canyon. Just below the Coconino Overlook, the trail switchbacks through

97

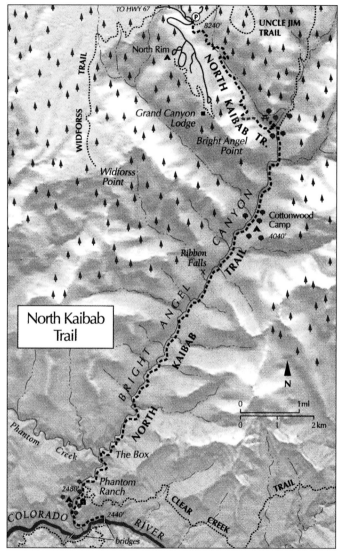

TO HWY 67

P
8240'

UNCLE JIM
TRAIL

North Rim

NORTH KAIBAB TR.

Grand Canyon
Lodge

Bright Angel
Point

WIDFORSS TRAIL

Widforss
Point

CANYON TRAIL

Cottonwood
Camp
4040'

Ribbon
Falls

BRIGHT ANGEL

**North Kaibab
Trail**

NORTH KAIBAB

N

0   1ml
0   1   2km

Phantom Creek

The Box

2480'

Phantom
Ranch

COLORADO   RIVER

2440'

bridges

CLEAR   CREEK

TRAIL

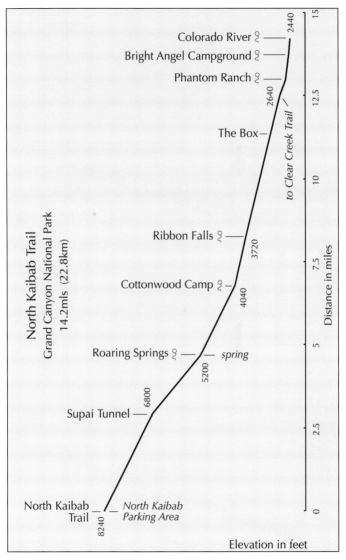

Colorado River   2440

Bright Angel Campground

Phantom Ranch   2640

to Clear Creek Trail

The Box

Ribbon Falls   3720

Cottonwood Camp   4040

Roaring Springs   5200   *spring*

Supai Tunnel   6800

North Kaibab Trail   8240   *North Kaibab Parking Area*

North Kaibab Trail
Grand Canyon National Park
14.2mls (22.8km)

Distance in miles

15   12.5   10   7.5   5   2.5   0

Elevation in feet

the Hermit Formation until it reaches the Supai Tunnel. The Supai Tunnel, built in the 1930s to replace the Old Bright Angel Trail, was blasted out of the rock in the 1930s by the California Conservation Corps.

In 0.5 miles you reach the Redwall Bridge, built after a 1966 flood wiped out this section of the trail. Crossing to the south side of the creek, the trail descends another 1.5 miles before it reaches the mouth of Bright Angel Canyon. From here the old overgrown Bright Angel Trail heads west back to the North Rim. A 0.25 mile side-trail leads to Roaring Springs, a popular day-hike destination. Cottonwood trees offer welcome shade above several picnic tables.

The trail follows Bright Angel Creek all the way to the Colorado River. The trail turns south on a moderate to easy grade 0.5 miles beyond the junction of the North Kaibab and Bright Angel Creek and across the bridge. The building here houses the caretaker who maintains the water supply for the North Rim. After 2 miles you come to Cottonwood campground, the first designated campsite on the North Kaibab Trail. In summer you'll find purified water and a ranger in residence. Water taken from Bright Angel Creek should be purified.

After Cottonwood camp the trail descends gradually for 7 miles and 1500ft to the Colorado River. Your first 1.8 miles brings you to the turn-off to Ribbon Falls, a spectacular 100ft high waterfall. The waterfall creates a perfect spot for a shower, an oasis in the otherwise dry and dusty descent. Continuing from Ribbon Falls, the canyon walls slowly narrow. Here several cacti and one non-native palm tree grow, while the overall vegetation appears typical of a desert. Passing next through the narrow canyon walls of the Box, you'll soon pass the Clear Creek trailhead veering east. Finally, you arrive at Phantom Ranch and, soon, Bright Angel campground.

For most times of the year, Phantom Ranch must be reserved almost a year in advance; meals are available to walkers by reservation only. Reserve Bright Angel campground several months ahead through the BIC. From the campground, a short stroll brings you to both the Kaibab and Silver suspension bridges. Crossing the Colorado River, these two bridges link up with the South Kaibab and Bright Angel (River) trails. After a 4500ft climb you arrive at Grand Canyon Village on the South Rim.

See Chapter 5 for more detailed information on the corridor trails, backcountry reservation procedures and specifics on hiking regulations.

Nankoweap Trail

Start	Nankoweap trailhead at FS 610 (8800ft/1365m); Nankoweap trailhead at FS445 at Saddle Mountain (6455ft/1967m)
End	Colorado River (2802ft/841m)
Distance, one way	14.5 miles (23.2km) from FR610 or FR445
Times, one way	10–12hrs down, 15–17hrs up
Map	Point Imperial, Nankoweap Mesa (United States Geological Survey 7.5'); Grand Canyon National Park (TI); Kaibab National Forest (United States Forest Service)
Season	Late spring and autumn
Water	Nankoweap Creek, Colorado River
Difficulty	Extremely strenuous

Take Arizona Hwy 67 south from Jacob Lake, 26 miles to westbound Forest Road FR22 at De Motte Park, 1 mile south of Kaibab Lodge. Turn east and go 200yds to Forest Road FR611. Proceed 1.2 miles to Forest Road FR610. Bear right 13.5 miles to the Saddle Mountain trailhead. If accessed via Forest Road FR610, the Nankoweap Trail follows brushy Forest Service Trail 57 for 3.4 miles to the National Park Service trailhead. From this trailhead you negotiate 11 rocky, exposed and slippery miles as you descend 5000 vertical feet to the Colorado River.

Another way to access the Nankoweap Trail is via Hwy 89A east of Jacob Lake to Forest Road FR810. Go south on FR810 to Forest Road FR445, which takes you to the other Saddle Mountain trailhead. If you join from the north via Forest Road FR445, follow Forest Service Trail 57 for 3 mlesi heading south to the National Park Service trailhead.

Directions
From the rim, the Nankoweap drops below Saddle Mountain through the Supai and contours to the east a little over 3 miles to Tilted Mesa. The exposed trail narrows to several feet with drop-offs of 100ft. The Redwall is reached west of Tilted Mesa on a narrow, flat promenade above Nankoweap and Little Nankoweap canyons.

Descending through the steep Redwall, you needle your way through layers of scree and talus as you descend further through the limestone and shale formations. Pick your way through the rubble to the perennial water of Nankoweap Creek. Follow the creek bed downstream for 3 miles to the Colorado River.

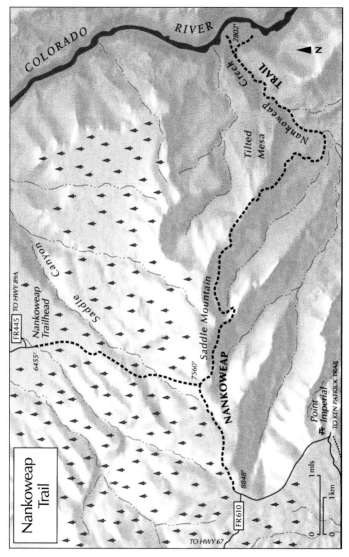

COLORADO RIVER

2802'

Creek

Nankoweap TRAIL

Tilted Mesa

Nankoweap Canyon

Saddle

Saddle Mountain

FR445 TO HWY 89A

Nankoweap Trailhead

6455'

7560'

NANKOWEAP

Point Imperial

TO KEN PATRICK TRAIL

8848'

FR 610

TO HWY 67

1 mls

1 km

Nankoweap Trail

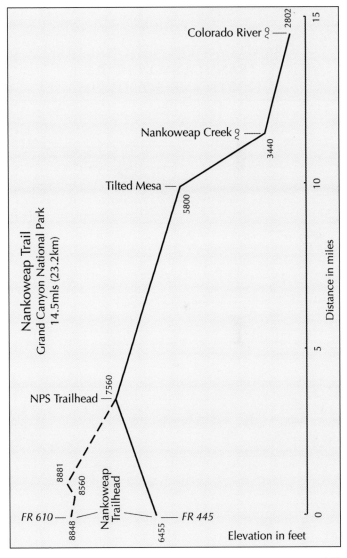

Nankoweap Trail
Grand Canyon National Park
14.5mls (23.2km)

Colorado River ♀ — 2802

Nankoweap Creek ♀ — 3440

Tilted Mesa — 5800

NPS Trailhead — 7560

8881

8560

FR 610 — 8848

Nankoweap Trailhead

FR 445 — 6455

Distance in miles

Elevation in feet

103

CHAPTER 8

GRAND CANYON NATIONAL PARK: TRANS-CANYON TRAILS, NORTH AND SOUTH RIM

...if you are pleased to see a stream running pure, glorifying a natural pavement;
if you are content to enjoy a river shore, leaving its design undisturbed;
if you think a wilderness river should be left dancing, alive and bringing life;
if you have come, even a little, under the spell of this place,
then this canyon we have seen only a little of
this Grand Canyon, is your Grand Canyon.

Roderick Nash and Ernest Braun

The Tonto Trail, the major east–west artery on the southern side of the Colorado River, sweeps an odd 85 or more miles between Red Canyon at Hance Rapids and Bass Canyon. Although not officially part of the Tonto Trail, the 15 mile Escalante Route between Tanner Canyon and Red Canyon adds additional miles to the walker's trans-canyon options.

Not usually walked in its entirety, the Tonto Trail opens up miles of canyon-walking between several convenient access points. Although appearing flat initially, walking the Tonto Trail involves crossing in and out of numerous drainages that indent into the Tonto Platform from the Colorado River. This creates some steep sections as you dip into creek beds and ascend the opposite side. The Tonto Trail supports gorgeous views from all of its sections.

The Tonto Trail which lies between Red Canyon and Bass Canyon is described here, along with the Escalante Route in the east-to-west direction. The section of the Tonto Trail between Garnet Canyon and Bass Canyon is not described here. The Clear Creek Trail, north of the Colorado River, is described from west to east.

Since both the Tonto and Clear Creek trails undulate with little change in elevation, travel on these trails rates as moderate. However, remember that many of the access rim-to-river trails that are connected together by the Tonto Trail merit strenuous or extremely strenuous ratings. The meandering of the Escalante Route is sometimes less than obvious – cairns mark the way in several places. However, use of the route over recent years has shaped it into a more obvious trail.

South Rim Trans-Canyon Trails

SOUTH RIM, TRANS-CANYON TRAILS				
Trail	Distance (miles) one way	Distance (km) one way	Rating	Difficulty
Escalante Route: Tanner Canyon to New Hance Trail at Red Canyon	12.0	19.2	Route	Ex. Strenuous
Tonto Trail: New Hance Trail at Red Canyon to Hance Creek	6.4	10.2	Wilderness	Moderate
Tonto Trail: Hance Creek to Cottonwood Creek	5.0	8.0	Wilderness	Moderate
Tonto Trail: Cottonwood Creek to South Kaibab Trail	20.2	32.3	Wilderness	Strenuous
Tonto Trail: South Kaibab Trail to Indian Garden	4.1	6.6	Wilderness	Moderate
Tonto Trail: Indian Garden to Hermit Creek	14.5	23.2	Wilderness	Moderate
Tonto Trail: Hermit Creek to Boucher Creek	6.3	10.1	Wilderness	Moderate
Tonto Trail: Boucher Creek to Bass Canyon	30.0	48.0	Wilderness	Strenuous

Escalante Route: Tanner Canyon to New Hance Trail at Red Canyon

Start	Tanner Rapids (2680ft/817m)
End	New Hance Trail at Red Canyon (2608ft/795m)
Distance, one way	12 miles (19.2km)
Times, one way	10–12hrs

Maps	Cape Royal, Desert View (United States Geological Survey 7.5′); Grand Canyon National Park (TI)
Season	Spring and autumn
Water	Tanner Rapids, Unkar Delta, Escalante Creek, Seventy-Five Mile Creek, Papago Creek, Hance Rapids
Rating	Extremely strenuous

Directions

Head west from Tanner Rapids along the Colorado River on the sandy river-runners' trail that initially veers south, away from the river. Your path undulates over some buttes and up some wooden steps. In less than 1hr, your route crosses Cardenas Creek. Reaching Unkar Peninsula, you'll want to refill your water bottles – this is your last water until Escalante Creek.

Cross Unkar Peninsula and contour around the north and then west side of the butte that overlooks Unkar Delta. A short detour brings you to the top of the butte, which affords excellent views of the delta. Another detour further west to the canyon edge brings you to a thrilling overlook of Unkar Rapids.

Turn south and head upwards. Gaining elevation gradually over the next 1.5 miles, you rise to the end of an unnamed drainage west of Cardenas Creek. Cairns mark your route. Cross the drainage and turn northwest, gaining a steep 400ft of elevation as you cross around the east side of Butchart's Ridge. Gorgeous eastern views of the Colorado River, Unkar Delta and Tanner Rapids fill the skyline. You'll find a wonderful lunch stop, with sweeping views, at the point where the trail circles around the north end of the ridge. After your rest stop, the trail turns south and contours around the west side of the notch.

The National Park Service description of this route presents an alternative that passes directly west through Butchart's Notch. From the west side, the Butchart's Notch Route looks like quite a rocky scramble down back to the trail. Though Constance passed through here twice, she stayed low both times. This straightforward route presents no unusual challenges.

Back on the trail on the west of the Notch, you're now travelling southwest towards Escalante Creek. Cross over the east arm of Escalante Creek, continue west up the hill and descend into the west arm of Escalante Creek. Follow the rocky trail into the creek bed and head north down the creek. When you get to the 20ft drop-off, backtrack 20ft and follow the cairns west and north above the drainage. Descend into the drainage and, in 20mins, reach a fine camping spot at the Colorado River.

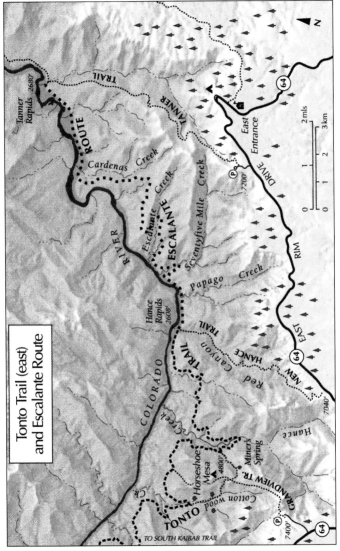

Tonto Trail (east)
and Escalante Route

Tanner Rapids 2600'
TANNER TRAIL
ROUTE
Cardenas Creek
Escalante Creek
Seventyfive Mile Creek
ESCALANTE
Papago Creek
RIVER
Hance Rapids 2608'
COLORADO
Red Canyon
NEW HANCE TRAIL
TRAIL
Hance
Miner's Spring
Horseshoe Mesa 4800'
Cottonwood
Cr
TONTO
GRANDVIEW TR.
TO SOUTH KAIBAB TRAIL

East Entrance
DRIVE
RIM
EAST
64
64
64

N

2 mls
3 km

7200'
7040'
7400'

Follow the cairns southwest and along the river until you are above Seventy-Five Mile Creek. Turn south and traverse above the creek for about 15mins until the cairns lead into the creek bed. Descend into the creek. A 20ft slide down a rocky ledge drops you into the drainage; you may want to lower your packs. If a pool of water lurks in the creek, this short climb may be difficult to negotiate in the west-to-east direction. Proceed down the drainage, lowering your packs in several spots if necessary, to Nevills Rapids at Seventy-Five Mile Creek.

Next, you may proceed west along the river if the water level is low. A rocky trail leads above the river west for 1 mile to Papago Creek. A chute that needs some scrambling goes down to the beach. Papago Creek offers poor camping choices.

West of Papago Creek, a steep 50ft high outcrop requires both hands to negotiate. You may wish to raise your packs up with some rope. Follow the cairns that mark the trail south and up another steep 300ft section, which winds in and out around large rocks. Finally, pass through a break in the rocks. Turn north and descend a steep and loose talus slope to the river, taking care not to dislodge rocks on to walkers below. Another 30mins along the river through the brush brings you to the New Hance Trail at Red Canyon. You'll find a fine camping spot located west of Red Canyon Wash under some trees, a bit back from the river.

Tonto Trail: New Hance Trail at Red Canyon to Hance Creek

Start	New Hance Trail at Red Canyon (2608ft/795m)
End	Hance Creek (3670ft/1119m)
Distance	6.4 miles (10.2km)
Times, one way	3–4hrs
Maps	Cape Royal (United States Geological Survey 7.5'); Grand Canyon National Park (TI)
Season	Spring, winter and autumn
Water	Hance Rapids, Hance Creek
Rating	Moderate

Directions

From Hance Rapids, at the foot of Red Canyon and the New Hance Trail, proceed west along the river for 20mins. The rocky trail takes off above the river and heads east before it turns south. Follow the cairns next as you turn south along the edge of Mineral Canyon. After 30mins, turn west and cross Mineral Canyon at Shady Overhang. This spot offers some shade for a rest stop or lunch. Climb up to the Tonto Platform and continue south to the head of Hance Creek, where you'll find perennial water. Miner's (Page) Spring, 30mins west, another perennial water source, offers a handy water source if you are ascending to the dry Horseshoe Mesa.

Tonto Trail: Hance Creek to Cottonwood Creek

Start	Hance Creek (3670ft/1119m)
End	Cottonwood Canyon (3680ft/1122m)
Distance	5 miles (8km)
Times, one way	2–3hrs
Maps	Cape Royal (United States Geological Survey 7.5'); Grand Canyon National Park (TI)
Season	Spring, winter and autumn
Water	Hance Creek
Rating	Moderate

Directions
Continue north on the west side of Hance Creek along the Tonto Trail. In 0.5 miles you pass the turn-off, east, up to Horseshoe Mesa and Miner's Spring. The Tonto Trail contours north around the base of Horseshoe Mesa. About 2 miles along, the Cave of the Domes Trail switchbacks south up the north side of the Mesa and links up with the Grandview Trail. Another 1 mile farther on you come to Cottonwood Canyon, where the Tonto Trail continues west towards Grapevine Canyon and the South Kaibab Trail. Camp here in the springtime at Cottonwood Creek, or along the creek bed. Another trail heads south up the west arm of Horseshoe Mesa.

Tonto Trail: Cottonwood Creek to South Kaibab Trail

Start	Cottonwood Creek (3680ft/1122m)
End	South Kaibab Trail at the Tipoff (3840ft/1170m)
Distance, one way	20.2 miles (32.3km)
Times, one way	10–13hrs
Maps	Phantom Ranch, Cape Royal (United States Geological Survey 7.5'); Grand Canyon National Park (TI)
Season	Spring, winter and autumn

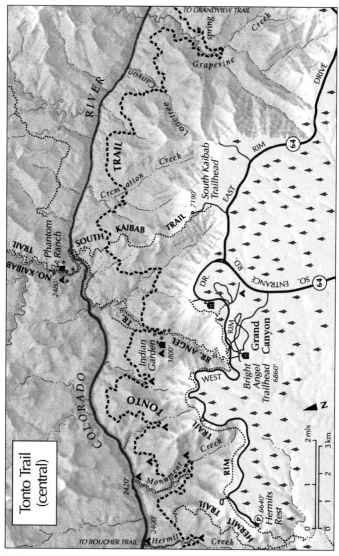

Tonto Trail
(central)

Water	Grapevine Canyon
Rating	Moderate

Directions

From Cottonwood Creek, the Tonto Trail winds 3.5 miles to Grapevine Creek. From the junction of the Cottonwood Creek Trail and the Tonto Trail, turn west and head north above Cottonwood Creek. Some fine campsites line the creek bed. Traverse around Mesa 3928 until you meet the imposing Grapevine Canyon. Stupendous views of the chasm greet you. Grapevine Canyon is the longest tributary drainage along the Tonto Plateau. Thus, the walk from one side to the other can be long and tedious in the heat. The trail skirts the southeast arm of Grapevine Creek before crossing the creek and heading northwest up the opposite side.

Grapevine Creek, supporting the only perennial water source along this section of the Tonto Trail, makes a great spot for a layover day. In spring, large pools of water invite swimmers, and cottonwood trees offer well-deserved shade.

From Grapevine Creek, now on the west side of the long arm of the creek, head north around the north side of Lyell Butte 5.8 miles to Boulder Creek, your next seasonal water source, often dry in early spring.

Lonetree Canyon, 2.8 miles further, marks your next seasonal water source and offers some shade. A further 3 miles along the Tonto Trail, you'll reach the south arm of Cremation Canyon. The first and third arms of Cremation Canyon offer the best dry camping spots. From the west arm of Cremation Canyon it's 1.5 miles along to the South Kaibab Trail at the Tipoff. Half a mile from the west arm, a large rock offers the only shade and protected camping spot. Spectacular views to the north grace this long section of the Tonto Trail. You can see Clear Creek Canyon, Zoroaster Temple, Sumner Butte, Bradley Point and, in the far distance, Bright Angel Canyon. The next perennial water flows from Pipe Spring, 1. 5miles west of the Tipoff.

Tonto Trail: South Kaibab Trail to Indian Garden

Start	South Kaibab Trail at the Tipoff (3840ft/1170m)
End	Indian Garden (3800ft/1158m)
Distance, one way	4.1 miles (6.6km)
Times, one way	2hrs
Maps	Grand Canyon, Phantom Ranch (United States

	Geological Survey 7.5'); Grand Canyon National Park (TI)
Season	All year
Water	Pipe Spring, Indian Garden
Rating	Moderate

Directions

A small sign at the Tipoff, where there is an emergency telephone and a toilet, marks the intersection of the Tonto Trail with the South Kaibab Trail. Fifteen minutes from the Tipoff, you get an overhead look at Phantom Ranch and Bright Angel Creek. Burro Spring, located 30mins further along, may be heard gurgling from the reeds just south of the trail. At about the halfway point, you cross Pipe Creek and its perennial spring. Winding your way west, you pass several small springs, which may be dry in autumn. Plateau Point juts out into your view farther west. Soon you greet civilisation at Indian Garden, with its buildings, campground, picnic tables, corral, toilets, and water.

Tonto Trail: Indian Garden to Hermit Creek

Start	Bright Angel Trail at Indian Garden (3800ft/ 1158m)
End	Hermit Creek (2960ft /902m)
Distance, one way	14.5 miles (23.2km)
Times, one way	7hrs
Maps	Grand Canyon (United States Geological Survey 7.5'); Grand Canyon National Park (TI)
Season	All year
Water	Hermit Creek, Monument Creek, Indian Garden
Rating	Moderate

Directions

From Indian Garden, continue west on the Tonto Trail. Passing the turn-off to Plateau Point, circle north of the Battleship to reach Horn Creek. Plan on carrying water if you've reserved a camping spot at Horn Creek, Salt Creek or Cedar

Camp. Cross north around Dana Butte to reach the campsite at Salt Creek. Continuing west, crossing around Point 3461 through the Inferno, you come to Cedar Spring, just north of the Alligator. One mile further on you reach Monument Creek. At the head of Monument Creek rises the magnificent spire of Tapeats Sandstone, after which the creek bed is named.

A trail, not on the United States Geological Survey maps, leads downhill 1 mile to Granite Rapids, where there are fine campsites all along the beach. On the eastern edge of the beach, splindly mesquites shield a splendid camp spot. Fine swimming can be found in the upper east wing of Monument Creek.

From Monument Creek, cross north of Cope Butte through two saddles to reach the junction of the Tonto Trail with the Hermit Trail. The Hermit Trail heads south and up to the rim past Cathedral Stairs and Santa Maria Spring.

One mile farther west on the Tonto Trail brings you to the campsites at Hermit Creek. Food should be protected from rodents by hanging packs from the overhead bars. The entire creek bed, especially south, makes for fine exploration, with sculptured walls, rushing water and swimming pools. From here a 1hr, 600ft descent north down the rocky creek bed brings you to Hermit Rapids, a highly recommended overnight destination, and more scenic than Hermit Camp.

Tonto Trail: Hermit Creek to Boucher Creek

Start	Hermit Creek (2980ft/908m)
End	Boucher Creek at Boucher Canyon (2760ft/841m)
Distance, one way	6.3 miles (10.1km)
Times, one way	3–4hrs
Maps	Grand Canyon (United States Geological Survey 7.5'); Grand Canyon National Park (TI)
Season	All year
Water	Boucher Creek, Hermit Creek
Rating	Moderate

Directions

Heading west again, you pass on the west slope of Hermit Creek, curving around the point that separates Travertine Canyon and Hermit Creek. Here you gain fine views of the Inner Gorge and back to Hermit Creek. Above you lurk the points of

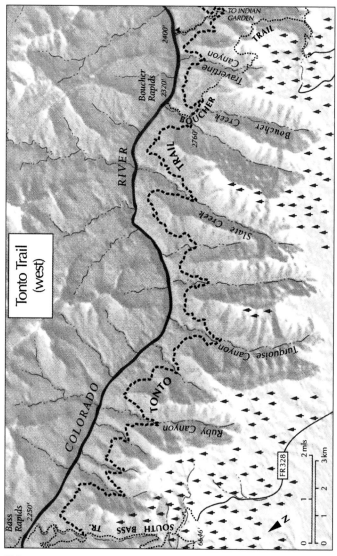

Tonto Trail (west)

TO INDIAN
GARDEN

2400'

Boucher
Rapids
2320'

Travertine
Canyon

TRAIL

BOUCHER

Boucher Creek

2760'

TRAIL

RIVER

Slate Creek

Turquoise Canyon

TONTO

Ruby Canyon

COLORADO

FR 328

2 mls

3 km

SOUTH BASS TR.

6646'

Bass
Rapids
2250'

N

Hermits' Rest, Pima Point and Mohave Point. Next you enter the dry Travertine Canyon, as you enter and exit via several rocky ledges.

The Tonto Trail undulates across the rolling plateau and pleasant walking predominates. Traverse around the north side of Whites Butte. Looking back, you are rewarded with fine views of Hermit Rapids as well as the Hermit Trail. You come now to the junction of the Tonto Trail with the Boucher Trail. Continue for 20mins, heading west on the Tonto Trail to Boucher Creek, where there are several used campsites and year-round water. A rocky 30mins descent from here down Boucher Creek brings you to Boucher Rapids.

Tonto Trail: Boucher Creek to Bass Canyon

Start	Boucher Canyon (2760ft/841m)
End	Bass Canyon (3200ft/975m)
Distance, one way	30 miles (41.6km)
Times, one way	15–20hrs
Maps	Grand Canyon, Havasupai Point, Shiva Temple, (United States Geological Survey 7.5'); Grand Canyon National Park (TI)
Season	Spring
Water	Bass Rapids, Boucher Creek
Rating	Strenuous

If you use good judgement and care, this remote section of the Tonto Trail poses no special difficulties. However, only seasoned canyoneers should attempt this section. Like many sections of the Tonto Trail, spring offers the best chance to take advantage of seasonal water sources. Be sure to check with the BIC before you start on your trip.

The Tonto Trails remains up on the platform across this remote section, except when shortcutting drainages. There are some steep rocky descents into the creek beds, usually marked by cairns, followed by short steep ascents out of the beds to reach the Tonto Platform again.

Directions

Heading west from the perennial water source at Boucher Creek, your first stop should be Slate Canyon, 5 miles away. Leaving Slate Canyon, contour around through Agate and Sapphire canyons. Your next seasonal water source is 12 miles from Boucher Creek, at Turquoise Canyon, a good choice for an overnight stop.

Continuing west, you greet your next seasonal water source at Ruby Canyon, after passing through Shaler and Le Conte plateaus. River-runners have named these numerous side-canyons 'the gems'. You'll pass Jasper and then Jade canyons before reaching Ruby Canyon. Next you'll greet Quartz Canyon, then Emerald Canyon and two unnamed drainages before coming to Serpentine Canyon. A further 4 miles brings you to Bass Canyon. Going north for 1 mile on the South Bass Trail brings you to Bass Rapids.

If you are planning to join these two rim-to-river trails, it is prudent to descend the South Bass Trail and ascend the steep Boucher Trail or more gradual Hermit Trail. The South Bass trailhead is located 29 miles from Grand Canyon Village on Rowe Well Road and 4 miles north of Pasture Wash ranger station on Forest Service Road 328. This unmaintained, rutted road floods at any time of year – high-clearance 4x4 vehicles are recommended. The Hermit's Rest car park, located 8 miles west of Grand Canyon Village on West Rim Road, provides convenient access to the Boucher Trail.

The Tonto Trail terminates 15 miles west of Bass Canyon at Garnet Canyon. Very experienced canyon-walkers with rock-climbing skills will want to explore the Royal Arch Route and Apache Trail, and visit Elves Chasm.

NORTH RIM TRANS-CANYON TRAILS

NORTH RIM TRAILS				
Trail	Distance (miles) one way	Distance (km) one way	Rating	Difficulty
Clear Creek Trail	8.8	14.0	Wilderness	Moderate

Clear Creek Trail

Start	Clear Creek trailhead at North Kaibab Trail (2649ft/805m)
End	Clear Creek (3420ft/1042m)
Distance, one way	8.8 miles (14km)
Maps	Phantom Ranch (United States Geological Survey 7.5'); Grand Canyon National Park (TI)
Season	All year

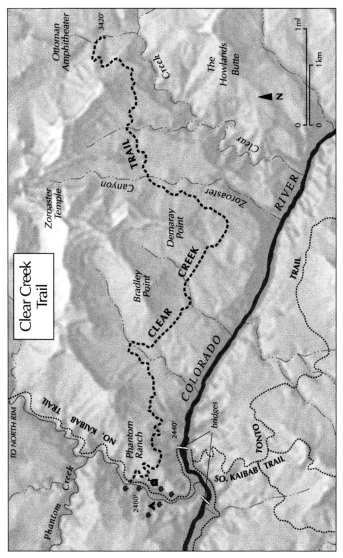

Clear Creek Trail

Water	Bright Angel Creek, Clear Creek
Rating	Moderate

Directions

The Clear Creek Trail leaves the North Kaibab Trail 0.3 miles northeast of Phantom Ranch. The first 1.5 miles brings you to Phantom Overlook, where you can rest on a bench and enjoy the views of Phantom Ranch below. For the first 2 miles the trail criss-crosses steeply on a well-formed path 1500ft up above the river to the base of Sumner Butte. Great river views back to the Colorado River suspension bridges and Phantom Ranch complement the walk once you have reached the plateau.

Camp only after you reach the rim and remember to carry water. If you've been unable to get a campsite at Bright Angel campground, this makes a great if not better alternative to the crowds at the canyon bottom.

Now begin your 6 mile level traverse to the east side of Clear Creek. You cross in and out of several drainages as you pass to the south of Bradley and Demaray points. In the last mile you drop 500ft to the Clear Creek drainage. Pleasant campsites dot the side of the creek among the cottonwoods. In all, you've walked almost 9 miles from Phantom Ranch. Popular day-hikes from this point include a trip to the Colorado River to the south, or north to Cheyava Falls.

CHAPTER 9

GRAND CANYON NATIONAL PARK: SOUTH AND NORTH RIM TRAILS

I am part of all that I have met;
Yet all experience is an arch wherethro'
Gleams that untravell'd world, whose margin fades
For even and for ever when I move.

Alfred Lord Tennyson

SOUTH RIM TRAILS

SOUTH RIM TRAILS				
Trail	Distance (miles) one way	Distance (km) one way	Rating	Difficulty
Rim Trail	9.0	14.4	Rim	Easy
Shoshone Point Trail	1.0	1.6	Rim	Easy

Rim Trail

Start	Hermit trailhead at Hermits' Rest (6640ft/2023m)
End	Yavapai Point (6640ft/2024m)
Distance, one way	9 miles (14.4km)
Times, one way	4hrs
Maps	Grand Canyon, Phantom Ranch (United States Geological Survey 7.5'); Grand Canyon National Park (TI); Grand Canyon National Park (EP)
Season	All year
Water	Hermits' Rest
Rating	Easy

Winding its way along the South Rim from Hermits' Rest to Mather Point, the 9 mile Rim Trail can be reached from any of its major South Rim viewpoints. Some

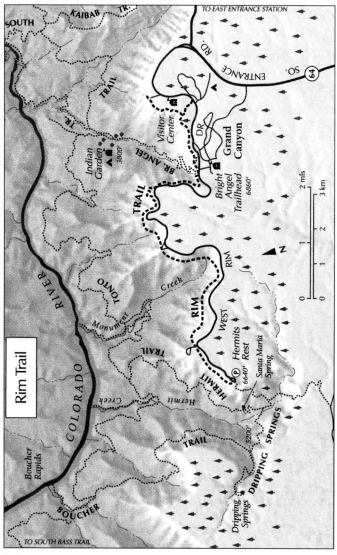

Rim Trail

consider it one of the finest of the Grand Canyon walks, with its splendid and dramatic views of different parts of the canyon.

Except for a limited period during winter, you must take the shuttle bus to points along the trail. Cars are not allowed along the West Rim Road for most of the year. Try taking the bus to Hermits' Rest and walking east on the trail towards Grand Canyon Village. The Rim Trail makes a fine short trip, using the bus to access the different viewpoints, or a longer day-walk. Note, though, that the bus stops only at Mohave and Hopi points on its return journey.

Paved and mostly wheelchair accessible for 3.5 miles between Yavapai and Maricopa points, the rest of the trail alternates between rocky sections, groomed trail and broken pavement. Lightweight shoes will suffice for its entire length, although in many places boots are more suitable. Children should be kept clear of the canyon's precipitous edge.

Directions

The Rim Trail heads east from Hermits' Rest, passing first by Pima Point. From here you can see sections of the Hermit Trail as it winds its way down Cathedral Stairs. Hermit and Boucher rapids are also visible. From Hermits' Rest to Maricopa Point the Rim Trail passes close to the rim, with dangerous drop-offs. The section between Hermits' Rest and Maricopa Point is much less used than the eastern section.

The 4 mile section between Pima Point and Mohave Point boasts spectacular views. From Pima Point, continue southeast along the rim and you soon pass above the Abyss, a deep chasm that indents into the rim at the south end of Monument Creek. This impressive amphitheatre cuts a deep void into the layers of rock. From this section of the trail you can see the Tonto Trail as it undulates east to west along the Tonto Platform. East of the Abyss, the Trail turns north towards Mohave Point. The Tonto Trail is visible, traversing the Tonto Platform, and you can see Hermit and Granite rapids.

Between Mohave and Maricopa Point you pass the Powell Memorial, built to honour the early Grand Canyon explorer, J Wesley Powell. Views are now to the east where you can see the Bright Angel Trail snaking its way from Indian Garden to the rim. Pass the Rim Trail Overlook, which gives you a bird's-eye view of Bright Angel Trail. Soon the numbers of visitors increase as you descend to reach the bus stop at the end of West Rim Road.

Next, heading into the main and busiest section of the village, you pass the Bright Angel trailhead, the busy Bright Angel Lodge and El Tovar Hotel, and Vercamp's Curios. Views are across the wide canyon and, at your feet, cottonwoods shade the verdant Indian Garden. The next part of the trail heads to Yavapai Point and Observation Station, overlooking Garden Creek, as it follows the wooded edge of the South Rim. Proceeding now further eastwards, the trail passes

Mather Point, with some of the best and most expansive views of the Grand Canyon, especially at sunset. The large car park here also services the new visitor centre nearby. Finally the trail continues to Pipe Creek Vista.

Shoshone Point Trail

Start	East Rim Drive (7200ft/2195m)
End	Shoshone Point (7300ft/2225m)
Distance, one way	1 mile (1.6km)
Time, one way	20mins
Maps	Phantom Ranch (United States Geological Survey 7.5'; Grand Canyon National Park (TI); Grand Canyon National Park (EP)
Season	All year
Water	None
Difficulty	Easy

Directions
The Shoshone Point Trail starts from an unmarked lay-by 1.75 miles east of Yaki Point along East Rim Drive. From the car park, walk through the locked gate on to the dirt road. One mile through the pine forest brings you to picnic tables and the canyon's edge. The area can be rented from the park service for special occasions, and it is often closed to passing visitors. Shoshone Point juts out from the rim and offers excellent views down to Grapevine and Cremation creeks. To the west, the South Kaibab Trail switchbacks down the east side of O'Neill Butte. You can visually follow much of the South Kaibab to Grandview Loop.

NORTH RIM TRAILS
The main North Rim of the Grand Canyon lures visitors with several fine walks, starting from near the main visitor centre. The lofty North Rim provides a cool alternative to the soaring temperatures of the lower canyon. In recent years the number of visitors to this faraway haven has increased, especially after glowing reports in numerous travel magazines. Cape Royal, Point Imperial and Bright Angel Point boast some of the most outstanding and unusual canyon views. Don't miss them!

From the main North Rim, only the North Kaibab Trail drops below the rim. As it winds its way down Roaring Springs Canyon, rising walls block views from the trail. This corridor trail (see chapter 7) makes up part of the major artery for walkers wanting to walk across the canyon.

To reach the North Rim, follow Arizona Hwy 67 south from Jacob Lake, Arizona for 31 miles to the North Rim Entrance Station. The Cape Royal Road/Point Imperial Road veers east 9.5 miles from the Entrance Station. The park road heads 2.5 miles further south to Grand Canyon Lodge and the visitor centre.

NORTH RIM TRAILS				
Trail	Distance (miles) one way	Distance (km) one way	Rating	Difficulty
Cape Royal Trail	0.3	0.5	Rim	Easy
Cliff Springs Trail	0.5	0.8	Rim	Easy
Cape Final Trail	2.0	3.2	Rim	Easy
Ken Patrick Trail	10.0	8.0	Rim	Moderate
Bright Angel Point Trail	0.5	0.4	Rim	Easy
Transept Trail	1.5	2.4	Rim	Easy
Widforss Trail	5.0	8.0	Rim	Easy
Uncle Jim Trail	2.5	4.0	Rim	Easy

Cape Royal Trail

Start	Cape Royal car park (7800ft/2377 m)
End	Cape Royal (7865ft/2397m)
Distance, one way	0.6 miles (1km)
Time, one way	10mins
Maps	Cape Royal (United States Geological Survey 7.5'); Grand Canyon National Park (TI)
Season	Mid-May to mid-October
Water	None
Difficulty	Easy

From the Cape Royal/Point Imperial road junction with the park road, turn east and proceed 14.3 miles to the end of the road at Cape Royal.

From the car park at the end of the Cape Royal Road, this short trail passes Angel's Window to the end of Cape Royal. A short detour guides you to a viewpoint above this large erosive gap in the canyon's limestone layer.

Directions

Continuing on to Cape Royal, the stunning view extends almost 360° to include Vishnu Temple, Freya Caste, Wotans Throne, Coronado Buttes and the Colorado River, 70 miles below Lee's Ferry. From this point, the Colorado River winds another 18 miles to Phantom Ranch and 207 miles west to Lake Mead. On the far southern rim, you can see the Desert View Lookout and Horseshoe Mesa at the base of the Grandview Trail. In the far distance, the San Francisco peaks line the horizon.

Cliff Springs Trail

Start	Cape Royal Road (7700ft/2347m)
End	Cliff Springs (7500ft/2286m)
Distance, one way	1 mile (1.6km)
Time, one way	20mins
Maps	Walhalla Plateau (United States Geological Survey 7.5'); Grand Canyon National Park (TI)
Season	Mid-May to mid-October
Water	None
Difficulty	Easy

From the Cape Royal/Point Imperial road Y-junction with the park road, turn east and proceed 13.7 miles to the Cliff Springs trailhead on the east side of the road. You will be 0.6 miles north of the end of the road at Cape Royal. This trail starts from the east side of the Cape Royal Road.

Directions

Cross the road and begin your descent. In 100yds you'll pass the old Anasazi granary. Continue to drop through pine trees to meet a rocky draw and reach a series of Kaibab cliffs. Here numerous springs converge and drip into pools. Contour around the ledges and boulders until you arrive at an obvious end point with fine views of Cape Royal. Retrace your steps to the car.

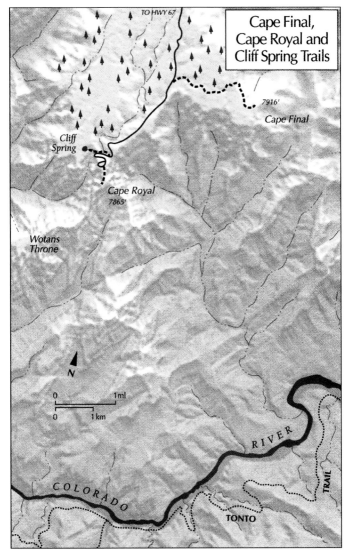

Cape Final,
Cape Royal and
Cliff Spring Trails

TO HWY 67

7916'

Cape Final

Cliff
Spring

Cape Royal
7865'

Wotans
Throne

N

0   1 ml
0   1 km

RIVER

COLORADO

TRAIL

TONTO

Cape Final Trail

Start	Cape Royal Road (7800ft/2377m)
End	Cape Final (8000ft/2438m)
Distance, one way	2 miles
Time, one way	1hr
Maps	Walhalla Plateau (United States Geological Survey 7.5'); Grand Canyon National Park (TI)
Season	Mid-May to mid-October
Water	None
Difficulty	Easy

This pleasant day or overnight walk starts from a small lay-by off the Cape Royal Road, 11.7 miles north of the Y-junction with the Point Imperial Road and 2.5 miles south of the end of the road at Cape Royal. If you wish to spend the night, don't forget to pick up a backcountry permit and carry water.

Directions
From the car park, follow the Cape Final Trail east through the pine trees – the road undulates through the forest. After 1 mile, at the clearing, your first canyon views include the Little Colorado River, Lava Creek and towered Siegfried Pyre. Turning south in the trees, you amble along this level trail to the south side of Cape Final. Your views from here include Unkar Creek and Delta along the Escalante Route. In the distance the Painted Desert, the South Rim and the Coconino Plateau mark the horizon. Retrace your steps back to the road.

Ken Patrick Trail

Start	Point Imperial (8803ft/2683m)
End	Cape Royal Road (8440ft/2572m)
Distance, one way	3 miles (4.8km)

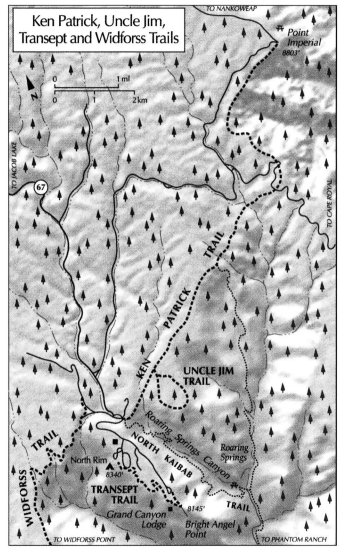

Ken Patrick, Uncle Jim,
Transept and Widforss Trails

TO NANKOWEAP

Point
Imperial
8803'

TO JACOB LAKE

67

TO CAPE ROYAL

N

0   1 ml
0   1   2 km

KEN PATRICK TRAIL

UNCLE JIM
TRAIL

Roaring Springs Canyon

Roaring
Springs

WIDFORSS   TRAIL

North Rim
8340'

NORTH KAIBAB

TRANSEPT
TRAIL

Grand Canyon
Lodge

8145'

Bright Angel
Point

TRAIL

TO WIDFORSS POINT

TO PHANTOM RANCH

Time, one way	1.5hrs
Maps	Point Imperial (United States Geological Survey 7.5'); Grand Canyon National Park (TI)
Season	Mid-May to mid-October
Water	None
Difficulty	Moderate

The 10 mile long Ken Patrick Trail connects the North Kaibab trailhead with Point Imperial. Its most scenic 3 mile section, described here, follows the canyon rim.

Point Imperial, the highest point on either rim, marks one of the finest views in all of the Grand Canyon. Flat-topped Mt Hayden adorns the foreground views. In the distance you can make out the mouth of the Little Colorado, Marble Platform, Cedar Mountain and Humphrey's Peak 12,633ft (3851m), the highest point in Arizona.

From the Cape Royal Road/Point Imperial Road junction with the park road, turn east and go 5.4 miles to the Y-junction. Continue north for 2.7 miles to Point Imperial.

Directions
From the west end of the Point Imperial car park, walk down the stairs and enjoy the fine views of Mt Hayden. In the distance you can see the Little Colorado River, the Painted Desert and the San Francisco Peaks. The trail, with its ups and downs, passes through the forest and then descends 100ft on switchbacks below the road. Then the trail ascends away from the road into the forest. Continuing southwest, the trail continues with its undulations just west of the rim. You can see Nankoweap Creek and the general path of the Nankoweap Trail. In a little over 2 miles the trail curves east and continues up and down to reach the Cape Royal Road. Continue southwest for 7 miles to the North Kaibab trailhead, or retrace your steps back to your car at Point Imperial.

Trail into the Grand Canyon

Grand Canyon from Desert View area

Bright Angel Point Trail

Start	Grand Canyon Lodge (8161ft/2487m)
End	Bright Angel Point (8250ft/2515m)
Distance, one way	0.5 miles (0.8km)
Time, one way	10mins
Maps	Bright Angel Point (United States Geological Survey 7.5′); Grand Canyon National Park (TI); Grand Canyon National Park (EP)
Season	Mid-May to mid-October
Water	None
Difficulty	Easy

Beginning at Grand Canyon Lodge at the north end of Hwy 67 and the park road, this short trail straddles a ridge across Roaring Springs Canyon and Transept Canyon, ending at Bright Angel Point. Bright Angel Point presents one of the finest Grand Canyon views, with Deva, Brama, Angel's Gate and Zoroaster Temples prominently displayed in the foreground.

Directions

From this point, you can follow the course of the North Kaibab Trail down Roaring Springs Canyon until it connects with Bright Angel Canyon at Roaring Springs and then continues to the Colorado River. On the distant South Rim you can identify Yaki Point at the start of the South Kaibab Trail, and some of the hotels.

Transept Trail

Start	North Rim Campground (8000ft/2438m)
End	Grand Canyon Lodge (8161ft/2487m)
Distance, one way	1.5 miles (2.4km)
Time, one way	40mins

Maps	Bright Angel Point (United States Geological Survey 7.5'); Grand Canyon National Park (TI); Grand Canyon National Park (EP)
Season	Mid-May to mid-October
Water	None
Difficulty	Easy

This popular 1.5 mile trail links Campsite 15 at the North Rim Campground with the Bright Angel Lodge. Although views are partially blocked by pine trees and shrubs, its undulating course overlooks Transept Canyon for its entire length.

From Jacob Lake, Arizona, drive south along Arizona Hwy 67 for 31 miles to the North Rim Entrance Station. Continue south on the park road for 21 miles to the turn-off to the campground and the general store.

Widforss Trail

Start	Widforss Trailhead (8000ft/2438m)
End	Widforss Point (8250ft/2515m)
Distance, one way	5 miles (8km)
Time, one way	2hrs
Maps	Bright Angel Point (United States Geological Survey 7.5'); Grand Canyon National Park (TI); Grand Canyon National Park (EP)
Season	Mid-May to mid-October
Water	None
Difficulty	Easy

Apart from a short climb at the beginning of the walk, the mostly level trail makes a fine, easy day-trip. Overnight camping is allowed; be sure to pick up a back-country permit and carry water. A self-guiding brochure describes the first half of the walk.

Drive 4 miles north of Grand Canyon Lodge to the turn-off for the Widforss trail-head. Turn west and follow the dirt road 1 mile to the car park. From the Cape Royal Road/Point Imperial road junction with the park road, proceed 0.25 miles south to the turn-off to the Widforss trailhead.

Directions

The first 0.5 miles winds through typical North Rim forests of pine, fir and aspen trees. Views open up along the first half of the trail as it passes the edge of Transept Canyon. From some of the viewpoints, you get glimpses of Grand Canyon Lodge on the far side of the canyon. At 2.5 miles, the halfway point, the route passes through heavy forest and then, surprisingly, opens up to panoramic vistas. The trail stops 0.5 miles southeast of Widforss Point itself and overlooks Haunted Canyon.

Uncle Jim Trail

Start	North Kaibab Trailhead (8241ft/2515m)
End	Uncle Jim Point (8031ft/2448m)
Distance, one way	2.5 miles (4km)
Time, one way	1.5hrs
Maps	Bright Angel Point (United States Geological Survey 7.5'); Grand Canyon National Park (TI); Grand Canyon National Park (EP)
Season	Mid-May to mid-October
Water	None
Difficulty	Easy

The North Kaibab trailhead is 0.9 miles south of the Cape Royal Road/Point Imperial Road junction on the park highway and 2 miles north of Grand Canyon Lodge.

Directions

Starting from the North Kaibab trailhead, this trail overlaps for its first 2 miles with the Ken Patrick Trail. At first traversing along the rim of Roaring Springs Canyon, the trail turns south, soon reaching the junction with a 1.5 mile loop. Joining the loop in either direction you cross level terrain and then greet a viewpoint above the North Kaibab Trail and Roaring Springs Canyon. Continue around to complete the loop and return to the car park on the first section of the trail. Walkers share this waterless trail with mules.

CHAPTER 10

GRAND CANYON NATIONAL PARK: LONG-DISTANCE ROUTES

*I am glad I shall never be young without
wild country to be young in.
Of what avail are forty freedoms without
a blank spot on the map!*

Aldo Leopold

Once you have a few miles of Grand Canyon hiking under your boots, perhaps on the corridor trails or the Grandview Trail, you'll want to explore more of the park by connecting several of the rim-to-river trails. Constance gives some information and personal ideas about the trips below. See chapter 6 (South Rim, Rim-to-River trails) and chapter 8 (Trans-Canyon trails) for descriptions of the individual trails that make up the loops. The Kanab Canyon–Thunder River Loop is described in detail at the end of this chapter.

GRAND CANYON NATIONAL PARK: LONG-DISTANCE ROUTES				
Trail	Distance (miles) one way	Distance (km) one way	Rating	Difficulty
Boucher Trail to Hermit Trail Loop	23.0	36.8	Wilderness	Ex. strenuous
Hermit Trail to Bright Angel Trail Loop	22.9	36.6	Wild/Corr.	Strenuous
North to South Rim: North Kaibab Trail to Bright Angel Trail	23.3	37.2	Corridor	Moderate
South Kaibab Trail to Bright Angel Trail	16.3	26.1	Corridor	Moderate
Grandview Trail to South Kaibab Trail	27.8	44.4	Wild/Corr.	Strenuous
Escalante Route: Tanner Trail to Grandview Trail	33.0	52.8	Wilderness	Ex. strenuous
Kanab Canyon to Thunder River Route	50.5	80.8	Route	Ex. strenuous

The suggested routes and trails below give you ideas for several overnight trips in Grand Canyon National Park. Walkers with no previous experience in the Grand Canyon should try the corridor trails, South Kaibab to Bright Angel Loop and the trans-canyon North Kaibab to Bright Angel trip.

Combining the rim-to-river trails with sections of the Tonto Trail and Escalante Route make splendid overnight trips. Experienced beginners can consider the Hermit to Bright Angel Loop. A step up from these trips is an overnight trip on Horseshoe Mesa on the Grandview Trail or the Grandview Trail to South Kaibab Trail trip. More experience is recommended for the Boucher to Hermit Loop or Escalante Route, Tanner Trail to Grandview Trail or New Hance Trail. Only experienced canyoneers should attempt the Kanab Canyon to Thunder River Loop.

Boucher Trail to Hermit Trail Loop

Start	Hermits' Rest (6640ft/2023m)
End	Hermits' Rest (6640ft/2023m)
Distance, one way	23 miles (36.8km)
Times	3–4 days
Maps	Grand Canyon (United States Geological Survey 7.5'); Grand Canyon National Park (TI); Grand Canyon National Park (EP)
Season	All year
Water	Boucher Creek, Boucher Rapids, Hermit Creek
Rating	Extremely strenuous

The Boucher Trail, one of the more difficult rim-to-river trails, has become more popular in recent years. Sections are exposed and one short part requires down-climbing.

This loop takes advantage of Hermits' Rest as a convenient trailhead for the 3–4 day-walk. When it is running, take the shuttle bus to the end of the West Rim Drive from Grand Canyon Village at the South Rim. At other times of the year, you can drive yourself to the car park at the end of the road.

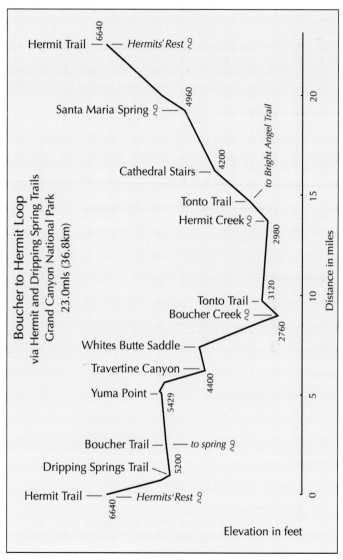

Boucher to Hermit Loop
via Hermit and Dripping Spring Trails
Grand Canyon National Park
23.0mls (36.8km)

Hermit Trail — 6640 — *Hermits' Rest* ♀

Santa Maria Spring ♀ — 4960

to Bright Angel Trail

Cathedral Stairs — 4200

Tonto Trail —
Hermit Creek ♀ — 2980

Tonto Trail — 3120
Boucher Creek ♀ — 2760

Whites Butte Saddle —
Travertine Canyon — 4400
Yuma Point — 5429

Boucher Trail — *to spring* ♀
Dripping Springs Trail — 5200
Hermit Trail — 6640 — *Hermits' Rest* ♀

Distance in miles

Elevation in feet

Directions

Descend the Boucher Trail, walk west to east on the Tonto Trail and ascend the Hermit Trail. The section of the Tonto Trail that connects Boucher Canyon with Hermit Creek undulates across the Tonto Trail on a straightforward course and presents no difficulties. The popular Hermit Trail, trodden upon by hikers as much as a corridor trail, resembles a maintained trail. You'll find the Hermit Trail takes a more gradual ascent than the steep Boucher Trail. Extra days can be spent at Boucher Creek, Hermit Creek or Hermit Rapids.

Hermit Trail to Bright Angel Trail Loop

Start	Hermits' Rest (6640ft/2023m)
End	Bright Angel Trailhead (6860ft/2091m)
Distance, one way	22.9 miles (36.6km)
Backpacking times	3–4 days
Maps	Grand Canyon, Phantom Ranch (United States Geological Survey 7.5'); Grand Canyon National Park (TI); Grand Canyon National Park (EP)
Season	All year
Water	Hermit Creek, Hermit Rapids, Monument Creek, Indian Garden
Rating	Moderate

The Hermit to Bright Angel Loop has become one of the Grand Canyon's most popular overnight trips.

This popular trip is not a true loop at all, but starts at Hermits' Rest and ends at the Bright Angel trailhead near Kolb Studio. A bus or taxi will connect you back to your car. You must camp in one of the several designated sites along the way. A good step up from the corridor trails, this long-distance trail can be easily handled by first-time canyon walkers with some backpacking experience. Most walkers choose to descend the Hermit Trail. Pleasant layover days can be spent at Hermit Rapids or Granite Rapids.

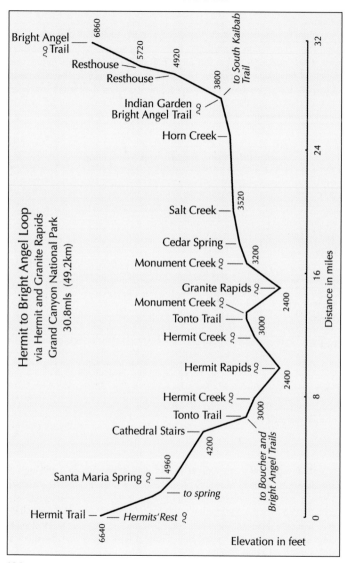

Hermit to Bright Angel Loop
via Hermit and Granite Rapids
Grand Canyon National Park
30.8mls (49.2km)

Bright Angel ♀ Trail — 6860

Resthouse — 5720

Resthouse — 4920

to South Kaibab Trail

Indian Garden ♀ Bright Angel Trail — 3800

Horn Creek —

Salt Creek — 3520

Cedar Spring —

Monument Creek ♀ — 3200

Granite Rapids ♀

Monument Creek ♀ — 2400

Tonto Trail — 3000

Hermit Creek ♀ —

Hermit Rapids ♀ — 2400

Hermit Creek ♀ —

Tonto Trail — 3000

Cathedral Stairs —

to Boucher and Bright Angel Trails

4200

Santa Maria Spring ♀ — 4960

to spring

Hermit Trail — Hermits' Rest ♀

6640

Distance in miles

32

24

16

8

0

Elevation in feet

Cross-canyon: North Kaibab Trail to Bright Angel Trail

Start	North Kaibab Trailhead (8241ft/2515m)
End	Bright Angel Trailhead (6860ft/2091m)
Distance, one way	23.3 miles (37.2km)
Backpacking times	3–4 days
Maps	Grand Canyon, Phantom Ranch, Bright Angel Point (United States Geological Survey 7.5′); Grand Canyon National Park (TI); Grand Canyon National Park (EP)
Season	Mid-May to mid-October
Water	Supai Tunnel, Roaring Springs, Cottonwood Camp, Phantom Ranch, Bright Angel Campground, Colorado River, Indian Garden
Difficulty	Moderate

This popular trip links the North Rim with the South Rim. It utilises the only bridges that cross the Colorado River near Phantom Ranch and Bright Angel Campground. You must make the long, although pleasant, 5hr drive between the South Rim and North Rim.

Trans-canyon hikers are allowed to use North Rim campground, located near the general store, without a prior reservation. Check at the campground entrance for information and location of your site. You must obtain the usual backcountry permit for your walk.

Though many people feel this is a 'must-do', and then can claim they have 'walked the Grand Canyon', Constance personally found it disappointing. This trail is partially paved and dotted with buildings. The trails are heavily used by day-walkers, backpackers, runners, and mules alike. Constance logged many, many miles in other more scenic, less crowded, true wilderness areas of the Grand Canyon.

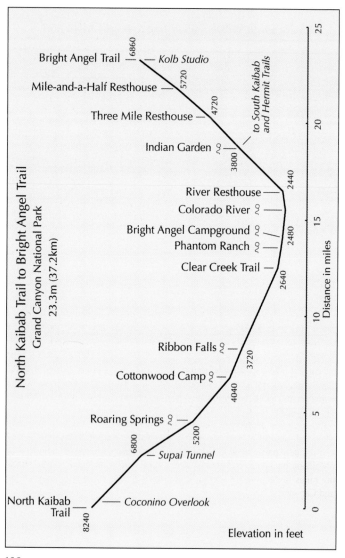

North Kaibab Trail to Bright Angel Trail
Grand Canyon National Park
23.3m (37.2km)

Bright Angel Trail — 6860 — *Kolb Studio*

Mile-and-a-Half Resthouse — 5720

Three Mile Resthouse — 4720

Indian Garden — 3800

to South Kaibab
and Hermit Trails

River Resthouse — 2440

Colorado River — 2480

Bright Angel Campground

Phantom Ranch

Clear Creek Trail — 2640

Ribbon Falls — 3720

Cottonwood Camp — 4040

Roaring Springs — 5200

6800 — *Supai Tunnel*

North Kaibab
Trail — — *Coconino Overlook*
8240

Distance in miles

Elevation in feet

South Kaibab Trail to Bright Angel Trail

Start	South Kaibab Trailhead near Yaki Point (7190ft/2192 m)
End	Bright Angel Trailhead (6860ft/2091m) at Kolb Studio
Distance, one way	16.3 miles (26.1km)
Backpacking time	2–3 days
Maps	Phantom Ranch (United States Geological Survey 7.5'); Grand Canyon National Park (TI); Grand Canyon National Park (EP)
Season	All year
Water	Bright Angel Campground, Indian Garden
Rating	Moderate

This extremely popular 2–3 day walk makes up the park's most popular overnight trip.

The walk is accessible all year around, and water is available on the ascent at Indian Garden all year and at Three-Mile and One-and-a-Half-Mile rest houses during the summer. Extra days may be spent exploring the North Kaibab Trail or Clear Creek. This route can be walked as a backpacking trip, staying at Bright Angel campground or at Indian Garden on the walk out. Lighten your load by staying in the cabins or dormitories at Phantom Ranch. An additional night may be spent at Indian Garden on the ascent if you are backpacking.

Although this is the most popular overnight trip in the park and the South Kaibab is a spectacular trail, the Bright Angel is disappointing. The National Park Service recommends that all first-time canyon hikers keep to the corridor trails. If not hiking in the heat of summer, you may want to consider returning to the rim on the more scenic South Kaibab Trail.

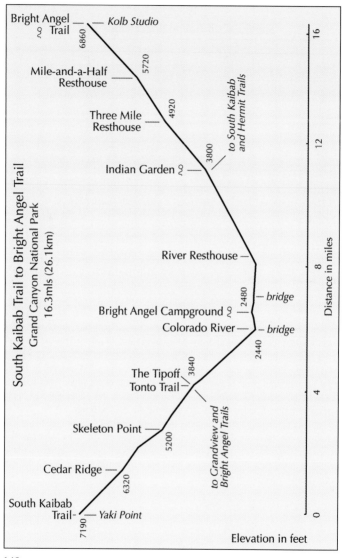

South Kaibab Trail to Bright Angel Trail
Grand Canyon National Park
16.3mls (26.1km)

Bright Angel
♀ Trail — Kolb Studio
6860

5720

Mile-and-a-Half
Resthouse

4920

Three Mile
Resthouse

3800

Indian Garden ♀

to South Kaibab
and Hermit Trails

River Resthouse —

2480 — bridge

Bright Angel Campground ♀

Colorado River — — bridge

2440

3840

The Tipoff
Tonto Trail —

to Grandview and
Bright Angel Trails

Skeleton Point —

5200

Cedar Ridge —

6320

South Kaibab
Trail — — Yaki Point

7190

Distance in miles

16

12

8

4

0

Elevation in feet

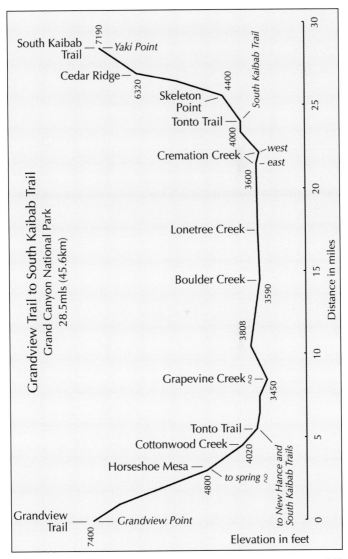

South Kaibab Trail — *Yaki Point* — 7190

Cedar Ridge — 6320

South Kaibab Trail

Skeleton Point — 4400

Tonto Trail — 4000

Cremation Creek — *west* / *east* — 3600

Lonetree Creek —

Boulder Creek — 3590

3808

Grapevine Creek — 3450

Tonto Trail —

Cottonwood Creek — 4020

Horseshoe Mesa — *to spring*

4800

to New Hance and South Kaibab Trails

Grandview Trail — *Grandview Point*

7400

Grandview Trail to South Kaibab Trail
Grand Canyon National Park
28.5mls (45.6km)

Distance in miles

Elevation in feet

Grandview Trail to South Kaibab Trail

Start	Grandview Trailhead at Grandview Point (7400ft/2256m)
End	South Kaibab Trailhead near Yaki Point (7190ft/2192m)
Distance	27.8 miles (44.4km)
Backpacking time	4 days
Maps	Grandview Point, Cape Royal, Phantom Ranch (United States Geological Survey 7.5'); Grand Canyon National Park (TI); Grand Canyon National Park (EP)
Season	Autumn, winter and spring
Water	Grapevine Creek
Rating	Strenuous

This walk offers a fine introduction to canyon-walking, without the challenges and steep descents of either the Boucher, Tanner or New Hance trails. It is possible to continue this trip by heading further west on the Tonto Trail to the Hermit Trail, or at the South Kaibab Trail descending to Indian Garden. This walk is best attempted in the spring. Although Grapevine Creek has perennial water, spring offers the best chance of water in Cottonwood and Lonetree creeks. Otherwise, water will have to be carried after Grapevine Creek.

Escalante Route: Tanner Trail to Grandview Trail

Start	Tanner Trailhead at Lipan Point (7349 feet/2240m)
End	Grandview Trailhead at Grandview Point (7400ft/2256m)
Distance	33.3 miles (52.8km)

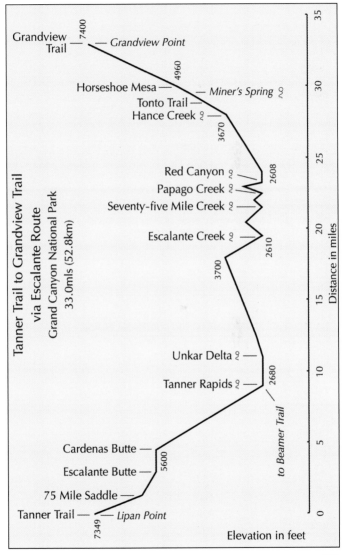

Tanner Trail to Grandview Trail
via Escalante Route
Grand Canyon National Park
33.0mls (52.8km)

Grandview
Trail
7400
— Grandview Point

4960

Horseshoe Mesa —
— Miner's Spring ♀
Tonto Trail —
Hance Creek ♀
3670

Red Canyon ♀
Papago Creek ♀
Seventy-five Mile Creek ♀
2608
Escalante Creek ♀
2610
3700

Unkar Delta ♀ —
Tanner Rapids ♀ —
2680
to Beamer Trail

Cardenas Butte —
5600
Escalante Butte —
75 Mile Saddle —
Tanner Trail —   — Lipan Point
7349

Distance in miles

Elevation in feet

35
30
25
20
15
10
5
0

Backpacking times	4–6 days
Maps	Cape Royal, Desert View (United States Geological Survey 7.5′); Grand Canyon National Park (TI); Grand Canyon National Park (EP)
Season	Spring and late autumn
Water	Colorado River at Tanner Rapids, Escalante Creek, Papago Creek, Red Canyon, Hance Creek, Miner's Spring
Rating	Extremely strenuous

This splendid multi-day walk provides a challenging trip for those not averse to some scrambling, steep descents and talus-hopping. The Escalante Route (see chapter 8) is less travelled than the Tonto Trail and provides the walker with a wilderness experience using convenient South Rim access points.

Kanab Canyon to Thunder River Route

Start	Sowats Point (6200ft/1890m) to Colorado River (2000ft/609m)
End	Indian Hollow (6380ft/1945m)
Distance	50.5 miles (80.8km)
Times	7–9 days
Maps	Tapeats Amphitheatre, Powell Plateau, Grama Spring, Kanab Point, Jumpup Point, Fishtail Mesa (United States Geological Survey 7.5′)
Season	Spring and late autumn
Water	Kanab Creek, Colorado River, Fishtail Rapids, Deer Creek, Deer Creek Spring, Tapeats Creek, Thunder River
Rating	Extremely strenuous

This splendid multi-day trip for experienced canyon backpackers is one of the most spectacular routes in the park. According to author and well-known canyon explorer George Steck, you pass by many of the canyon 'must-see' points. In dry conditions, passenger cars can navigate the road to Sowats Point, although in the spring there may be mud and deep ruts, so a 4x4 may be necessary. A car shuttle between Indian Hollow and Sowats Point makes your trip easier. The trip will be described in a counter-clockwise direction, the easiest and most practical way to walk the loop.

Although Kanab Creek is marked with a trail on the Grand Canyon National Park Trails Illustrated Map (TI), there is no obvious trail here and 'route' is a much more accurate classification. Only serious canyoneers should travel here. You should know how to swim, and be comfortable with bouldering, scrambling and route-finding. Seasonal water may be available in Kwagunt Hollow, Jumpup Canyon, west up Indian Hollow from Jumpup Canyon, and in upper Kanab Canyon. Water flows year round in Kanab Creek.

To reach Sowats Point, take Hwy 67 for 26 miles to FR422. Drive 18 miles west towards Dry Park to FR425. Turn west and drive for 6.5 miles south to FR233. Turn west again and drive another 8.5 miles to the car park for entrance into the Kaibab National Forest.

Forest Road FR422 can also be accessed from Fredonia, Arizona. Drive 1 mile east on Hwy 89A and then turn south on to FR422. Continue south on FR422, past Big Springs, turning west on FR425 and west again on FR233 to Sowats Point.

Directions

About 200yds before Sowats Point on FR233, the trail descends west at a sign into the Kaibab National Forest. Pass the Kaibab National Forest entrance sign-in register and head west around the southwest side of Sowats Point. The steep, slippery trail descends through the Kaibab, Toroweap, and Coconino formations and, in 2 miles, reaches a group of cottonwood trees. The easiest and most scenic access into Jumpup Canyon heads straight west, cross-country from the trees descending into the drainage of Kwagunt Hollow. The trail, however, continues north to Sowats Canyon, an alternative access into Jumpup Canyon.

Kwagunt Hollow, easily negotiated with some scrambling and boulder-clambering, joins Jumpup Canyon after 3 miles. After reaching Jumpup Canyon, turn south on flat terrain as you pass through the several miles of narrows. Early in the season there may be water in Kwagunt Hollow, Jumpup Canyon or at the junction of Kanab Creek and Jumpup Canyon. In dry years, or later in the season, water

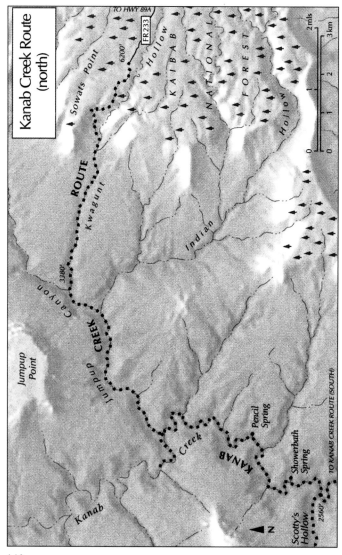

Kanab Creek Route (north)

TO HWY 89A

FR 233

6200'

Sowats Point

Hollow

KAIBAB

NATIONAL

FOREST

Hollow

ROUTE

Kwagunt

Indian

3380'

JUMPUP CREEK

Canyon

Jumpup

Jumpup Point

Jumpup

Creek

Pencil Spring

KANAB

Showerbath Spring

Kanab

2560'

Scotty's Hollow

TO KANAB CREEK ROUTE (SOUTH)

N

2 mls

3 km

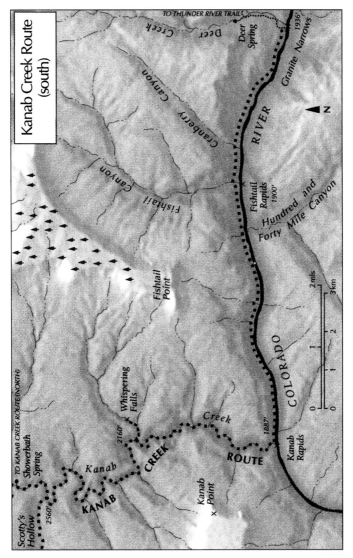

Kanab Creek Route
(south)

TO THUNDER RIVER TRAIL

Deer Creek

Deer Spring

1936'

Granite Narrows

Cranberry Canyon

RIVER

N

Fishtail Canyon

Fishtail Rapids 1900'

Hundred and Forty Mile Canyon

Fishtail Point

2 mls

3 km

COLORADO

TO KANAB CREEK ROUTE (NORTH)

Showerbath Spring

Whispering Falls

2160'

Creek

CREEK

ROUTE

1887'

Kanab

2560'

Kanab Point

Kanab Rapids

Scotty's Hollow

KANAB

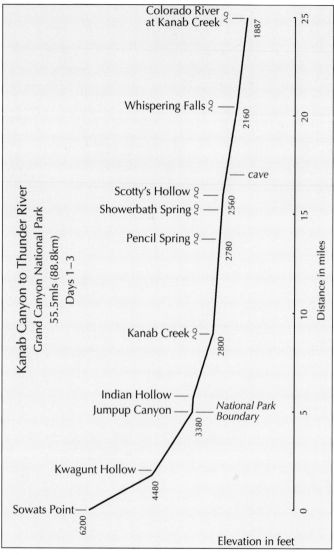

Kanab Canyon to Thunder River
Grand Canyon National Park
55.5mls (88.8km)
Days 1–3

Colorado River at Kanab Creek 1887

Whispering Falls 2160

cave

Scotty's Hollow
Showerbath Spring 2560

Pencil Spring 2780

Kanab Creek 2800

Indian Hollow
Jumpup Canyon — *National Park Boundary* 3380

Kwagunt Hollow 4480

Sowats Point 6200

Distance in miles

Elevation in feet

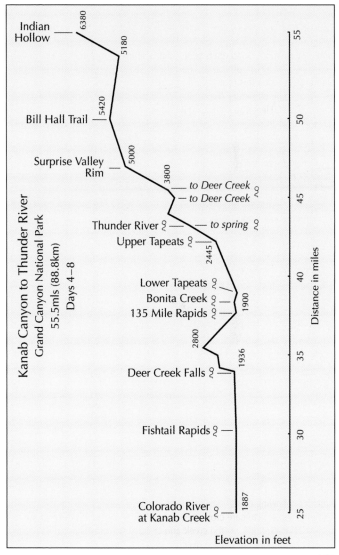

Elevation in feet

may not be found until you have descended into Kanab Creek for several miles. Jumpup Canyon rises 1000ft up from the creek bottom; at the narrowest point, the walls are only 20ft apart. Indian Hollow joins from the west after 1 mile. When Jumpup Canyon is dry, there is often water 30mins up Indian Hollow. The Jumpup Narrows, dangerous during the flash-flood season, presents one of many outstanding sights on this route.

Your route continues down Jumpup Canyon through the splendid narrows to Kanab Creek. Here you enter Grand Canyon National Park and overnight permits are required. In rainy years, water may be available in upper Kanab Creek. The first perennial water is Pencil Spring, clearly marked on the Kanab Point 7.5 minute quad, around 3 miles from the Jumpup/Kanab junction. This horizontal display of dripping ferns juts out from overhanging rocks. Around 1.5 miles farther on you reach overhanging Showerbath Spring, where the creek has undercut the bank to support a green and red array of plants.

One mile further on, the terrain becomes more difficult as larger boulders, swimming pools, and rushing water block easy passage and provides challenging walking. At Scotty's Hollow, where the canyon makes a 180° turn, you'll find a convenient camping spot. Scotty's Castle is the name given to the tower that adorns the 180° turn. If you have excess energy you can hike up Scotty's Hollow. Just a few minutes up the canyon, a waterfall cuts through the rocks and creates a splendid series of small bathing pools.

Continuing down the canyon, your route is slowed by tedious negotiation around large boulders and pools of water. Canyon walls rise steeply from the sides of the creek. Less than 1 mile from Scotty's Hollow, a large cave, providing shelter from the rain, juts into the canyon walls on the east side of the creek. Four hours down the canyon from Scotty's Hollow, be sure to stop at the next major drainage that joins from the east. Long remembered by any visitor, a 10mins walk up this major drainage brings you to the Whispering Falls. Here water has carved a passage through a rock slide, adorned with flowers and falling into a deep clear pool. Though the water is definitely 'whispering', it is clearly not a 'falls'. In *Grand Canyon Loop Hikes I*, George Steck calls it the Slide of Susurrus, perhaps a more accurate description.

Continuing down the creek your passage soon eases, and in 1hr you pass some interesting Muav ledges on the true left of the creek. In another couple of hours the difficulties lighten even more as you reach the Colorado River. Fine camping spots can be found 10mins before reaching the river, just before the creek's final swing east. At the river, the east side of the creek supports additional camping spots. Take care crossing over to them; if the mud is deep or the river is high, backtrack north up the creek and cross to the other side of the creek first before continuing south to the river.

To continue to Deer Creek, Thunder River and Tapeats Creek, your route bears east along the Colorado River to Fishtail Rapids. From the mouth of Kanab Creek it is two days of boulder-hopping to reach Deer Creek, and this shadeless, hot and tedious section between Kanab Creek and Fishtail Rapids tests even the most rugged canyoneer. The rocks are blisteringly hot and jagged, so despite the heat you may consider wearing lightweight gloves and long pants. Give strong consideration to walking this section in the cool morning. The route, taking anywhere from 4–7hrs, follows just above the river for the entire day. Constance went through this section three times and each time it was challenging. Difficulty depends on where the boulders have fallen and been placed as a result of the previous winter and the fluctuating water levels of the Colorado River. After the struggle, you will be glad to find a sandy and somewhat shaded stopping point at Fishtail Rapids.

After a night at Fishtail Rapids, continue east along the river for another 4hr trip, although considerably easier than your previous day's toils. There is a trail for much of the way, often veering several hundred feet above the Colorado River as it avoids cliffs and outcropping that make staying close to the river impassable. Within 1.5hrs you come to Steck's 'Siesta Spring', a flow of water coming from one of the Cranberry Canyon drainages. It was a mere trickle when Constance last passed by, even in a very wet year. Just after the drainage, you head high, away from the river. The trail drops back to the river east of a wash on a crumbling rocky slope. The last mile ends easily, as you walk on rocks next to the river to Deer Creek Falls, no doubt a welcome sight.

Join the trail to Deer Creek up into Surprise Valley, where you can continue on to the Thunder River Trail and Tapeats Creek, described in chapter 7. An alternate route traverses from Deer Creek above the river, high above the rapids to Bonita Creek and the Lower Tapeats campsite. It may be difficult to ascend Tapeats Creek in the spring; crossing may be extremely dangerous until the winter water levels lessen into the summer.

ZION
NATIONAL PARK

Chapter 11

VISITING ZION NATIONAL PARK

Nothing can exceed the wondrous beauty of Zion...
in the nobility and beauty of the sculptures
there is no comparison

Clarence E Dutton, 1880

Zion National Park offers visitors some amazing scenery; its sheer canyon walls are dramatic and vividly coloured with deep reds and blinding white faces. Contorted, weirdly eroded strata with incredible bastions and turrets of multicoloured rock create a landscape of sometimes-unbelievable designs. Blasted and carefully crafted from this natural amphitheatre are some stunning trails and routes. With walks, hikes and new canyoning trips to suit all abilities, Zion National Park is a true paradise for outdoor enthusiasts.

Accessed from Las Vegas and Salt Lake City, Zion is the busiest of Utah's national parks. Most of the park's three million visitors a year spend their time in Zion Canyon, often enjoying a short day-walk. The park, however, encompasses 229 square miles, complete with hiking trails, springs for water, sweeping views and deep canyons. Visits to its high, cool plateaux guide the walker far away from the valley crowds.

GETTING THERE

Salt Lake City, Utah, and Las Vegas, Nevada, offer the closest major airports and numerous car-rental options. Rental cars are also available in St George and Cedar City, Utah, but it is more practical to obtain cars from the larger cities of Salt Lake City or Las Vegas. Zion National Park makes a 3hr, 158 mile car trip from Las Vegas; a 6hr, 325 mile trip from Salt Lake City; and a 1hr, 42 mile trip from St George, Utah. In addition, Zion is a 2hr, 86 mile drive from Bryce Canyon National Park; a 5hr, 253 mile drive from the South Rim of the Grand Canyon; a 3hr, 120 mile ride from the North Rim of the Grand Canyon; and a 6hr, 284 mile ride from Death Valley, California.

You reach Zion by going north from Las Vegas or south from Salt Lake City on Interstate 15 towards St George. Just north of St George, take the Hurricane exit to Utah Route 9. Drive through the small towns of Hurricane, Virgin and Rockville and continue 37 miles to Springdale, just south of the park entrance.

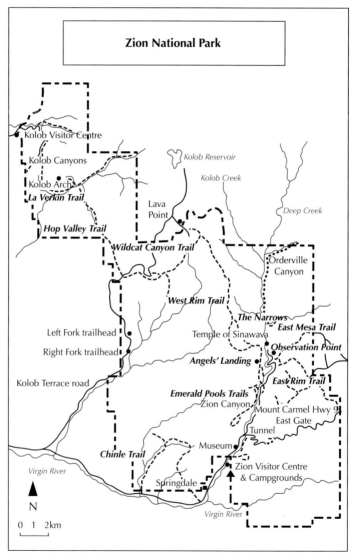

Zion National Park

Kolob Visitor Centre

Kolob Canyons

Kolob Arch

La Verkin Trail

Hop Valley Trail

Kolob Reservoir

Kolob Creek

Deep Creek

Lava Point

Wildcat Canyon Trail

Orderville Canyon

West Rim Trail

The Narrows

East Mesa Trail

Left Fork trailhead

Right Fork trailhead

Temple of Sinawava

Observation Point

Angels' Landing

East Rim Trail

Kolob Terrace road

Emerald Pools Trails

Zion Canyon

Mount Carmel Hwy 9

East Gate

Tunnel

Chinle Trail

Museum

Zion Visitor Centre & Campgrounds

Virgin River

Springdale

N

0 1 2km

Virgin River

Coming from the east of Zion on US 89, turn west at Mount Carmel junction on Utah Route 9 to reach the park's East Entrance. It is 13 miles past the Checkerboard Mesa to the visitor centre via the Zion Mount Carmel tunnel, a major engineering feat built in the 1920s.

Public transport to Zion National Park is not available.

ENTRANCE FEES

A fee of $20 is charged per vehicle and this is valid for seven days. Note that transiting cars are also charged this fee to drive from Mount Carmel to Springdale. To visit the northern Kolob Canyons only, a fee of $10 is levied per vehicle. For $40 one can obtain an annual pass for the park. Golden Eagle Passport and all other annual passes are valid here.

Note that to transit the Mount Carmel Tunnel, all large vehicles/RVs (in excess of 7ft 10in wide or over 11ft 4in high) need an escort. This costs US$15 in addition to the entrance fee, and is valid for two journeys through the tunnel in a seven-day period. Vehicles higher than 13ft and various other larger vehicles, as well as bicycles and pedestrians, are prohibited.

GETTING AROUND – ZION VALLEY SHUTTLE SERVICE

Zion National Park provides an excellent shuttle bus service, which runs every 6mins from 6.45am to 10pm during spring and autumn within the main Zion Canyon along the Virgin River. From the Zion Canyon Visitor Centre, it is 6 miles to the end of Zion Canyon Scenic Drive. In summer, from late May to early September, shuttles run from 5.45am to 11pm. The visitor centre, car park and shuttle bus terminal are close to the Watchman Campground. Buses also link Springdale (Majestic View stop) to the Zion Canyon Theatre near the visitor centre, and the south entrance to the main canyon area, from 5.30/6.30am until 10.15/11.15pm, depending on the season. Private cars are not permitted in the main Zion Canyon area in season, except for those staying at Zion Lodge. From the Zion Canyon Visitor Centre it is 40 miles to Lava Point, and 45 miles to the Kolob Canyons Visitor Centre on the west side of the park. These parts of the park do not currently have any shuttle service.

WEATHER AND SEASONS

The park, lodge and campgrounds remain open all year, although many park services, such as ranger talks, hikers' shuttles and tram rides, run only between April and October. Spring or autumn make the best time for a visit, when temperatures are ideal and there are fewer visitors.

The Southwest Desert trails and most Zion Canyon trails remain open all year. Valley trails, such as the Riverside Trail, Emerald Pools and

Average Valley Temperatures (°C/°F)/Rainfall (cm/in) Zion National Park

Month	Av. High	Av. Low	Av. Rainfall	Thunder-storm	Partly wet days
Jan	11 (52)	-2 (29)	4.1 (1.6)	0	7
Feb	13 (57)	-1 (31)	4.1 (1.6)	0	7
Mar	18 (63)	2 (36)	4.3 (1.7)	0	8
Apr	22 (73)	6 (43)	3.3 (1.3	1	6
May	28 (83)	11 (52)	1.8 (0.7)	4	5
Jun	34 (93)	16 (60)	1.5 (0.6)	5	3
Jul	38 (100)	20 (68)	2.0 (0.8)	14	5
Aug	36 (97)	19 (66)	4.1 (1.6)	15	6
Sep	33 (91)	16 (60)	3.6 (1.4)	5	4
Oct	26 (78)	9 (49)	2.5 (1.0)	2	4
Nov	17 (63)	3 (39)	3.1 (1.2)	0	5
Dec	12 (53)	1 (34)	3.8 (1.5)	0	6

Weeping Rock are also open all year. High country trails are accessible usually from mid to late April until October. Each year the amount of winter snow determines the exact beginning and end of the high-country walking season.

The most unpredictable wet weather occurs in the spring. March is the rainiest month, yet it can snow into April. Wildflowers dot the high country from late April into early June. Be aware, however, that the rivers and streams overflow in spring and narrow-canyon-walking may be dangerous. Thunderstorms can produce flash floods and limit canyon-walking, peaking in July and August.

Zion and the surrounding areas bake in the scorching summer heat, although higher elevations are moderated and experience slightly cooler temperatures. Summer temperatures soar in the valley, often exceeding 100°F, with the high country averaging around 75°F. The high plateaus stay cooler and remain pleasant for walking when the lower elevations broil.

Autumn brings cool temperatures, and brilliant colours highlight the high-country trees in late September and the valley in late October.

In winter, when the higher elevations can only be accessed using snowshoes or skis, the Chinle Trail makes a fine outing. Lava Point is often snowbound until early to mid May. Those trails that connect the valley floor with the rim, such as the East and West Rim trails and Observation Point Trail, may be blocked by snow during the winter (and early spring). In particular, the upper sections of these trails may be icy and dangerous to traverse.

LODGING

Zion Lodge, the only accommodation inside the park, offers year-round motel-style rooms and cabins. Here the Virgin River flows peacefully near your footsteps; you can almost touch the red canyon walls outside your door. A restaurant, gift shop, dining room, snack bar and post office offer limited visitor services. Reservations, made through Xanterra Parks and Resorts (see Appendix B), should be made several months in advance, especially for the busy spring and summer seasons. Xanterra Parks and Resorts maintains a full selection of available rooms and cabins through their telephone reservation service (888) 297 2757, or try 435 772 7700. Limited Zion Lodge reservations are available on the Internet; see www.zionlodge.com.

Springdale has plenty of better-class hotels and motels, but book ahead. To the east, Mount Carmel, Orderville and Glendale have some choices. Further out are Kanab and Fredonia, both small, pleasant towns with motels. For the western side of the park, La Verkin has a motel. Hurricane is another choice. For the Kolob Canyons area, the closest places are Leeds (Motel, RV and camping), Toquerville and Kanarraville. Other larger places, like St George and Cedar City, have good accommodation options but are further away. See Appendix C for suggestions.

CAMPING

Zion's South and Watchman campgrounds lie near the park's south entrance. Reservations are accepted for the Watchman campground. It is open all year round and charges $16 or $18, with hook-ups, per vehicle. Riverside sites are $20. Reservations are accepted up to five months in advance, online at www.reservations.nps.gov, or tel 800 365 2267. The South campground operates on a first-come first-served basis and charges $16 per site. Lava Point, on the Kolob Terrace Road, has six spaces on a primitive campground without water. Campgrounds fill early in summer.

Nearby Springdale offers a small private campground with showers. La Verkin also has a campground.

FOOD

Zion Lodge has restaurants and a snack bar. In Springdale there are plenty of eateries of all standards. Grocery stores are located in Springdale, Mount Carmel and Kanab; in La Verkin is a large Farmers Market superstore with attached snack bar.

VISITOR SERVICES

Zion Canyon Visitor Centre provides information, a museum, books, weather reports and visual displays. Park-orientation video shows are offered free at the Zion Museum centre every half hour. Both Zion Canyon and Kolob Canyons visitor centres issue backcountry permits.

For advance information contact Zion National Park, Springdale, Utah 84767-1099, tel 435 772 3256, fax 435 772 3426, email: ZION_park_information@nps.gov, www.nps.gov/zion.

ZION NATURAL HISTORY ASSOCIATION

The Zion Natural History Association, a non-profit-making organisation, helps to maintain park land and preserve its resources. Members are entitled to discounts on purchases at visitor centres at all national parks and monuments. Books, T-shirts, posters etc. on sale at the visitor centre help finance this organisation. Tel 800 635 3959 or 435 772 3264, fax: 435 772 3908, www.zionpark.org.

INTERPRETATIVE PROGRAMMES

Ranger-led activities feature various topics, from geology, plant and animal life to human history. Programmes, which run from May to October, vary from walks, talks at the centre, and campfire programmes at the campgrounds. Schedules are posted at the visitor centre and campgrounds.

OTHER FACILITIES

Limited general supplies are most readily available on Utah Route 9 in Springdale, just outside the south entrance to the park. You will find motels, post office, laundrette, showers, bank, restaurants, small grocery stores, petrol stations and limited backpacking and camping supplies.

TIME ZONES

The state of Utah, including Zion National Park and Bryce Canyon National Park, operates on mountain standard time (MST). Daylight savings time (MDT or mountain daylight time), when the clocks are pushed ahead 1hr, stays in effect between early April and late October. Utah runs 1hr ahead of Nevada, which operates on Pacific standard time (PST) and Pacific daylight time (PDT).

EMERGENCY/MEDICAL SERVICES

A 24hr service is available on tel 772 3322 or 911. In Springdale is the Zion Canyon Medical Clinic, tel 772 3226. St George, Cedar City and Kanab have the closest hospitals.

SOME USEFUL WEBSITES

www.nps.gov/zion
www.zion.national-park.com
www.zionnationalpark.com
www.desertusa.com/zion
www.go-zion.com
www.go-utah.com/Zion-National-Park
www.utah.com/zion
www.zioncanyoneering.org

CHAPTER 12

WALKING IN ZION NATIONAL PARK

*We are the pilgrims master, we shall go
Always a little further; it may be
Beyond the last blue mountain barred with snow*

James Elroy Flecker

With three distinct areas, Zion offers an exceptional variety of hiking. The most popular Zion Canyon valley has easy access and every grade of walk. To the west the country is more open, with colourful crags and canyons. Further to the northwest, the quieter area of the Kolob Canyons hides some impressive secrets. Each of the areas is cleverly linked by some longer, more demanding trails.

OVERNIGHT PERMITS

The permit system in Zion has been restructured recently and some further changes may be anticipated. Overnight camping is prohibited in many of Zion's canyons, so it would be wise to contact the Backcountry section at the visitor centre, tel 435 772 0170, www.nps.org/zion.

Permits are required for all overnight trips in the backcountry. This includes through-hikes of the Virgin River and its tributaries, as well as 'routes' like the Subway canyon. Reservations can be made on www.nps.gov/zion, but at least

40% of permits are reserved for on-the-spot bookings. These permits can be obtained either the day before or the same day at the visitor centres in Zion Canyon and Kolob Canyon. Some new canyoning and rock-climbing routes were added to the system in 2006. Limits on the number of permits for camping in Timber Creek and La Verkin Creek, Hop Valley, Potato Hollow and the West Rim apply. For the Narrows, only 80 people per day are now permitted.

Permits are also required for day-hikes in any of the canyons requiring artificial aid, such as the Left Fork of North Creek (the Subway), Kolob Creek, Pine Creek, Keyhole Falls or Orderville Canyon. These 'canyoneering' permits allow 50 per day. Descriptions of these off-trail canyon 'routes,' which are beyond the scope of this guide, can be found in books available at the visitor centres.

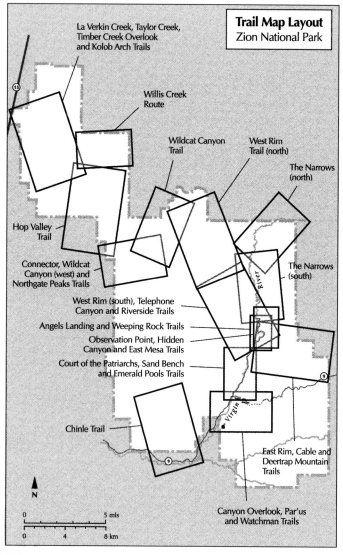

La Verkin Creek, Taylor Creek, Timber Creek Overlook and Kolob Arch Trails

Willis Creek Route

Wildcat Canyon Trail

West Rim Trail (north)

The Narrows (north)

Hop Valley Trail

Connector, Wildcat Canyon (west) and Northgate Peaks Trails

The Narrows (south)

West Rim (south), Telephone Canyon and Riverside Trails

Angels Landing and Weeping Rock Trails

Observation Point, Hidden Canyon and East Mesa Trails

Court of the Patriarchs, Sand Bench and Emerald Pools Trails

Chinle Trail

East Rim, Cable and Deertrap Mountain Trails

Canyon Overlook, Par'us and Watchman Trails

Trail Map Layout
Zion National Park

River

Virgin

N

| 0 | | 5 mls |
| 0 | 4 | 8 km |

Court of the Patriarchs (Zion Valley)

General view of colourful rocks east of Zion National Park

Green Zion Valley near Zion Lodge

FEES

Fees are based on the group size. Charges are as follows: 1–2 persons cost $10, 3–6 people $15, and 7–12 people $20.

DAY-WALKING

Permits are not required for most day-walking. You will need a permit, however, if you wish to complete the Narrows walk downstream from Chamberlain's Ranch to the Temple of Sinawava in one day. Permits are best obtained at the visitor centre the day before your hike. You do not need a permit to do the day-walk Up The Narrows, upstream from the Temple of Sinawava.

HIKING THE NARROWS

People come from all over the world to hike the Zion Narrows (chapter 18). This unique experience presents its own risks and rewards. No trail exists and you must walk in the riverbed through deep water. Flash floods and hypothermia present constant dangers. A sample of narrows-walking can be obtained by walking Up The Narrows to Orderville Canyon (chapter 15).

An overnight trip in the Narrows offers time to enjoy astounding scenery in this unique environment. Day-walks for the entire 16 mile Narrows trip are permitted only during the long, light days of summer. The most practical and enjoyable time to walk the Narrows is from July through to early October, when the water temperature rises, the flow of water lessens and speed slows. If walking between July and August, be sure to check the weather forecast and be aware of the possibility of flash floods.

SHUTTLE SERVICES

At the time of writing, no fixed shuttles operate from the main Zion visitor centre to other areas such as the western Kolob Canyons area of the park (to Lee Pass), to all roadheads off the Kolob Terrace Road (e.g. Hop Valley, Wildcat Canyon and Lava Point roadheads), to the East Entrance on Utah State Hwy 9 or to Chamberlain's Ranch at the start of the Narrows walk. From mid-April through to mid-October, contact the Zion Lodge travel desk or the visitor centre for information on private shuttle services. Especially during the busy summer season, reservations should be made several weeks in advance.

GROUPS

The National Park Service encourages small groups. To minimise environmental impact, groups of more than twelve must divide into smaller groups and visit different areas. This does not apply to Emerald Pools, Angels' Landing, Observation Point and the lower narrows before Orderville Canyon, all within the main Zion Canyon area.

MAPS

All trails in Zion appear on the plastic-coated Trails Illustrated (TI) Zion National Park map, scale approx 1:37,700, 30 'X25', with contour intervals of 50ft. This (map number 214) may be all you will need. A cheaper map is the Zion Topographical Map, scale 1:37,700, 39 'X25'; this is paper and not so durable. United States Geological Survey (USGS) 7.5 minute maps provide excellent additional detail. You may obtain the 7.5 minute series, possibly from the Zion Natural History Association, or more likely from the United States Geological Survey (USGS) (see Appendix B).

WATER SOURCES

Backcountry water must be treated, boiled or purified. All washing, either of dishes, clothing or yourself, should take place at least 200ft from any water source. Zion springs, the most reliable water sources, are found throughout the backcountry. Year-round water sources appear on this book's maps, fact panels and route profiles.

WAYMARKING

Signs stand at almost all trail junctions in the park. Though some of the backcountry receives limited use, most trails are distinct and easy to follow.

FLASH FLOODS

Thunderstorms many miles upstream cause huge torrents of water to rush down creek beds, washes and canyon bottoms. Especially during the peak flash-flood season from July through to August, any threat of rain should warn you against walking in narrow canyons. Heed the flash-flood warnings as well if you are day-walking upstream from the Temple of Sinawava to Orderville Canyon (chapter 15).

INSECTS, BIRDS, REPTILES AND MAMMALS

Deerflies proliferate along creeks in summer. Tiny, irritating insects abound in mid to late spring. Both can persist into autumn. Mosquitoes predominate during the summer months. Repellent, long sleeves and long trousers provide protection.

So far, 271 species of birds have been spotted in Zion. Rare or endangered birds are the peregrine falcon, Mexican spotted owl and willow flycatcher.

Non-poisonous snakes are sometimes seen in Zion, including the garter, gopher and whip snakes. The western rattlesnake, Zion's only poisonous reptile, strikes only when frightened or provoked. Leave them alone and they will slither away. Lizards are common, but a canyon treefrog is less common.

Mule deer are quite easily seen, and desert bighorn sheep may also be spotted. Of the 75 mammals living in the park, the most elusive – perhaps luckily – is the mountain lion, which is occasionally seen in Zion. There is little to fear – an attack is very unlikely, since they prefer to avoid confrontation. If you see a lion, do not run away, or it will think you are prey. In the event of a lion approaching, wave, shout and throw rocks. Try to look larger – spread your arms wide.

CHAPTER 13

ZION NATIONAL PARK:
KOLOB CANYONS TRAILS

Only a fool can predict the weather.

Unknown

The Kolob Canyons section of Zion National Park, making up its northwest border, hosts many fewer visitors than the busy eastern Zion Canyon. To reach this area from the Zion National Park South Entrance, take Utah Hwy 9 west through Virgin and Rockville for 22 miles to Hwy 17, then turn north. Proceed 6 miles to Interstate 15, turn north and, in 13 miles, take Exit 40 to Kolob Canyons. Allow 1hr driving time from Zion Canyon.

KOLOB CANYONS TRAILS			
Trail	Distance (miles) one way	Distance (km) one way	Rating
Timber Creek Overlook	0.5	0.8	Easy
Middle Fork of Taylor Creek	2.5	4.0	Moderate
La Verkin Creek	7.0	11.2	Moderate
Kolob Arch	0.3	0.5	Moderate
Willis Creek Route	4.5	7.2	Moderate
Hop Valley	6.7	10.7	Moderate

Timber Creek Overlook

Start	End of Kolob Canyons Road (6250ft/1905m)
End	Timber Creek Overlook (6369ft/1941m)
Distance, one way	0.5 miles (0.8km)
Time, one way	20mins
Maps	Kolob Arch (United States Geological Survey 7.5′); Zion National Park (TI)

Season	April through to November
Water	None
Rating	Easy

Directions

From the car park, 5.3 miles east of the Kolob Canyons visitor centre at the end of Kolob Canyons Road, the trail heads south across a knoll. In 0.5 miles it reaches a lookout over the Timber Creek drainage. Splendid views east to Shuntavi Butte and Timber Top Mountain greet you.

You can see the path of the La Verkin Creek Trail as it rounds Gregory Butte. Retrace your steps to your car.

Middle Fork of Taylor Creek Trail

Start	Taylor Creek parking area (5480ft/1670m)
End	Double Arch Alcove (6050ft/1844m)
Distance, one way	2.5 miles (4km)
Time, one way	1hr
Maps	Kolob Arch (United States Geological Survey 7.5′); Zion National Park (TI)
Season	April through to October
Water	None
Rating	Moderate

Starting from the Taylor Creek car park, 2 miles east of the Kolob Canyons visitor centre on Kolob Canyons Road, this walk visits the less popular, but no less scenic, western section of the park. The Middle Fork of Taylor Creek is limited to day use only. Camp only in the North Fork of Taylor Creek.

Directions

From the Taylor Creek car park the trail heads east and descends 80ft down steps to reach Taylor Creek. Follow the creek east and upstream as you continually cross the creek in and out of the water. In another 0.75 miles, you pass the run-down Larsen Cabin, used for logging settlements at the turn of the last century. From the cabin, dramatic views to Tucupit Point tower 1500ft above the creek. In

0.25 miles the North Fork of Taylor Creek branches north; camping is allowed 0.5 miles north of the confluence.

Continuing along the Middle Fork, the trail roughens as the canyon narrows. Now you ascend gradually as you enter the canyon between Tucupit Point and Paria Point. Next the red-walled canyons rise above the deteriorated 1930 Fife Cabin. The canyon bends south, ending at Double Arch Alcove. Here, a recess in the rock forms an overhanging cliff and an alcove; water drips from its interior. Retrace your steps to the car park.

La Verkin Creek Trail

Start	Lee Pass (6060ft/1847m)
End	Hop Valley Trail (5360ft/1634m)
Distance, one way	7 miles (11.2km)
Time, one way	3–4hrs
Maps	Kolob Arch (United States Geological Survey 7.5'); Zion National Park (TI)
Season	April through to November
Water	La Verkin Creek, Beatty Spring
Rating	Moderate

This popular 14 mile round trip, often completed in one day, begins from Lee Pass, 3.8 miles east of the Kolob Canyons visitor centre on Kolob Canyons Road. Some walkers make a short trip to the small waterfall and pools located near the Corral, 4.8 miles from Lee Pass. Bearcat Canyon and Hop Valley, further down La Verkin Creek, merit an overnight stay. If you plan to camp, you must pick up a backcountry permit at the Zion Canyon visitor centre or at the Kolob Canyons visitor centre. Camp only in designated sites along Timber and La Verkin Creeks and in Hop Valley.

Directions

From the car park at Lee Pass, the trail heads south and descends 500ft steeply through sage brush. In 1 mile you meet the cottonwood-lined Timber Creek drainage, where you'll see the first of the area's designated campsites. As you follow the creek, splendid eastern views to Shuntavi and Gregory buttes mark the horizon. Your route descends gradually as you round the edge of Shuntavi Butte

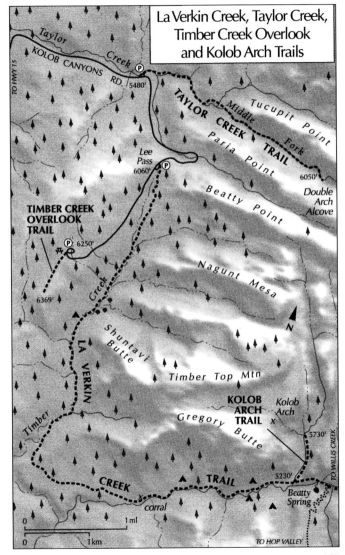

La Verkin Creek, Taylor Creek, Timber Creek Overlook and Kolob Arch Trails

TO HWY 15

Taylor Creek

KOLOB CANYONS RD.

℗ 5480'

TAYLOR CREEK TRAIL

Tucupit Point

Middle Fork

Paria Point

Lee Pass 6060'

℗

Beatty Point

6050'

Double Arch Alcove

TIMBER CREEK OVERLOOK TRAIL

℗ 6250'

Nagunt Mesa

Creek

6369'

N

LA VERKIN

Shuntavi Butte

Timber Top Mtn

KOLOB ARCH TRAIL

Kolob Arch x

Timber

Gregory Butte

5730'

TO WILLIS CREEK

CREEK

TRAIL

5230'

corral

Beatty Spring

0 _____ 1 ml

0 _____ 1 km

TO HOP VALLEY

167

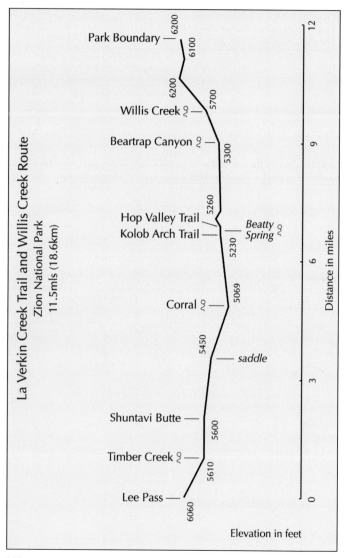

La Verkin Creek Trail and Willis Creek Route
Zion National Park
11.5mls (18.6km)

Park Boundary — 6200
6100
6200
Willis Creek ⚲ — 5700
Beartrap Canyon ⚲ — 5300
5260
Hop Valley Trail
Kolob Arch Trail — *Beatty Spring* ⚲
5230
5069
Corral ⚲ —
5450
saddle
Shuntavi Butte —
5600
Timber Creek ⚲ — 5610
Lee Pass — 6060

Distance in miles
12   9   6   3   0

Elevation in feet

and approach a low saddle. Now there are views to the east and south down the La Verkin Creek drainage. From the saddle, you soon approach a fine lunch stop at a small waterfall, and slickrock pools carved from the bedrock known as the Corral. Continuing up the drainage on the creek's true left and north side past several designated campsites, the walls of Gregory Butte to the north and Neagle Ridge to the south rise from the drainage. One hour further through grassy meadows along the sandy creek bed brings you to the Kolob Arch Trail.

From the Kolob Arch Junction, the La Verkin Creek Trail continues upstream and in 0.2 miles fords to the true right or south side of the creek. Just after crossing the creek, Beatty Spring, a perennial water source, drips down a rock wall. Pass several more campsites and ascend 50ft up a hill, and in 5mins you'll reach a trail junction and the end of the La Verkin Creek Trail. The Willis Creek Route continues straight ahead and the Hop Valley Trail ascends to the east.

Kolob Arch Trail

Start	Kolob Arch Trail (5230ft/1594m)
End	Under Kolob Arch (5730ft/1747m)
Distance, one way	0.3 miles (0.5km)
Time, one way	20mins
Maps	Kolob Arch (United States Geological Survey 7.5'); Zion National Park (TI)
Season	April through to November
Water	La Verkin Creek
Rating	Moderate

Directions

Turning north from the La Verkin Creek Trail, ascend along the true left of a small stream among numerous boulders. Just 0.5 miles from the main trail, three small drainages intersect below a flat bench. A sign marks the end of the trail at a viewpoint; travel beyond this point is not allowed. Far up and to the west spans the sprawling 292ft Kolob Arch, rivalling 291ft Landscape Arch in Arches National Park for the title of the world's largest free-standing arch. From this point, the arch appears quite small, and many visitors leave disappointed with the view.

Willis Creek Route

Start	Junction of Hop Valley Trail and La Verkin Creek Trail (5360ft/1633m)
End	Park Boundary (6200ft/1890m)
Distance, one way	4.5 miles (7.2km)
Time, one way	3hrs
Maps	Kolob Arch, Kolob Reservoir (United States Geological Survey 7.5'); Zion National Park (TI)
Season	April through to October
Water	Willis Creek
Rating	Moderate

Willis Creek can be explored as an extra day from the Kolob Arch area when backpacking across Zion National Park. Access Willis Creek only from the western La Verkin Creek. Some older maps show a now-closed trail crossing private land west of Kolob Reservoir and then joining the Willis Creek Trail from its eastern park boundary. Eastern access through the private land west of Kolob Reservoir requires special written permission.

Directions

From the Hop Valley Trail junction east of Beatty Spring, continue north up La Verkin Creek. Even in the spring the water levels are usually low, and you should have no difficulty fording the creek. Several pleasant designated campsites line the creek bed. After a little over 1 mile, Herb's Point dominates to the north, and in 2 miles you reach Beartrap Canyon. Continuing up the canyon, you come to the junction of La Verkin Creek and Willis Creek, where your route turns east. Massive cliff walls rise above the creek. Water seeps through into the previously dry creek bed as you rise higher and higher up the drainage. A gate marks the park boundary and your turn-around point. You must retrace your steps back to La Verkin Creek.

The 30mins walk to the waterfall up Beartrap Canyon makes a worthwhile detour. The walls of the canyon slowly close in above you as the canyon narrows. A waterfall blocks your passage further up the canyon.

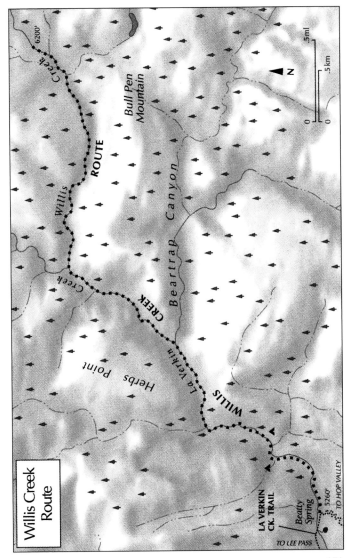

Hop Valley Trail

Start	Junction of Hop Valley Trail at La Verkin Creek (5360ft/1634m)
End	Kolob Terrace Road (6350ft/1935m)
Distance, one way	6.7 miles (10.7km)
Time, one way	4hrs
Maps	Kolob Arch, The Guardian Angels (United States Geological Survey 7.5'); Zion National Park (TI)
Season	Mid-April through to October
Water	Hop Valley
Rating	Moderate

The Hop Valley trailhead can be accessed from its western end at La Verkin Creek as described above, or from the east from the Hop Valley trailhead on the Kolob Terrace Road. To reach its eastern end, drive 13 miles north of Virgin, Utah, on the Kolob Terrace Road. If you are walking the Across Zion route (see chapter 18), you will be walking from La Verkin Creek to the Hop Valley trailhead from west to east as described here. If you are planning a day-walk to Kolob Arch, the most scenic route connects La Verkin Creek with the Kolob Terrace Road.

Directions

From the junction of the La Verkin Creek Trail, just up the hill from Beatty Spring, and at the start of the Willis Creek Route, turn uphill and east on the Hop Valley Trail. Climb 500ft up switchbacks to an overlook of Hop Valley, where you can see Gregory Butte and Timber Top Mountain behind you.

From here there are fine views to Hop Valley, as you descend through the trees to the bottom of the hill and to the valley bottom. You'll soon see some designated campsites on the north side of the creek. At this section of the valley, you will notice that the creek water disappears as it flows underground to form Beatty Spring in La Verkin Creek. When you reach the valley floor, follow one of the cattle trails south across the grassy, sometimes muddy bottom, along the sides of the creek. Pass through the gate into private property. Criss-cross the creek several times. As you wander down the pleasant sandy valley, you soon see Langston

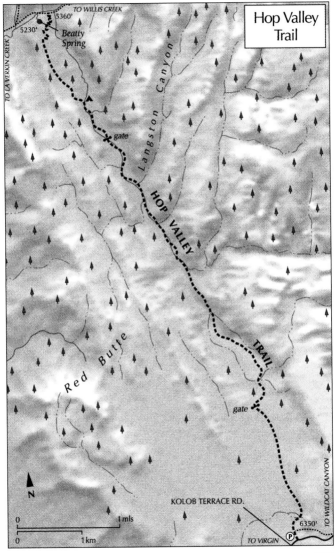

Hop Valley
Trail

TO WILLIS CREEK

TO LA VERKIN CREEK

5360'
5230'

Beatty Spring

Langston Canyon

gate

HOP VALLEY

Red Butte

TRAIL

gate

N

0   1 mls

0   1 km

KOLOB TERRACE RD.

TO WILDCAT CANYON

TO VIRGIN

6350'
P

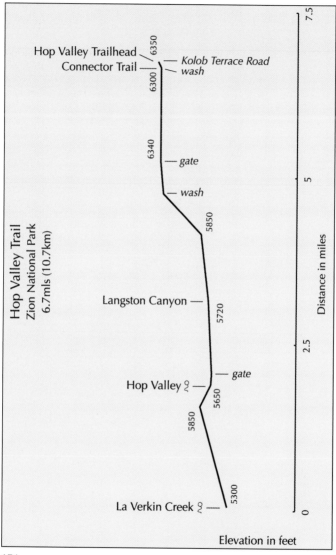

Hop Valley Trailhead
Connector Trail
6350
6300
Kolob Terrace Road
wash

6340
gate
wash

5850

Hop Valley Trail
Zion National Park
6.7mls (10.7km)

Langston Canyon
5720

gate
Hop Valley ♀
5650
5850

5300
La Verkin Creek ♀

Distance in miles

7.5

5

2.5

0

Elevation in feet

Canyon joining from the east. After reaching the end of the valley, you begin a gradual ascent of 500ft between the towering cliffs and two creek beds until you reach the upper plateau.

Cross the arid plateau, with its chaparral and other low-lying vegetation. Behind you are the red walls of La Verkin Creek. Red Butte rises to the west. In 1 mile another gate and fence mark your exit from private land. The vague road now winds south through the vegetation, as Firepit Knoll forms a helpful landmark to the east. Soon you cross a wash and a sign leading east to the Connector Trail. In 0.1 miles you reach the Hop Valley trailhead and Kolob Terrace Road.

CHAPTER 14

ZION NATIONAL PARK: WEST RIM TRAILS

Adventure is not in the guidebook
And Beauty is not on the map.

Jerry and Renny Russell

This stunning section of Zion National Park, most easily reached from Virgin, Utah, along Kolob Terrace Road, provides a variety of walking trails. From Zion National Park South Entrance, take Utah Hwy 9 south through Springdale and Rockville to the town of Virgin. Turn north on Kolob Terrace Road to reach all the roadheads. Even if you aren't planning to walk, take a few hours to drive this scenic road, far away from the valley crowds.

WEST RIM TRAILS			
Trail	Distance (miles) one way	Distance (km) one way	Rating
Connector Trail	4.0	6.4	Moderate
Wildcat Canyon	5.8	9.3	Moderate
Northgate Peaks	2.2	3.5	Easy
West Rim Trail	14.2	22.7	Strenuous

Connector Trail

Start	Hop Valley Trailhead (6350ft/1935m)
End	Wildcat Canyon Trail (6950ft/2118m)
Distance, one way	4 miles (6.4km)
Time, one way	2hrs
Maps	The Guardian Angels (United States Geological Survey 7.5') (trail not marked on map); Zion National Park (TI)
Season	Mid-April through to October
Water	None
Rating	Moderate

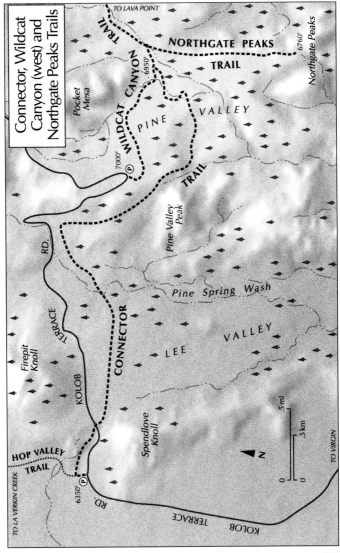

Connector, Wildcat Canyon (west) and Northgate Peaks Trails

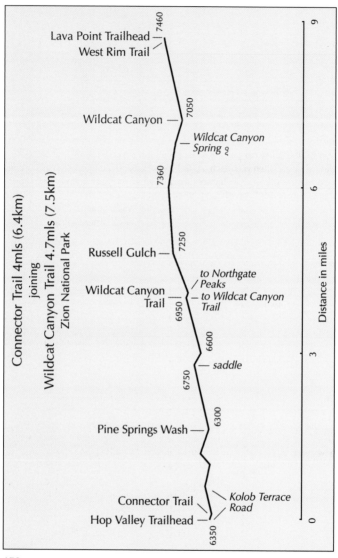

Connector Trail 4mls (6.4km)
joining
Wildcat Canyon Trail 4.7mls (7.5km)
Zion National Park

Lava Point Trailhead — 7460
West Rim Trail

Wildcat Canyon — 7050

Wildcat Canyon Spring ♀

7360

7250

Russell Gulch —

Wildcat Canyon Trail — 6950

to Northgate / Peaks
to Wildcat Canyon Trail

6600

— *saddle*

6750

Pine Springs Wash — 6300

Kolob Terrace Road

Connector Trail —
Hop Valley Trailhead — 6350

Distance in miles

9

6

3

0

The Connector Trail, allowing walkers to cross Zion on foot without having to walk along the Kolob Terrace Road, provides a convenient, albeit hot and dry, link between the Kolob Terrace Road and the Wildcat Canyon Trail.

The Hop Valley Trail starts from the car park 13 miles north of Virgin, Utah, off the Kolob Terrace Road.

Directions

From the Hop Valley car park, walk north 0.1 miles on the trail that heads to Hop Valley. Turn east when you reach the old creek bed and the signpost. In 0.25 miles the trail crosses the Kolob Terrace Road to enter the north end of Lee Valley. Spendlove Knoll juts up to the south and Firepit Knoll to the north. After 45mins and 1.5 miles the trail passes through Pine Spring Wash. In another 1.3 miles you reach a pine-tree-laden saddle north of Pine Valley Peak, where you are rewarded with a fine view of North Guardian Angel. Continue east for 1 mile until the Connector Trail joins the Wildcat Canyon Trail, about 1 mile from the Wildcat Canyon parking area and 0.1 miles west of the Northgate Peaks Trail, where there is fine camping in its pine forest.

Water along the Connector Trail may be sparse to non-existent. In spring, Pine Springs Wash may harbour several unexpected water pockets. Ask the park service if anyone has reported them. The closest perennial water flows from Wildcat Canyon Spring several miles ahead. If you are walking across the park on the Across Zion trip, you may wish to collect water either near the Hop Valley trailhead or, better yet, off the trail at the Wildcat Canyon and Northgate Peaks Trail junction.

Wildcat Canyon Trail

Start	Wildcat Canyon Trailhead (7000ft/2134m)
End	Lava Point Trailhead (7460ft/2274m)
Distance, one way	5.8 miles (9.3km)
Time, one way	3hrs
Maps	Kolob Reservoir, The Guardian Angels (United States Geological Survey 7.5'); Zion National Park (TI)
Season	Mid-April through to October

| Water | Wildcat Canyon Spring |
| Rating | Moderate |

The Wildcat Canyon car park is located 16 miles north of Virgin on Kolob Terrace Road.

Directions

From the car park, walk east on the old road through the pine forest. In 0.5 miles the Connector Trail to Hop Valley joins from the southwest. In another 0.1 miles the Northgate Peaks Trail turns south. Bear northeast and head steadily uphill past Russell Gulch. You reach your high point around 1.5 miles from the trail junction and begin your descent into Wildcat Canyon. From the high point in another 0.5 miles you come to Wildcat Canyon Spring, clearly visible on the west side of the trail, where a sign reads 'Purify Water'. Wildcat Canyon offers poor camping. Another 0.5 miles further on the trail, you cross dry Wildcat Creek and begin a 1 mile ascent to the West Rim Trail. At the trail junction on the top of the hill you join the West Rim Trail. Turn south towards Zion Canyon or walk north 0.1 miles to the Lava Point car park.

Northgate Peaks Trail

Start	Wildcat Canyon Trailhead (7000ft/2134m)
End	Lookout to North Guardian Angel (6760ft/2060m)
Distance, one way	2.2 miles (3.5km)
Time, one way	1hr
Maps	The Guardian Angels (United States Geological Survey 7.5') (trail not on map); Zion National Park (TI)
Season	Mid-April through to October
Water	None
Rating	Easy

This remote, little-used trail offers many fine, dry camping spots on its level, pine-studded plateau.

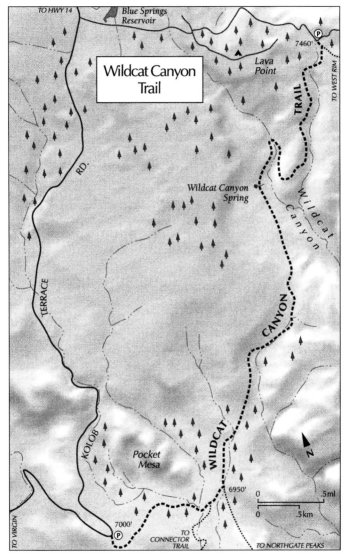

Wildcat Canyon Trail

TO HWY 14

Blue Springs Reservoir

Lava Point

7460'

TRAIL

TO WEST RIM

RD.

Wildcat Canyon Spring

Wildcat Canyon

TERRACE

CANYON

KOLOB

Pocket Mesa

WILDCAT

N

6950'

7000'

TO VIRGIN

TO CONNECTOR TRAIL

TO NORTHGATE PEAKS

0   .5ml
0   .5km

The Wildcat Canyon car park off Kolob Terrace Road, 16 miles north of Virgin, Utah, provides the easiest access to this pleasant trail.

Directions

From the Wildcat Canyon trailhead proceed east for 1 mile to the junction with the Connector Trail. Continue straight ahead and go 0.1 miles to the Northgate Peaks Trail Junction and turn south. The Wildcat Canyon Trail heads northeast.

Heading south from the trail junction, you notice immediately a well-worn path dropping to the west. This path leads into Russell Gulch to the popular off-trail route descending the Left Fork and passing through the Subway. Remaining on the main trail, continue straight ahead through the pine forest. Eventually the trees thicken and block your view. Later the vistas open up as the trail ends at a lava-formed viewpoint. Northgate Peaks line either side of your gaze and North Guardian Angel stands directly in front of you. Numerous canyons and gorges of the central park area make up the rest of the landscape. Checkerboarding adorns many of the stone faces and domes. In the far distance you can identify the Bishopric and Inclined Temple, and the drainages of the Right and Left Fork.

West Rim Trail

Start	Lava Point Trailhead (7460ft/2274m)
End	Grotto picnic area (4298ft/1310m)
Distance, one way	14.2 miles (22.7km)
Time, one way	7hrs
Maps	Kolob Reservoir, Temple of Sinawava, The Guardian Angels (United States Geological Survey 7.5′); Zion National Park (TI)
Season	Mid-April through to October
Water	West Rim (Cabin) Spring
Rating	Strenuous

One of Zion's most spectacular walks and its most popular backpacking route, the West Rim Trail can be walked as an overnight trip or a long day-walk. Three springs at Potato Hollow, Sawmill Springs and West Rim (Cabin) Spring provide water. Camp only in designated sites dotting the West Rim and Potato Hollow area.

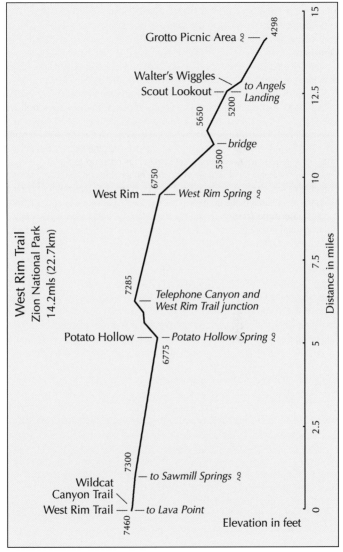

Grotto Picnic Area ⚲ — 4298

Walter's Wiggles
Scout Lookout — ⎯ to Angels
Landing
5200

5650

⎯ bridge
5500

West Rim ⎯ West Rim Spring ⚲
6750

7285

Telephone Canyon and
West Rim Trail junction

Potato Hollow ⎯ ⎯ Potato Hollow Spring ⚲
6775

7300 ⎯ to Sawmill Springs ⚲

Wildcat
Canyon Trail
West Rim Trail ⎯ ⎯ to Lava Point
7460

West Rim Trail
Zion National Park
14.2mls (22.7km)

15

12.5

10

7.5

Distance in miles

5

2.5

0

Elevation in feet

The overnight trip, included in the Across Zion itinerary (see chapter 18), allows more time to admire the first-class views of many distant parts of the park. The least strenuous and most scenic trip starts from the Lava Point trailhead and descends to the valley floor. The hardy can start from the Grotto picnic area and ascend 3000ft to the West Rim. This second alternative misses some of the finest park views from the West Rim Trail and south from Potato Hollow.

To reach the trailhead from Virgin, Utah, take the Kolob Terrace Road 21 miles to the Lava Point turn-off and turn east. Proceed 1 mile to where three roads intersect. Take the middle road directly east and to the north of the road to Lava Point. The West Rim Trail begins 1.25 miles down this road at the trail register and vehicle barrier. Contact Zion Lodge or the visitor centre to find out if there is any convenient shuttle service to Lava Point.

Directions

From the West Rim trailhead, follow the flat jeep road south, soon crossing the junction with the Wildcat Canyon Trail. After 1 mile from the start, a trail branches west to Sawmill Springs. A short detour down a small hill brings you to the spring in a lovely meadow.

The main trail continues on top of the plateau, unfortunately marred by many lightning strikes and fires. The sandstone finger of Horse Plateau juts out over the North Fork of the Virgin River and the cliffs of Goose Creek. Views of North and South Guardian Angel open up to the west. After 4 miles the trail descends a gully to grassy Potato Hollow, where you'll admire fine views towards the Narrows and the Virgin River. You may want to reserve a designated campsite here in the vicinity of Potato Hollow Spring and leave the scenic West Rim Trail for the morning.

Leaving Potato Hollow, you climb steeply south, enjoying splendid views north to Imlay Canyon, Sleepy Hollow and Greatheart Mesa. Reaching the top of a ridge, the trail drops a bit as spectacular southern views to the Inclined Temple, Ivins Mountain and the Right Fork become evident. As you descend a narrow ridge, these views grab your attention before you finally reach the bottom of a small saddle. Climbing steeply again 400ft up the ridge from Potato Hollow, you come to the junction of the Telephone Canyon Trail and West Rim Trail.

The Telephone Canyon Trail, a shorter but much less scenic alternative to the West Rim Trail, branches east to meet the West Rim Spring Junction. The dramatic West Rim Trail turns west and begins its scenic meandering along the edge of the West Rim. The views from this trail are some of the most spectacular in the park. White and red sandstone rock formations mix among finger-like valleys and bald-topped plateaux. The first views take in South Guardian Angel and the Right Fork of North Creek. The trail then veers southeast and crosses southern Horse Plateau. Turning south you gaze down into Heaps Canyon and the Inclined Temple. Three

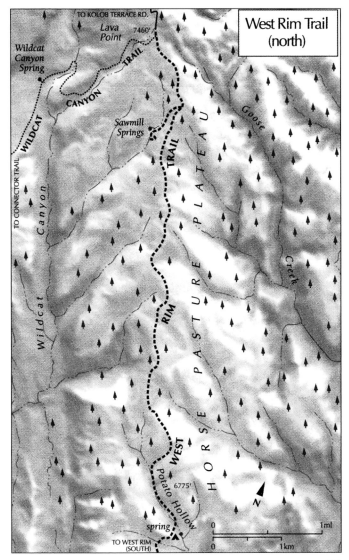

West Rim Trail (north)

TO KOLOB TERRACE RD.

Lava Point 7460'

Wildcat Canyon Spring

WILDCAT CANYON TRAIL

TO CONNECTOR TRAIL

Sawmill Springs

Wildcat Canyon

WEST RIM TRAIL

HORSE PASTURE PLATEAU

Goose Creek

6775'

Potato Hollow

spring

TO WEST RIM (SOUTH)

N

0   1ml

0   1km

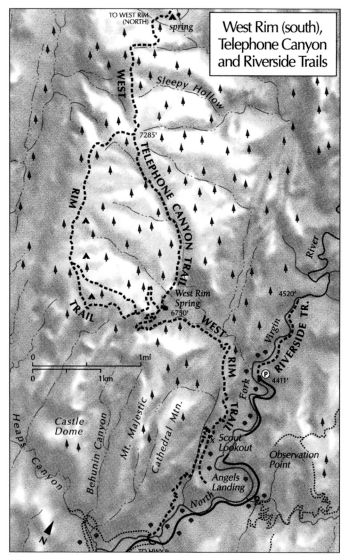

TO WEST RIM (NORTH)

spring

West Rim (south), Telephone Canyon and Riverside Trails

Sleepy Hollow

7285'

WEST

RIM

TELEPHONE CANYON TRAIL

TRAIL

West Rim Spring

6750'

WEST

RIM

River

4520'

RIVERSIDE TR.

0   1mi

0   1km

TRAIL

Virgin

Fork

P 4411'

Heaps Canyon

Castle Dome

Behunin Canyon

Mt. Majestic

Cathedral Mtn.

Scout Lookout

Observation Point

Angels Landing

North

Fork

N

TO HWY 9

186

other grand flat-topped mesas ornament your distant views. As you meander east, Behunin Canyon comes into view and you can see Castle Dome to the south and further east the flat top of Mount Majestic and Cathedral Mountain.

Numbered campsites are scattered along this section of the West Rim. Soon the trail switchbacks down 300ft to meet the Telephone Canyon Trail and nearby West Rim (Cabin) Spring. This small spring, trickling out of the rock 100yds east down the edge of a 700ft cliff, served a park service cabin until the cabin burned down in the 1970s. This spring provides your last water source until you reach Zion Valley.

Returning to the junction near the spring, you begin another dramatic section of the trail. Here you skirt the edge of the rim on a wide path next to high Navajo sandstone cliffs. Made of either rock or pavement, the trail winds its way along switchbacks 1.5 miles down to the valley floor. Take care in the spring, when ice or snow can make this section treacherous. Looking back you can see the high, water-stained West Rim cliffs you have just descended.

Reaching the floor below the West Rim, you descend 0.5 miles into a dry wash and cross a bridge. Continuing north from the bridge, you turn abruptly south and begin a 150ft climb that soon tops out with fine views north to the Mountain of Mystery and across the valley to the Great White Throne and Red Arch Mountain. The trail winds down to Scout Lookout and reaches the base of Angels' Landing. Hopefully, you will have allowed for a detour to the top of Angels' Landing. Here you feel back at civilisation, as you will meet many day-walkers ascending from Zion Canyon.

See the description in chapter 15, Zion Canyon Trails, for the climb of Angels' Landing and for the last section of the West Rim Trail from Scout Lookout to the Grotto picnic area.

ZION NATIONAL PARK: ZION CANYON TRAILS

Silence alone is worthy to be heard.

Henry David Thoreau

ZION CANYON TRAILS			
Trail	Distance (miles) one way	Distance (km) one way	Rating
Gateway to the Narrows or Riverside Trail	1.0	1.6	Easy
Up the Narrows to Orderville Canyon	3.2	5.1	Strenuous
Weeping Rock	0.2	0.3	Easy
Hidden Canyon	1.0	1.6	Moderate
Observation Point	3.7	5.9	Strenuous
Angels' Landing via Scout Lookout	2.5	4.0	Strenuous
Lower Emerald Pool	0.6	1.0	Easy
Middle Emerald Pool	1.0	1.6	Easy
Upper Emerald Pool	1.3	2.1	Moderate
Court of the Patriarchs	0.02	0.03	Easy
Sand Bench Horse Trail	3.4	5.4	Easy
Par'us	2.0	3.2	Easy
The Watchman	5.8	9.3	Moderate

Gateway to The Narrows or Riverside Trail

Start	Temple of Sinawava (4411ft/1344m)
End	Virgin River (4490ft/1368m)
Distance, one way	1 mile (1.6km)
Time, one way	20mins

Maps	Temple of Sinawava (United States Geological Survey 7.5'); Zion National Park (TI)
Season	All year
Water	Virgin River
Rating	Easy

Zion's most popular walk, Gateway to the Narrows or the Riverside Trail, is a paved, wheelchair-accessible trail following the Virgin River 1 mile up the narrowing canyon.

The trail starts from the northernmost end of the Zion Canyon Scenic Road at the Temple of Sinawava. Heading upstream on the true left of the Virgin River below steep cliffs, you are flanked by the towering Pulpit to the west and the red-faced Temple of Sinawava to the east. Hanging gardens of wildflowers line the path in the spring. On a hot summer's day you can cool your feet in the river.

If no flash-flood danger exists, you can continue upstream from the trail's end. The route snakes through the Virgin River to Orderville Canyon, 2.2 miles ahead. This part of the walk overlaps with the last section of the Narrows Route, described next under 'Up The Narrows to Orderville Canyon.'

Up The Narrows to Orderville Canyon

Start	Temple of Sinawava (4418ft/1347 m)
End	Orderville Canyon (4610ft/1405m)
Distance, one way	3.2 miles (5.1km)
Time, one way	3hrs
Maps	Temple of Sinawava (United States Geological Survey 7.5'); Zion National Park (TI)
Season	June through to October
Water	Virgin River
Rating	Strenuous

This trip, starting from The Temple of Sinawava at the end of the Zion Canyon Road and overlapping with the last section of the Narrows Route, offers a splendid example of canyon-walking. If you don't want to backpack or attempt the whole of the Narrows in a single day, this route provides a sneak peak at some narrows-walking. You may be inspired to return later for the complete trip.

Water temperatures chill the hardiest walkers – even in summer – so be sure to carry warm clothing on this trip. Protective clothing, available for rent in Springdale, provides extra warmth; special shoes prevent slipping on the rocks. The name 'Up the Narrows' may confuse you, since this walk does not include the true 'narrows' section of the Virgin River located between Deep Creek and Orderville Canyon. (See chapter 18, Zion National Park, Long-distance Routes, for a more complete description of equipment needed and risks associated with canyon-walking.)

Directions
Starting at the Temple of Sinawava car park, follow the Gateway to the Narrows Trail (Riverside Trail) for 1 mile to the end of the concrete path. Continue straight ahead and enter the Virgin River. Fighting the current, weave back and forth across pebbly side-bars and sandy beaches to find shallow crossing areas.

Carving a 2000ft channel down from the Markagunt Plateau, the Virgin River has created grottoes, side-canyons, springs and waterfalls. Mystery Canyon, 1 mile north of the end of the concrete trail, presents itself as a trickle of water from the east side of the canyon. Orderville Canyon, the first major canyon to join the Virgin River, enters from the east, 2.2 miles from the start. Though its upper reaches can only be explored with specialist equipment, you can wander a short way upstream before your passage is blocked.

Returning to the Virgin River at Orderville Canyon, the 'Narrows' section begins 0.5 miles north of the junction and continues for 2 miles upstream beyond this point. Do not enter this section during bad weather, thunderstorms or in the event of any risk of flash floods. Return to the parking area by retracing your steps downstream.

Weeping Rock

Start	Weeping Rock car park (4350ft/1326m)
End	Weeping Rock (4450ft/1356m)

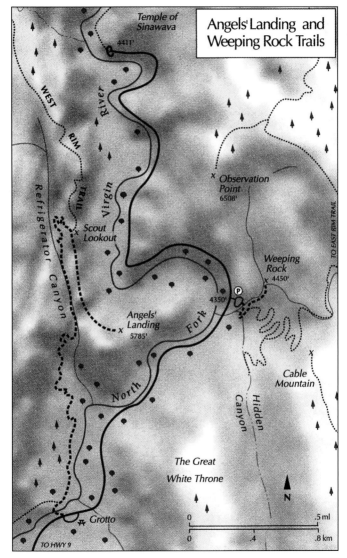

Angels' Landing and Weeping Rock Trails

Temple of Sinawava

4411'

WEST

RIM

TRAIL

Virgin

River

Refrigerator Canyon

Scout Lookout
x

x Observation Point
6508'

TO EAST RIM TRAIL

Weeping Rock
4450' x

P
4350'

x Angels' Landing
5785'

North Fork

Cable Mountain x

Hidden Canyon

The Great White Throne

N

Grotto

TO HWY 9

| 0 | | .5 ml |
| 0 | .4 | .8 km |

Distance, one way	0.2 miles (0.3km)
Time, one way	10mins
Maps	Temple of Sinawava (United States Geological Survey 7.5'); Zion National Park (TI)
Season	All year
Water	None
Rating	Easy

From the Weeping Rock car park, 4.4 miles up Zion Canyon Scenic Drive, follow the trail south over the creek. Interpretative signs describe the vegetation. In 5mins the trail forks; the East Rim Trail continues east and up from here.

Directions
The trail continues north to an overlook under Weeping Rock. Rain 'weeps' from a spring in the sandstone roof of the alcove above you. Retrace your steps to the car, or turn east at the junction to continue to Observation Point and Hidden Canyon.

Hidden Canyon and Observation Point

Start	Weeping Rock car park (4350ft/1326m)
End	Hidden Canyon (5100ft/1554m) or Observation Point (6508ft/1984m)
Distance, one way	to Hidden Canyon 1 mile (1.6km); to Observation Point 3.7 miles (5.9km)
Time, one way	3hrs to Observation Point
Maps	Temple of Sinawava (United States Geological Survey 7.5'); Zion National Park (TI)
Season	June through to October
Water	None
Rating	Moderate

These trails, cut into the sandstone in the 1930s, show off imposing views of the Zion Canyon, just as splendid as their better-known cross-canyon counterparts.

Swirling rock formations on the road out to the east entrance to Zion National Park

Upper and Middle waterfalls (Emerald Pools Trail, Zion)

Incredible rock formations on the Canyon Overlook Trail (Zion)

Zigzag path to Walter's Wiggles (Angel's Landing Trail, Zion)

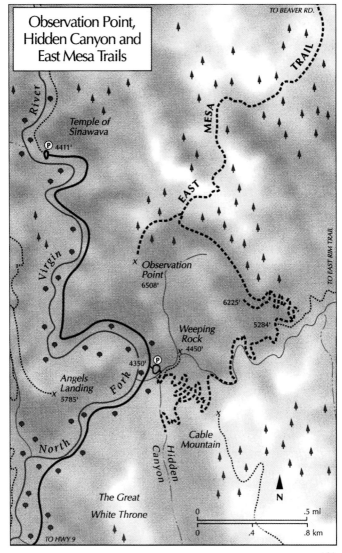

Observation Point,
Hidden Canyon and
East Mesa Trails

TO BEAVER RD.

EAST MESA TRAIL

River

Temple of
Sinawava

P 4411'

Virgin

x Observation
Point
6508'

6225'

5284'

Weeping
Rock
4450' x

TO EAST RIM TRAIL

4350'
P

Angels
Landing
5785' x

North Fork

x

Cable
Mountain

Hidden Canyon

The Great
White Throne

N

0   .5 ml

.4   .8 km

TO HWY 9

Starting from the Weeping Rock car park, 4.4 miles up Zion Canyon Scenic Drive, these two hikes may be completed separately or together. The hike to Observation Point offers a wonderful alternative to the crowded hike to Angels' Landing or Scout Lookout.

Directions

From the car park follow the interpretative trail south, and in 5mins continue east at the junction that turns to Weeping Rock. Ascend the cliffs below Cable Mountain in a series of switchbacks. In 30mins the trail to Hidden Canyon branches south. A traverse along the slickrock walls leads to the mouth of Hidden Canyon, sandwiched between the Great White Throne and the sheer walls of Cable Mountain. Potholes formed by rainwater wear grooves into the canyon walls. Continuing 0.5 miles upstream from the mouth of the canyon brings you to a small arch.

Back on the trail to Observation Point, climb past the turn-off to Hidden Canyon. After several more switchbacks, you enter cool Echo Canyon, weaving amidst the red-walled cliffs and washes until you reach a signed junction. The trail to Observation Point continues west and East Rim Trail branches east. Snow or ice may block the upper sections of this trail in spring. Cutting into the sandstone, the trail rises steeply as it climbs to a high plateau to meet the East Mesa Trail. Turn south and soon reach Observation Point. Outstanding views of the Great White Throne, Cable Mountain, the West Rim, Angels' Landing and Zion Canyon greet you. Retrace your steps to the car.

Angels' Landing via Scout Lookout

Start	Grotto picnic area (4290ft/1308m)
End	Angels' Landing (5790ft/1765m)
Distance, one way	2.5 miles (4km)
Time, one way	2hrs
Maps	Temple of Sinawava (United States Geological Survey 7.5'); Zion National Park (TI)
Season	March through to November
Water	None
Rating	Strenuous

This famous walk to Angels' Landing distinguishes itself as the most popular day-walk in Zion.

Begin from the Grotto picnic area, 0.5 miles north of Zion Lodge on the Zion Canyon Scenic Drive.

Directions

From the picnic tables, cross the road and take the footbridge to the true right of the Virgin River. Just after crossing the river, the trail to Emerald Pools veers southwest. The path to Angels' Landing follows the river north amidst a jumble of boulders.

Ahead you can see the trail as it switchbacks upward through the sandstone. Leaving the switchbacks behind, enter cool Refrigerator Canyon. The famous 21 switchbacks of Walter's Wiggles follow, as you climb the last 1000ft to Scout Lookout. This section was blasted into solid rock during construction by the Civilian Conservation Corps (CCC) in 1926. Fine views down the sheer walls into Zion Canyon greet you. Scout Lookout, a popular turn-around point for many day-walkers, marks the turn-off to Angels' Landing. Three miles further along this trail, together with a steep ascent, brings you to West Rim (Cabin) Spring and the West Rim Trail and Telephone Canyon Trail junction.

Angels' Landing, clearly viewed from here, makes a highly recommended and exciting detour. However, if you are afraid of heights or are accompanied by small children, do not attempt it. Forego your ascent also in wet, icy conditions or thunderstorms. From Scout Lookout, the trail appears more treacherous than it truly is and many a frightened walker turns back here. Chains and wide steps protect the entire path.

From Scout Lookout, follow the trail south, first up over a notch and across a narrow spine to the north side of the landing. Next ascend an extremely steep sandstone ridge, equipped with chains, rails and wide steps. Steep drop-offs mark both sides of the trail. Continue upward and hold on tightly. Reaching the upper knife-edge of the landing, you are rewarded with views across the Zion Valley to the Great White Throne, Cable Mountain, the South Zion Valley and the Observation Point Trail as it winds its way up to the rim from Weeping Rock. Carefully retrace your steps to Scout Lookout and back to the Grotto picnic area.

Emerald Pools

Start	Zion Lodge (4276ft/1303m)
End	Upper Emerald Pool (4520ft/1378m) via Lower and Middle Pools

Distance, one way	0.6 miles (1km) to Lower Pool; 1 mile (1.6km) to Middle Pool; 1.3 miles (2.1km) to Upper Pool
Time, one way	10mins to Lower Pool; 20mins to Middle Pool; 45mins to Upper Pool
Maps	Temple of Sinawava (United States Geological Survey 7.5′); Zion National Park (TI)
Season	All year
Water	None
Rating	Moderate

There are three emerald pools to visit; all are accessible by linked trails.

From the Emerald Pools car park, across from Zion Lodge, cross the Virgin River on a bridge to the west and true right of the river. Just across the river, the fork that bears north marks the easiest, wheelchair-accessible path to the Lower Pool. A turn south accesses a loop trail to the Upper and Middle Pools and the Sand Bench Trail.

Directions

Taking the north fork toward the Lower Pool, you wander among a forest of trees until you reach an overhang. In the spring, Heaps Canyon Creek drips into the Lower Pool and forms the Emerald Pools. From the Lower Pool a steeper, more difficult trail leads in 0.2 miles to the Middle Pool, and in another 0.3 miles to the Upper Pool.

Back at the first junction, if you wish to visit the Middle and Upper pools, follow the southern fork until it turns sharply to the north and in 1 mile leads you to the Middle Pool. As you climb up the trail, you are rewarded with views across the canyon to the Great White Throne and Red Arch Mountain. To the north you see the Spearhead and to the east Lady Mountain. Passing near the Middle Pool, a narrow trail climbs to the Upper Pool. Cross the field of boulders and its many intersecting paths. From here sandstone cliffs rise from three sides and after rain a waterfall drops into the Upper Pool.

From any of the pools you can retrace your steps to the car park, or head north for 0.8 miles to the Grotto picnic area. Fine views of Observation Point, the Great White Throne and Angels' Landing line this path. A 0.6 mile, almost flat trail, paralleling Zion Drive, connects Zion Lodge and the Grotto picnic area. From the picnic area walk east towards the ranger's residence, and follow the path south through the trees until it emerges from the forest near Zion Lodge.

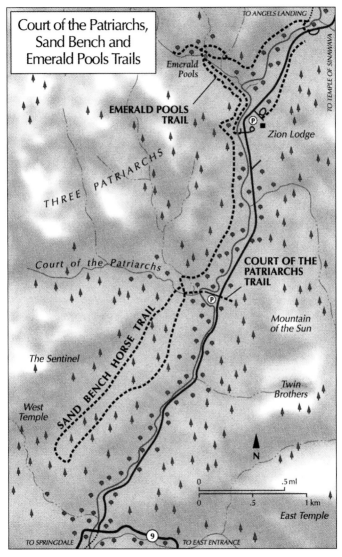

Court of the Patriarchs, Sand Bench and Emerald Pools Trails

TO ANGELS LANDING

TO TEMPLE OF SINAWAVA

Emerald Pools

EMERALD POOLS TRAIL

Zion Lodge

THREE PATRIARCHS

Court of the Patriarchs

COURT OF THE PATRIARCHS TRAIL

Mountain of the Sun

The Sentinel

SAND BENCH HORSE TRAIL

Twin Brothers

West Temple

N

0 .5 ml

0 .5 1 km

East Temple

TO SPRINGDALE

9

TO EAST ENTRANCE

Court of the Patriarchs

Start	Court of the Patriarchs car park (4250ft/1295m)
End	Court of the Patriarchs viewpoint (4290ft/1308m)
Distance, one way	0.02 miles (0.03km)
Time, one way	5mins
Maps	Springdale East (United States Geological Survey 7.5'); Zion National Park (TI)
Season	All year
Water	None
Rating	Easy

This popular paved trail, open all year, offers fine views of the entire Zion Canyon.

Directions

From the Court of the Patriarchs car park, 2.2 miles up Zion Canyon Scenic Drive from Utah Route 9, the concrete trail ascends east from the road until it ends at a canyon overlook. You see the Sentinel, Court of the Patriarchs, Mt Moroni, and far down the valley to Angels' Landing. Return to the car park by retracing your steps.

Sand Bench Horse Trail

Start	Court of the Patriarchs car park (4250ft/1295m)
End	Corral (4600ft/1402m)
Distance, semi-loop	3.4 miles (5.4km)
Time, one way	2hrs
Maps	Springdale East (United States Geological Survey 7.5'), Zion National Park (TI)
Season	All year
Water	None
Rating	Moderate

Horses frequent this dusty trail from spring through to autumn.

From the Court of the Patriarchs car park, 2.2 miles up Zion Canyon Scenic Drive, take the road to the west side of the road, pass the water tank and cross the Virgin River

Directions

On the far side, turn south and climb above the river until you reach the fork in the trail. The north fork brings you to the Emerald Pools and the south fork quickly connects you to the Sand Bench Loop. Before you stands the Court of the Patriarchs, with the red cliffs of the Three Patriarchs, and Mt Moroni soars above you.

Begin a 500ft climb on the southwest fork around the loop. The Streaked Wall dominates the view ahead of you; the Watchman looms across the canyon. At the south end of the loop you come to a picnic table, a rest area and a corral. As you circle north, you are rewarded with views of the Mountain of the Sun, the East Temple and the Twin Brothers. Combine this hike with the Emerald Pool Trail into a half-day hike.

Par'us Trail

Start	South Campground (4000ft/1219m)
End	Zion Canyon Drive at Utah State Hwy 9 (4000ft/1219m)
Distance, one way	2 miles (3.2km)
Time, one way	1hr
Maps	Springdale East (United States Geological Survey 7.5'); Zion National Park (TI)
Season	All year
Water	Virgin River
Rating	Easy

This is a flat, 2 mile walk on a paved, wheelchair-accessible trail shared with bicycles.

The route starts west of the Virgin River at the South Campground. Fine views north to the Towers of the Virgin, the Streaked Wall, and lower Zion Canyon stretch out before you. The trail ends when it intersects the Zion Canyon Scenic Drive.

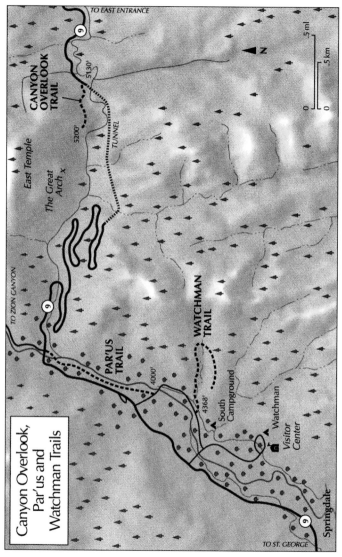

Canyon Overlook,
Par'us and
Watchman Trails

TO EAST ENTRANCE

9

5130'

CANYON OVERLOOK TRAIL

5200'

TUNNEL

East Temple

The Great Arch

9

TO ZION CANYON

PAR'US TRAIL

4000'

WATCHMAN TRAIL

4368'

South Campground

Watchman

Visitor Center

9

Springdale

TO ST. GEORGE

N

.5 ml

.5 km

The Watchman

Start	Watchman car park, east of South Campground (3900ft/1189m)
End	Viewpoint (4368ft/1331m)
Distance, around loop	5.8 miles (9.3km)
Time, one way	3hrs
Maps	Springdale East (United States Geological Survey 7.5′); Zion National Park (TI)
Season	All year
Water	None
Rating	Moderate

To reach the Watchman trailhead, drive 0.25 miles from the South Entrance and turn east into the Watchman Campground. Just past the self-pay station, take the service road northeast for 400yds to the Watchman Trail car park.

Directions
From the car park, the trail ascends a knoll below Bridge Mountain and the Watchman. As you near the base of the Watchman, the trail ascends the mountain via switchbacks. Fine views open up westward across the Virgin River to the Towers of the Virgin and southward to the town of Springdale. Be sure to supervise children near the steep drop-offs. Once on the top, continue around the loop from the viewpoint and retrace your steps to the car park.

CHAPTER 16

ZION NATIONAL PARK: EAST RIM TRAILS

Today looked so easy yesterday.

Gary Ladd

EAST RIM TRAILS			
Trail	Distance (miles) one way	Distance (km) one way	Rating
Canyon Overlook Trail	0.5	0.8	Easy
East Rim Trail	9.8	15.7	Moderate
East Mesa Trail	2.5	4.0	Easy
East Boundary to Echo Canyon Trail	0.6	1.0	Easy
Stave Spring Junction to Cable Mountain Trail	2.9	4.6	Easy
Stave Spring Junction to Deertrap Mountain Trail	3.2	5.1	Easy

Canyon Overlook Trail

Start	Mount Carmel Tunnel (5130ft/1563m)
End	Canyon Overlook (5200ft/1584m)
Distance, one way	0.5 miles (0.8km)
Time, one way	20mins
Maps	Springdale East (United States Geological Survey 7.5′); Zion National Park (TI)
Season	All year
Water	None
Rating	Easy

From the South Entrance of Zion National Park, north of Springdale, Utah, take State Hwy 9 through the Mount Carmel Tunnel. The Canyon Overlook Trail begins just east of the tunnel from the north side of the road. There are several lay-bys along the road for parking.

Directions

Ramble up a short series of uneven steps. In 5mins you'll reach several walkways with iron railings. Proceed under numerous rock overhangs beside steep drop-offs. Be cautious, especially if accompanied by small children. The trail weaves back and forth among pine trees, ending at a lookout with fine views of the West Temple and East Temple, Towers of Virgin and the south Zion Canyon. Retrace your steps to your car.

East Rim Trail

Start	East Entrance (5740ft/1750m)
End	Weeping Rock (4360ft/1329m)
Distance, one way	9.8 miles (15.7km)
Time, one way	4hrs
Maps	The Barracks, Temple of Sinawava, Springdale East (United States Geological Survey 7.5'); Zion National Park (TI)
Season	May through to October
Water	Stave Spring
Rating	Moderate

This splendid, lightly used Zion trail connects the park's East Entrance with the Zion Valley at Weeping Rock. The walk can be completed as a day-trip or as an overnight, including side-trips to Cable and Deertrap mountains (chapter 18). Views from the east side of Zion Canyon offer a different perspective on the valley from those seen on the popular West Rim walks. Stave Spring, 5.5 miles from the start, provides the only reliable water along the route.

To reach the East Rim Parking Area, take Utah State Hwy 9 for 13 miles to the Zion National Park East Entrance. The East Rim Trail starts from the parking area, 150yds west of the East Entrance.

Directions

From the trailhead next to the ranger's residence, pass by the register station to the dusty trail. Following Clear Creek Wash, you climb as the trail bends north into

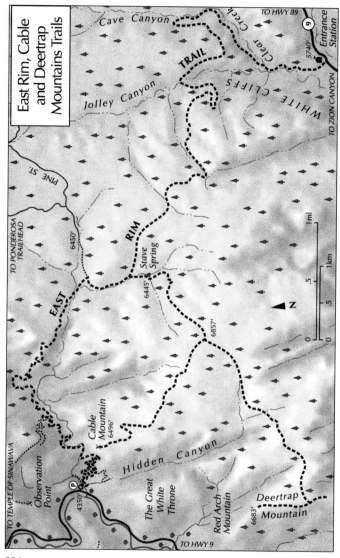

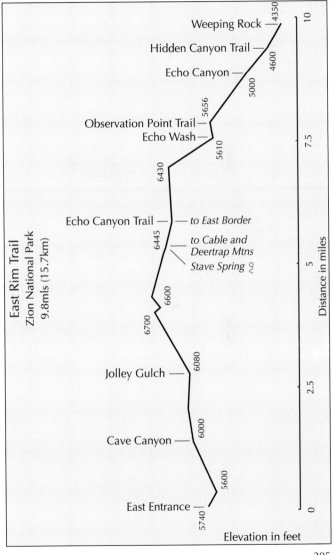

East Rim Trail
Zion National Park
9.8mls (15.7km)

Weeping Rock — 4350
Hidden Canyon Trail —
Echo Canyon — 5000
4600
Observation Point Trail — 5656
Echo Wash — 5610
6430
Echo Canyon Trail — — *to East Border*
6445
*to Cable and
Deertrap Mtns
Stave Spring* ♀
6600
6700
Jolley Gulch — 6080
Cave Canyon — 6000
5600
East Entrance — 5740

Distance in miles

10

7.5

5

2.5

0

Elevation in feet

Cave Creek. Turning south, you pass high above Cave Creek to gain fine views of the Checkerboard Mesa, Jolley Gulch and the White Cliffs of Zion. Next heading westward, the trail crosses dry Jolley Gulch and climbs gradually to a hilltop dotted with pine, juniper and manzanita. A short gradual descent brings you to the small but reliable Stave Spring. One hundred and fifty yards beyond the spring, you come to the trail junction for the Deertrap Mountain Trail leading to Cable and Deertrap mountains. Turn west if you are planning this splendid side-trip.

Overnight walkers will want to collect water here; camp at least 0.5 miles from the spring. If continuing on to Deertrap and Cable mountains, some nice camping sites dot the plateau along the Deertrap Mountain Trail. Or, if you are heading directly to the valley, the trees and foliage above Echo Canyon shelter lovely camping spots.

Bear east if you are continuing on the East Rim Trail. In 0.2 miles the trail to the Ponderosa trailhead veers to the east. The East Rim Trail, now signed as the Echo Canyon Trail, continues west from this junction across the flats and through hoards of sagebrush to the head of an unnamed side-canyon. Traversing above this canyon past several campsites, you are greeted with splendid views of the West Rim. Then the trail drops precipitously off the East Rim and zigzags on a rock-strewn path into Echo Canyon. Looking upward and south, you can make out the cable works on the edge of Cable Mountain.

Follow the cairns across several side-canyons until you reach the junction with the trail to Observation Point. The Observation Point Trail ascends west and the route to the valley and the Weeping Rock trailhead continues south downhill. (See the description of the Observation Point Trail (chapter 15) for an account of the final 2 miles down to the valley.) Upon reaching the Weeping Rock trailhead, catch the shuttle back.

East Boundary to Echo Canyon Trail

Start	East Boundary from Pine Street (6450ft/1966m)
End	Echo Canyon Trail (6400ft/1951m)
Distance, one way	0.6 miles (1km)
Time, one way	20mins
Maps	Temple of Sinawava, Springdale East (United States Geological Survey 7.5'); Zion National Park (TI)
Season	May through to October

Water	None
Rating	Easy

From the East Entrance to Zion National Park, take Utah State Hwy 9 east for 2.5 miles, then turn north on North Fork Country Road. Follow this road for 5.4 miles, then turn left into the Zion Ponderosa Ranch and Resort. Pass under the entrance sign and continue straight ahead on to the narrow, dirt Twin Knolls Road. Proceed for 0.8 miles then turn left on to Buck Road. Take the immediate right fork and drive for 0.6 miles, turning left at the next fork. Continue on this road to Pine Street and park on the side of the road. Walk 0.5 miles west on Pine Street down the rocky rutted road past several summer homes to the park boundary.

Directions
From the park gate, take the trail west running gradually downhill through a grove of ponderosa pines. A few minutes more will bring you into an open meadow and to a trail junction. Turn south to go to Cable and Deertrap mountains. Turn north to join the East Rim Trail to Weeping Rock and Echo Canyon.

East Mesa Trail

Start	East Boundary from Beaver Road (6520ft/1987m)
End	Observation Point (6500ft/1981m)
Distance, round trip	2.5 miles (4km)
Time, one way	1hr
Maps	Temple of Sinawava (United States Geological Survey 7.5'); Zion National Park (TI)
Season	May through to October
Water	None
Rating	Easy

Follow the directions to Zion Ponderosa Ranch and Resort (see East Boundary to Echo Canyon Trail above) and pass under the main entrance sign. Continue straight ahead on Twin Knolls Road. Drive 0.8 miles and turn right on to Beaver Road. Proceed as far as you can on the rutted road. Park the car on the shoulder and continue on foot for about 0.5 miles to the fenced park entrance.

Directions

From the hiker's gate, the trail, an old dirt road, crosses a high plateau dotted with ponderosa pines. The trail ascends gently, with views to the north all the way to the Pink Cliffs of the Virgin Rim. After 1.5 miles, just before a knoll and the trail's high point, a side-path heads to an overlook of Mystery Canyon. Back at the main trail, you now turn south, with commanding views of Zion and Echo Canyons. The trail then skirts the edge of an unnamed canyon that joins the Virgin River in the north.

After traversing a low saddle, the trail descends gradually to reach the Observation Point Trail. Turn southwest, and in 0.3 miles you reach Observation Point, with its splendid views of the entire Zion Canyon, Angels' Landing and the West Rim. Though less scenic than the trail from Weeping Rock, this trail offers a much less strenuous way to enjoy Observation Point's splendid views.

The trail map to the East Mesa Trail can be found in chapter 15, Zion Canyon Trails, along with the map of the trail to Observation Point and Hidden Canyon.

Stave Spring Junction to Cable Mountain and Deertrap Mountain trails

Start	Stave Spring Junction (6445ft/1964m)
End	Cable Mountain (6496ft/1980m) and Deertrap Mountain (6683ft/2037 m)
Distance, one way	2.9 miles (4.6km) to Cable Mountain; 3.2 miles (5.1km) to Deertrap Mountain
Time, one way	1hr to Cable Mountain; 1.5hrs to Deertrap Mountain
Maps	Temple of Sinawava, Springdale East (United States Geological Survey 7.5'); Zion National Park (TI)
Season	May through to October
Water	Stave Spring
Rating	Easy

This trailhead, located just next to Stave Spring, can be reached via the East Rim Trail from the East Entrance, from Weeping Rock on the East Rim Trail or from the East Boundary via the Echo Canyon Trail. A combination of the East Rim Trail with detours to Cable and Deertrap mountains makes a pleasant overnight trip (see chapter 18, Zion National Park, Long-distance Walks). An 11 mile day-walk to Cable and Deertrap mountains can be completed in the summer from the East Boundary via the Echo Canyon Trail to Stave Spring Junction.

Directions

From the Stave Spring Trail Junction you meet the East Rim Trail coming from the Park's East Entrance, the trail from Weeping Rock and the Echo Canyon Trail. Stave Springs trickles from a pipe 150yds south of the junction. Continue southwest through a pine forest for 1.1 miles on the signed Deertrap Mountain Trail to the Y-junction of the trail for Cable and Deertrap mountains.

The left fork, the Deertrap Mountain Trail, heads 2.1 miles southwest across a barren mesa and several draws. A brisk climb leads to the top of the mesa, descends briefly and climbs again to another mesa. The trail soon arrives at the top of Deertrap Mountain. A northern spur ends at a promontory, with views of Angels' Landing and the Temple of Sinawava. The southern spur affords fine views of the East Temple and Twin Brothers.

Retrace your steps back to the Y-junction of the trail to Deertrap and Cable mountains. Turning northwest on the right fork towards Cable Mountain, you climb gently and are rewarded by northern views to the Pink Cliffs of the Virgin Rim. The trail then descends gradually 1.8 miles to meet the sandstone cliffs and the void of Zion Canyon. Ruins of the old Zion tramway rest near the cliff's edge. Between 1904 and 1926 it was used to transport logs into the Zion Canyon. Your view overlooks the Big Bend of the Virgin River, the Organ, Angels' Landing, and the West Rim.

Retrace your steps back to the Y-junction and then to the Stave Spring junction. Continue on to your final destination, whether you return to the East Entrance, Weeping Rock or to the East Boundary.

CHAPTER 17

ZION NATIONAL PARK: SOUTHWEST DESERT

There's a long trail a winding into the land of my dreams.

Stoddard King

The Southwest Desert area of Zion National Park hosts fewer visitors than any other area in the park. In winter, this area makes an excellent alternative to the snowy high-country trails. Unbearable heat plagues this area in summer. Several off-trail routes, such as Huber and Coalpits Wash, provide an opportunity for round-trip walks, rather than backtracking on the Chinle Trail.

SOUTHWEST DESERT TRAILS			
Trail	Distance (miles) one way	Distance (km) one way	Rating
Chinle Trail	8.1	13.0	Moderate
Huber Wash	2.4	4.0	Moderate

Chinle Trail

Start	Park Boundary on Utah Hwy 9 (4020ft/1230m)
End	Coalpits Wash (4100ft/1252m)
Distance, one way	8.1 miles (13km)
Time, one way	4–5hrs
Maps	Springdale West (United States Geological Survey 7.5'); Zion National Park (TI)
Season	Autumn, winter and spring
Water	Coalpits Wash
Rating	Moderate

This remote part of the park provides solitude not found in other parts. An excellent alternative to the Zion Valley during the cool winter months, these trails may

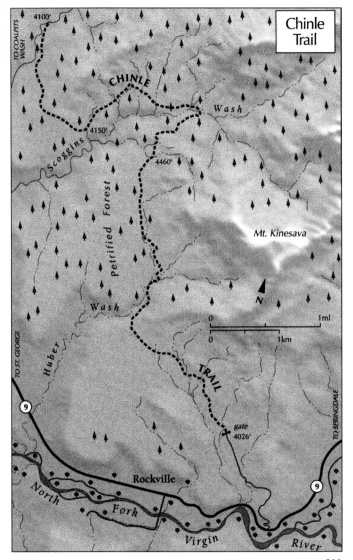

Chinle
Trail

TO COALPITS WASH

4100'

CHINLE

Wash

4150'

Scoggins

4460'

Petrified Forest

Mt. Kinesava

Wash

N

Huber

Wash

0 .... 1ml

0 .... 1km

TO ST. GEORGE

9

TRAIL

gate
4026'

TO SPRINGDALE

9

Rockville

North

Fork

Virgin River

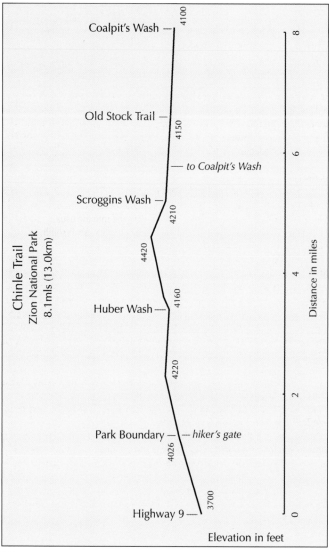

Chinle Trail
Zion National Park
8.1mls (13.0km)

Coalpit's Wash — 4100

Old Stock Trail — 4150

— *to Coalpit's Wash*

Scroggins Wash — 4210

4420

Huber Wash — 4160

4220

Park Boundary — — *hiker's gate*
4026

Highway 9 — 3700

Distance in miles

8

6

4

2

0

Elevation in feet

be walked as an overnight hike or as a day-trip. Elevation gain remains minimal and numerous campsites dot the route.

From the South Entrance to Zion National Park, drive 3.5 miles south on Utah State Hwy 9. Between Springdale and Rockville, turn north on to a dirt lay-by and park here. The dirt road crosses private land; close all gates behind you. From the highway, a 4x4 road heads north 1.2 miles to the Chinle trailhead. Walk or drive to the end of the road to the hiker gate and park boundary.

Directions

From the trailhead, follow the sandy path northwest, with fine views of the red cliffs of Mount Kinesava ahead of you. After a little over 1 mile, pass under the power lines and traverse a wash. After 3 miles, descend into the usually dry Huber Wash. You may wish to return to your car by taking Huber Wash south, although you'll have to walk a few miles along Utah Hwy 9.

From Huber Wash, ascend 150ft and traverse the eastern flanks of the Petrified Forest with its age-old wood. Petrified wood dots the landscape. (You may not collect samples in a national park.) Now Mount Kinesava rises even closer to the east, and to the northwest Cougar Mountain impresses with its surrounding cliffs. Continuing north, you now gain views of the east of the West Temple, an unusual view for park visitors. From Huber to Scroggins Wash, dry desert landscape characterises your walk. Now, veering west, climb above Scroggins Wash, then climb in and out of a gully before descending into the dry Scroggins Wash.

Just west of the wash, a cross-country route to Coalpits Wash follows a wash north through a gap in the ridge and joins another wash that descends into Coalpits Wash. From Coalpits Wash you can turn southwest to the end of the Chinle Trail and then loop back to your car.

Back at the Chinle Trail, ascend gradually through a small saddle. Turning southwest, you follow a wash and cross another small saddle and soon pass a sign marking the Old Scoggins Stock Trail. The Chinle Trail continues west and then terminates at Coalpits Wash. Detours include exploring upstream to the 1908 oil-well ruins; you should not camp here. Travel downstream past the small waterfall to the alcove and to the spring and overhanging garden, located just past where the creek turns south.

Huber Wash

Start	Hiker's Gate for Huber Wash Route (3700ft/1128m)
End	Chinle Trail at Huber Wash (4160ft/1268m)
Distance, one way	2.5 miles (4km)
Time, one way	2hrs
Map	Springdale West (USGS 7.5′); Zion National Park (TI)
Season	Autumn, winter and spring
Water	None
Rating	Moderate

From the South Entrance to Zion National Park, drive 6.1 miles west on Utah State Hwy 9 through Springdale and Rockville. Drive into the lay-by on the north side of the road and proceed to the hiker's gate. If you start at the Chinle Trail, you can loop these two walks together, walking a short way on Utah Hwy 9.

Directions

From the lay-by, pass through the hiker's gate. (Take care to close all gates along the route.) Follow the road past the transformer station. When the road forks, take the left fork down into the wash. Turn north and pass through the hiker's gate on the east side of the wash. Stay in the wash; mud may be under your feet after rain. As you proceed north, Mount Kinesava dominates your far view and the Petrified Forest ornaments the near view.

When the wash branches, proceed northeast. Soon you come to a jam of petrified logs. To bypass the dry fall, backtrack 150ft and climb up on the western shelf of the canyon. Look for a chimney that leads you up to the mesa. Backpackers may wish to raise their packs with 25ft of rope. Once on the mesa, follow the paths east to reach the Chinle Trail.

CHAPTER 18

ZION NATIONAL PARK: LONG-DISTANCE ROUTES

Prayer of the tired walker:
'If you pick 'em up,
O lord, I'll put 'em down.

Anonymous

LONG-DISTANCE ROUTES			
Trail	Distance (miles) one way	Distance (km) one way	Rating
Across Zion via Hop Valley and the West Rim	37.6	60.2	Moderate
The Zion Narrows	15.5	24.8	Strenuous
East Rim Trail via Cable Mountain and Deertrap Mountain	20.4	32.6	Moderate

Across Zion via Hop Valley and the West Rim

Start	Lee Pass (6060ft/1847m)
End	Grotto picnic area (4298ft/1310m)
Distance, one way	37.6 miles (60.2km)
	Times, one way: 4–5 days
Maps	Kolob Arch, Kolob Reservoir, Temple of Sinawava, the Guardian Angels (United States Geological Survey 7.5'); Zion National Park, Utah (TI)
Season	Late April through to October
Water	Beatty Spring, La Verkin Creek, Hop Valley, Wildcat Canyon Spring, Potato Hollow Spring, West Rim (Cabin) Spring
Rating	Moderate

The splendid Kolob Arch area of Zion National Park's northeastern section, much less visited than the busy eastern valley, conceals many of the park's hidden treasures.

From the Zion National Park South Entrance, take Utah Hwy 9, west, through Virgin and Rockville for 22 miles to Hurricane. Turn north on Hwy 17. Proceed for 6 miles to Interstate 15. Turn north and, after 13 miles, take Exit 40 to Kolob Canyons. Allow 1hr driving time from Zion Canyon.

Begin with a visit to the Kolob Canyon Visitor Centre, where you will find exhibits on the flora and fauna of the park. You may pick up backcountry permits here. Next, take Kolob Canyons Road 3.5 miles east to Lee Pass.

If you do not have enough time for the entire Across Zion itinerary, several shorter alternatives are recommended. The Kolob Arch area is a popular overnight trip. The Kolob Arch area can be reached from the west via La Verkin Creek and from the east via the more scenic Hop Valley. You can explore Timber and La Verkin creeks and make a short detour to the arch. Both routes boast diverse scenery. A valuable extra day allows time to explore Willis Creek and Beartrap Canyon.

The Across Zion trip covers the park's most splendid backcountry area. From Lee Pass you descend the La Verkin Creek Trail as it drops into the La Verkin and Timber Creek drainage and meets the Hop Valley Trail and Kolob Arch Trail. Turning east and crossing Hop Valley, you meet the Kolob Terrace Road. From here the 4 mile Connector Trail links up with the Wildcat Canyon Trail, and a short detour south brings you to fine, albeit waterless, camping on the Northgate Peaks Trail. A short spur trail leads you to the Northgate Peaks Overlook.

Directions

Retracing your steps to the Wildcat Canyon Trail, you pass Wildcat Canyon Spring. Descend into Wildcat Canyon and ascend out of the canyon to join the West Rim Trail near Lava Point. You next cross Horse Plateau and descend to Potato Hollow, where there are fine views of the Virgin River Canyon and the Narrows. Next, one of the most spectacular trails in the park takes you along the West Rim, with outstanding views of the Right Fork and Phantom Valley. Meeting the West Rim Trail at the West Rim (Cabin) Spring, you drop down to Scout Lookout, where another short detour will take you up the famous Angels' Landing. Finally wind your way down Walter's Wiggles to the Zion Valley at the Grotto picnic area.

The above trails – La Verkin Creek Trail, Hop Valley Trail, the Connector Trail, the Northgate Peaks Trail, the Wildcat Canyon Trail and the West Rim Trail – are described individually in chapters 13 and 14.

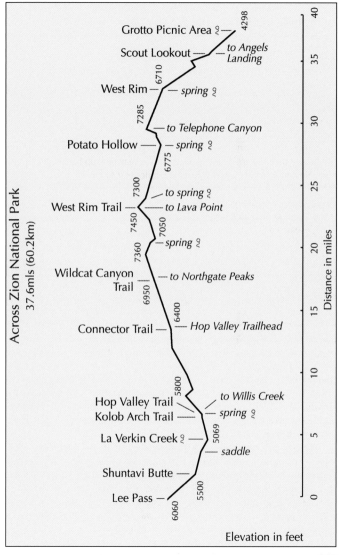

Across Zion National Park
37.6mls (60.2km)

Grotto Picnic Area ⚲ — 4298
Scout Lookout — — to Angels Landing
West Rim — 6710 — spring ⚲
7285
— to Telephone Canyon
Potato Hollow — — spring ⚲ — 6775
7300
West Rim Trail — — to spring ⚲
7450 — to Lava Point
7050
— spring ⚲
7360
Wildcat Canyon Trail — — to Northgate Peaks
6950
6400
Connector Trail — — Hop Valley Trailhead
5800
Hop Valley Trail — — to Willis Creek
Kolob Arch Trail — — spring ⚲
La Verkin Creek ⚲ — 5069
— saddle
Shuntavi Butte — 5500
Lee Pass — 6060

Distance in miles
40
35
30
25
20
15
10
5
0

Elevation in feet

The Zion Narrows

Start	Chamberlain's Ranch (5830ft/1777m)
End	Temple of Sinawava bus stop (4411ft/1344m)
Distance, one way	15.5 miles (24.8km)
Times, one way	12hrs or 2 days
Maps	Temple of Sinawava (United States Geological Survey 7.5'); Zion National Park (TI)
Season	Late June to October
Water	North Fork of Virgin River, Virgin River
Rating	Strenuous

This famous, highly recommended classic Zion walk, Utah's most renowned hike, can be completed in one long summer day or as an overnight trip. Overnight walkers are only allowed to walk downstream from Chamberlain's Ranch to the Temple of Sinawava. This 16 mile trip wanders through high sandstone cliffs, passing arches and waterfalls. The entire route meanders in the riverbed; there is no trail. Walking from the 'bottom up', starting at the Temple of Sinawava and proceeding north up the Virgin River to Orderville Canyon, is described in chapter 15.

Special National Park Service regulations apply for the Narrows walk. Permits are required for your walk from Chamberlain's Ranch to the Temple of Sinawava either for a day-walk or overnight walk. Obtain your permit at the Zion Canyon Visitor Centre. Camping spots are pre-assigned by the park service. The best time of year to walk the Narrows is late June to early October. Flash floods peak late July into August. Frigid water temperatures and swift currents limit canyon-walking during the colder months of the year. Protective gear and shoes are available for rent in Springdale.

Signs of possible flash floods include: changes in the water from clear to muddy; rising water; thunderstorms or sounds of thunder; a roar of water upstream. Seek higher ground immediately and do not try to out-run the flood. Stay on high ground until the high water subsides, sometimes up to 72hrs.

Danger lurks in the swift strong currents and deep pools of water. Take care when crossing the river and choose your wading spots with caution. Look for the shallow spots – wide areas are often shallower than narrow crossings. A walking stick aids in providing stability and helps check the depth of the water.

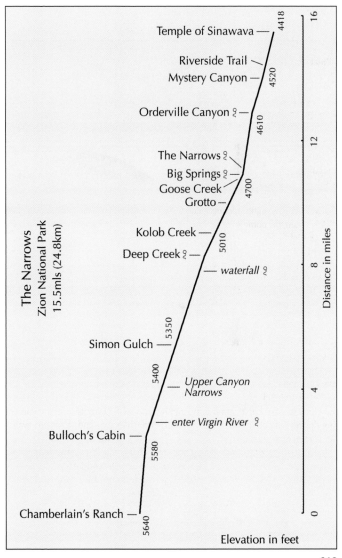

The Narrows
Zion National Park
15.5mls (24.8km)

Temple of Sinawava — 4418

Riverside Trail —
Mystery Canyon — 4520

Orderville Canyon ⚲ 4610

The Narrows ⚲
Big Springs ⚲
Goose Creek — 4700
Grotto —

Kolob Creek — 5010

Deep Creek ⚲

— *waterfall* ⚲

Simon Gulch — 5350

5400
— *Upper Canyon
Narrows*

— *enter Virgin River* ⚲

Bulloch's Cabin — 5580

Chamberlain's Ranch — 5640

Distance in miles

16

12

8

4

0

Elevation in feet

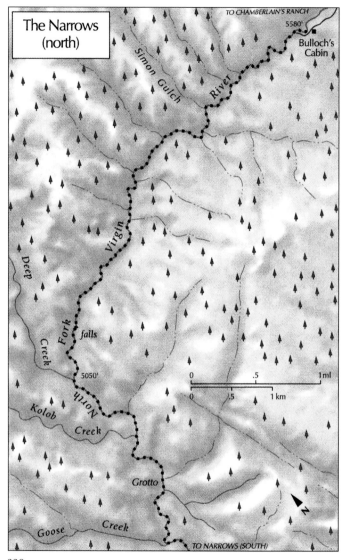

The Narrows
(north)

TO CHAMBERLAIN'S RANCH

5580'

Bulloch's
Cabin

Simon Gulch

River

Deep

Virgin

Creek

Fork

falls

North

5050'

Kolob

Creek

0   .5   1 ml
0   .5   1 km

Grotto

N

Goose   Creek

TO NARROWS (SOUTH)

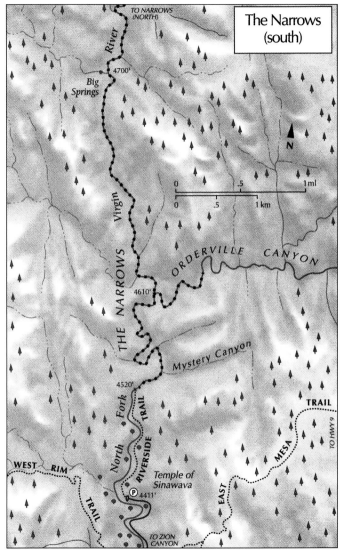

The Narrows
(south)

TO NARROWS
(NORTH)

River

4700'

Big
Springs

N

0   .5   1 ml

0   .5   1 km

Virgin

ORDERVILLE CANYON

THE NARROWS

4610'

Mystery Canyon

4520'

North Fork

RIVERSIDE TRAIL

TRAIL

TO HWY 9

WEST   RIM

Temple of
Sinawava

TRAIL

P   4411'

EAST   MESA

TO ZION
CANYON

Be prepared to swim. Chest deep holes exist. Wrap all your clothes in double stuff sacks or plastic bags. Bring warm clothing for chilly nights.

Ask Zion Lodge or the visitor centre if there is any private shuttle service operating to the start of the walk at Chamberlain's Ranch. If so, you will probably have to reserve your space several weeks ahead. Go as early as possible to allow the maximum amount of time in this unique setting. If you have two vehicles, you can shuttle one car to Chamberlain's Ranch. Use the shuttle bus from Temple of Sinawava to return to your car if you've left it at the visitor centre. Check with the National Park Service for other regulations.

See the Zion Adventure Company in Springdale, Utah, for information on flash-flood risk, equipment rental and current data on water depth, flow and temperature. Rentals are available for walking sticks, 'water tennies' and neoprene booties, waterproof backpacks and canyon drysuits.

To reach Chamberlain's Ranch, take Utah State Hwy 9 for 2.5 miles east from the Park's East Entrance. Turn left on North Fork Road and continue for 18 miles to the bridge over the North Fork River. Turn left after the bridge and drive 0.25 miles to the gate to Chamberlain's Ranch. Drive 0.5 miles to the river, where you can park; no camping is allowed. Please respect private property. Allow 1.5hrs for the drive from Zion Canyon to Chamberlain's Ranch.

Directions

Cross the river and begin your walk on the road along the river for the next 3 miles. The Chamberlains have requested that you do not walk in the riverbed until you reach the end of the road. Heading west, you pass through a pastoral setting amidst grazing cattle. After 2.5 miles you pass old Bulloch's cabin and, still on the old road, you begin to criss-cross the river from bank to bank. As soon as the road begins to fade, a well-worn trail marks your route along the shore, dotted with ponderosa pines. Slowly, cliffs begin to close in on the riverbed.

After another 2 miles, you come to the first true narrow section of the canyon. If you were planning to see narrows only below Big Springs, this part may come as a surprise. By now you are wading in the river and the red walls soar 500ft above you. Simon Gulch, entering from the north 6.5 miles from the start, breaks up the continuous canyon walls. Now the canyon becomes more and more enclosed by the towering walls. After 7.5 miles you meet a waterfall; take the passage on its south side. Five to six hours from the start, the canyon widens and you encounter Deep Creek, where the water level rises significantly. Most of the designated campsites are located on benches above the river, below this confluence. Look carefully for the campsite markers.

Now beyond Deep Creek, measure your progress downstream by noting the side-streams that join the Virgin River Canyon. Kolob Creek joins from the west,

3 miles below the confluence with Deep Creek. Half a mile from Kolob Creek, you pass The Grotto, an overhanging alcove used for a campsite. Next, 0.5 miles further on and easy to miss, narrow Goose Creek enters from the north. One mile more and you come to the impressive Big Springs as it pours over boulders, moss and other plants, the spring gurgling water at a rapid rate.

From Big Springs, south, you enter the true Narrows. There is no high ground for 2 miles until Orderville Canyon. Occasional flash floods rampage through this canyon – undercut canyon side-walls and debris attest to their power. Little sunlight graces this hidden area, as the sculptured canyon side-walls rise over 1000ft above your head. Be careful, as the deepest pools exist here. Look carefully for sandbars and visually scour the bottom as you place your feet. Enjoy the solitude and splendour of the narrow, fluted canyon walls.

Orderville Canyon, a fine side-canyon to explore, joins the Virgin River from the east, 2hrs below Big Springs. After 1 mile, deep pools and a waterfall block your way. From Orderville Canyon, south, you will meet day-hikers walking up the Virgin River from the Temple of Sinawava. One mile below Orderville Canyon, a stream of water from Mystery Canyon splashes down the canyon walls from the east side. A further 2 miles brings you the Riverside Trail. Finish with the last mile on the concrete trail that ends at the car park. The section between Orderville Canyon and the Temple of Sinawava is described in chapter 15.

East Rim Trail via Cable and Deertrap mountains

Start	East Entrance (5740ft/1750m)
End	Weeping Rock (4360ft/1329m)
Distance, one way	20.4 miles (32.6km)
Times, one way	10hrs or 2 days
Maps	The Barracks, Temple of Sinawava, Springdale East (United States Geological Survey 7.5'); Zion National Park, (TI)
Season	April and May, September to November
Water	Stave Spring
Rating	Moderate

This trip can be completed in one day, or as an overnight backpacking trip. It combines the East Rim Trail with visits to Cable and Deertrap mountains. The trailhead

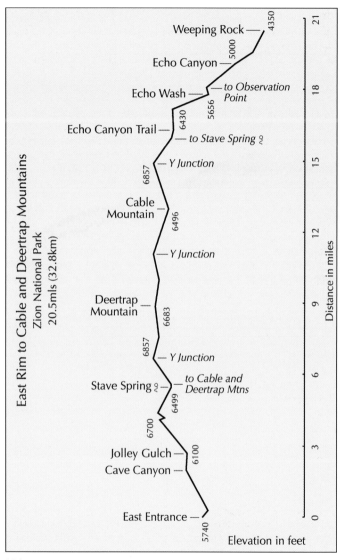

East Rim to Cable and Deertrap Mountains
Zion National Park
20.5mls (32.8km)

Distance in miles

Weeping Rock — 4350
5000
Echo Canyon —
Echo Wash — — to Observation Point
5656
Echo Canyon Trail — 6430
— to Stave Spring ⚲
— Y Junction
6857
Cable Mountain — 6496
— Y Junction
Deertrap Mountain — 6683
6857
— Y Junction
Stave Spring ⚲ — — to Cable and Deertrap Mtns
6499
6700
Jolley Gulch — 6100
Cave Canyon —
East Entrance —
5740
Elevation in feet

Amazing rock towers on the Peekaboo Trail (Bryce Canyon)

Wall of Windows (Peekaboo Trail, Bryce Canyon)

General view of hoodoos (Peekaboo Trail, Bryce Canyon)

Siân dwarfed by rocky towers on the Peekaboo Trail (Peekaboo Trail, Bryce Canyon)

Bryce Canyon overview (Rim Trail)

is next to the park's East Entrance. Finish at the Weeping Rock car park. The only water available is at Stave Spring.

You will find individual trail descriptions in chapter 16.

BRYCE CANYON NATIONAL PARK

CHAPTER 19

VISITING BRYCE CANYON NATIONAL PARK

Climb the mountains and get their good tidings. Nature's peace
will flow into you as sunshine flows into trees.
The winds will blow their own freshness into you,
and the storms their energy, while cares will
drop off like autumn leaves...

John Muir

You might have seen the photographs, but your first gaze over the rim into Bryce Canyon National Park will come as a stunning surprise. The multi-coloured collections of spires spread endlessly into the depths of the far distance and defy what you can imagine. Faraway views spread out over three states. It is hard to capture the many coloured hues with the amateur's photographic lens; memories are best preserved in the mind of the observer. Years of erosion, rain, snow and ice have shaped the limestone cliffs into acres of spires, towers and hoodoos coloured by red, rose and pink overtones. ('Hoodoos' is the collective name given to the colourful limestone and sandstone formations.) The green ponderosa pines and spruce forests accent these colours; the blue sky rounds out the magnificent vistas.

In winter, when the trails are closed with snow, you can enjoy the park only from its viewpoints. The canyon trails are usually closed by snow from November through to April. When a dusting of snow coats the ground, a magnificent contrast occurs between the blue sky, the red-pink walls and the green conifers. From late spring to the autumn the walker can experience the true feel of Bryce Canyon on foot; the true depth of its colours is best appreciated in the early morning or late afternoon.

The small, 56-square-mile park, made up of a series of horseshoe-shaped amphitheatres, is open all year round. Lodging and visitor services operate from April through to October. An 18 mile Rim Drive passes 13 overlooks; four spur roads provide access to its most distant points.

GETTING THERE

Visits to Bryce Canyon National Park are often combined with trips to Zion National Park and the North Rim (mid-May to mid-October) and the South Rim (open all year) of Grand

Canyon National Park. The best way to get around this area of the United States is to rent a car. There is no public transportation into the park.

Bryce Canyon National Park is 270 miles or 6hrs by car from Las Vegas and 256 miles or 6hrs from Salt Lake City by car. Zion National Park is a 78 mile, 2hr car ride. The North Rim of the Grand Canyon is 152 miles, about a 3hr ride from Bryce Canyon and the South Rim of the Grand Canyon is 300 miles.

Commercial airlines serve the major airports of Las Vegas (270 miles) and Salt Lake City (270 miles), as well as the smaller cities of Cedar City (87 miles) and St George (150 miles).

From Panguitch, Utah, head 7 miles south along Hwy 89 and turn east on to route 12. The road passes through the spectacular Red Canyon and continues east to the Bryce turnoff (route 63). Head south for 3 miles to the park entrance. From the east, via Capitol Reef National Park and Escalante National Monument, take Utah 12 to Utah 63 and turn south to the park entrance.

ENTRANCE FEES

A fee of $20 is charged per vehicle, and this is valid for seven days. A $10 fee is levied on pedestrians, cyclists and group members. An annual pass for Bryce is available for $30. Golden Eagle Passport and all other annual passes are valid here.

GETTING AROUND

There is no public transport, so renting a car offers the most flexibility when travelling in this part of the United States. Depending on your route, rental cars are available in Page, Flagstaff and Phoenix, Arizona and Las Vegas, Cedar City, Salt Lake City, and St George, Utah.

WEATHER AND SEASONS

Bryce Canyon National Park is open all year. However, from late autumn into early spring, many access roads and walking trails remain closed by snow. Road maintenance and snow-ploughing may lead to temporary road closures during the winter and early spring. Spring weather brings intermittent rain storms and some muddy trails. Night-time temperatures remain below freezing well into May. Pleasant summer temperatures predominate, due to the park's high elevation. Much of the yearly precipitation occurs in July and August, in the form of thundershowers. Autumn may be the best season to visit Bryce. The temperatures remain cool, the summer visitors have departed and the golden aspen trees accent the park's green and red background.

Snow, averaging 100in per year, blankets the area from early November to early May. Winter visits to the park can be rewarding, although temperatures can be very cold. Visitor numbers are low and rates at local motels are discounted.

Snow blocks the main park walking trails, but some snowshoe and cross-country ski trails invite visitors. The park service ploughs the main road all the way to Rainbow Point and viewpoints remain open.

LODGING

Within the park, Xanterra Parks and Resorts handles cabin and room reservations for the Bryce Canyon Lodge, tel (888) 297 2757, www.brycecanyonlodge.com. This historic lodge, renovated in 1989 and restored to its early 1930s style, is located off the park road between Sunrise and Sunset Points. You'll find a dining room, lounge and gift shop.

Ruby's Inn, just north of the park entrance, offers lodging all year. This sprawling Best Western complex is complete with pools, spas, convention centre, post office, ATM, general store, internet ($1 per 5mins), gift shop, art gallery, horseback riding and ski rentals.

Other options include the Bryce Canyon Resort at junction 12. Along the road to Panguitch is Foster Motel and Family Steakhouse, plus a bakery and shop, as well as the Bryce Canyon Pines motel and restaurant. Beyond Red Canyon to the west is Harold's Place, and in Panguitch there are plenty of motels from $30 upwards. Hatch, to the south, has limited lodgings. The small settlements of Tropic and Cannonville, to the east along Hwy 12, have some

motels and hotels. Further away, consider lodgings at Cedar City. Be aware that all places are full to capacity in the summer.

CAMPING

North and Sunset campgrounds offer pleasant, shaded, first-come, first-served sites inside the park. Campgrounds fill early in the busy summer months. Fees are $10 per night per site, plus a reservation fee of $9 for the North Campground. The North Campground can be reserved by calling 877 444 6777 or check www.ReserveUSA.com.

The Sunset Campground cannot be pre-booked. One group campsite is available by reservation only at the same contact points given above. Campground openings in the winter months may be variable – check with park headquarters before you arrive. Several private, National Forest and State Park campgrounds operate near the park.

At Bryce, Ruby's Inn has an RV campground. To the west is King's Canyon campground, and closer to Red Canyon is Bryce Canyon Country Store and campground. Opposite Harold's, east of the Red Canyon Indian Store, is the Red Canyon RV Park and Campground, with a few cabins as well as a small camping area for tents; PO Box 717, Panguitch, Utah 84759, tel 801 676 2690.

FOOD

All the main lodges have restaurants and snack areas. The general stores at and close to Ruby's Inn have reasonable food selections. Otherwise eat or buy basic essentials in Panguitch or Tropic.

VISITOR SERVICES

The Bryce Canyon Visitor Centre, located near the park entrance, presents exhibits, a slide show and gift shop. Backcountry permits may be obtained here. Hours are extended during the summer, spring and autumn. For advance information contact Bryce Canyon National Park, PO Box 640201, Bryce, Utah 84764-0201, tel 435 834 5322, fax 435 834 4102, brca_information@nps.gov; www.nps.gov/brca.

INTERPRETATIVE PROGRAMMES

Campfire programmes, offered by the National Park Service (NPS) during the summer, are held at North and Sunset campgrounds.

BRYCE CANYON NATURAL HISTORY ASSOCIATION

Bryce Canyon Natural History Association, a non-profit organisation, publishes educational materials, maps and slides of the park. Membership entitles you to the group's publications, as well as discounts at any

National Park or National Monument store throughout the country. Tel (888) 362 2642. See address in Appendix B.

OTHER FACILITIES

A grocery store, the General Store, a laundrette and showers, located next to Sunrise Point, operate during the summer season. Xanterra Parks and Resorts runs the dining room and gift shop in the Bryce Canyon Lodge.

SHUTTLE SERVICES

To date a long-planned shuttle service to relieve traffic congestion, improve road maintenance and allow for backcountry access has not been implemented.

TIME ZONES

The state of Utah, including Zion National Park and Bryce Canyon National Park, operates on mountain standard time (MST). Daylight savings time, (MDT or mountain daylight time), when the clocks are pushed ahead one hour, stays in effect between early April and October.

EMERGENCY

Call 435 676 2411 or 911.

Garfield County Sherriff, tel (435) 676 2678.

Garfield Memorial Hospital, tel (435) 676 8811.

CHAPTER 20

WALKING IN BRYCE CANYON NATIONAL PARK

Though we travel the world over to find the beautiful,
we must carry it with us or we find it not.

Ralph Waldo Emerson

Day-hikers and backcountry walkers find many options for exploration in Bryce Canyon National Park. The walks in the park's northern section, such as the Fairyland Loop, and in its central section, such as the Peekaboo Loop, give the visitor a splendid look at the park in a short half-day or whole-day walk. If time is short, try the Navajo Loop in combination with the Queen's Garden Loop; alternatively, just stroll along the 5.5 mile Rim Trail. Views of Bryce National Park's hoodoos and spires and expansive amphitheatres are most impressive in the northern and central sections of the park.

Overnight trips are limited to the 23 mile Under the Rim Trail or the short, 8 mile Riggs Spring Loop. The Under the Rim Trail, though less congested than trails in the northern section of the park, offers only limited views of the park's geologic formations and travel may be handicapped by lack of reliable water sources.

WALKING PERMITS

Day-walking requires no permits. Overnight permits for all backpacking in Bryce National Park may be obtained at the visitor centre. Reservations are not accepted.

GROUPS

Backcountry group camping sites support a limited number of walkers in only a few group sites.

MAPS

The Trails Illustrated/National Geographic map number 219 (TI) 1:37270 topographical map Bryce Canyon National Park provides all the information you will need. It can be purchased at local stores and at the park visitor centre. The United States Geological Survey (USGS 7.5') maps show more detail and are available through mail order from the USGS Denver office. 'Bryce Canyon Hiking Map', produced by the Bryce Canyon Natural History Association, is a cheaper and good alternative at just

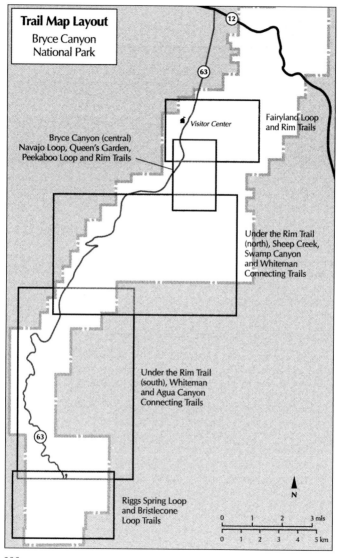

Trail Map Layout
Bryce Canyon
National Park

(12)

(63)

Visitor Center

Fairyland Loop
and Rim Trails

Bryce Canyon (central)
Navajo Loop, Queen's Garden,
Peekaboo Loop and Rim Trails

Under the Rim Trail
(north), Sheep Creek,
Swamp Canyon
and Whiteman
Connecting Trails

Under the Rim Trail
(south), Whiteman
and Agua Canyon
Connecting Trails

(63)

Riggs Spring Loop
and Bristlecone
Loop Trails

N

0   1   2   3 mls

0   1   2   3   4   5 km

Average Rim Temperatures (°C/°F) /Rainfall (cm/in) Bryce National Park

Month	Av. High	Av. Low	Av. Rainfall	Thunder-storm	Sunny days
Jan	3 (39)	-12 (9)	4.3 (1.7)	0	9
Feb	5 (41)	-10 (13)	3.6 (1.4)	0	7
Mar	8 (46)	-9 (17)	3.6 (1.4)	0	9
Apr	13 (56)	-4 (25)	3.0 (1.2)	1	10
May	19 (66)	1 (34)	2.0 (0.8)	5	12
Jun	25 (76)	3 (38)	1.5 (0.6)	6	17
Jul	28 (83)	9 (47)	3.6 (1.4)	14	16
Aug	27 (80)	7 (45)	5.7 (2.2)	19	16
Sep	23 (74)	2 (37)	3.6 (1.4)	7	18
Oct	18 (63)	-2 (29)	3.6 (1.4)	2	17
Nov	11 (51)	-7 (19)	3.0 (1.2)	0	11
Dec	6 (42)	-11 (11)	4.1 (1.6)	0	10

$1.99. It has a scale of 1:10,000 and covers all the major trails close to the visitor centre area, the most frequented zone of the park.

WEATHER AND SEASONS

The park trails open for backpacking and walking once the snow has melted, usually from mid-April through to October. Cool nights, many below freezing, predominate for over 200 nights per year. Winter visits are limited to driving along the main road, viewing the park from the automobile lay-bys, snowshoeing and cross-country skiing.

WATER SOURCES

Water at Bryce National Park is limited; the national park provides information on water sources. All back-country water should be treated.

Check with the National Park Service for up-to-date information on water availability and conditions. You may have to carry all the water you will need for your overnight trips.

WAYMARKING

Prominent signs mark all trail junctions in the backcountry and along day-routes.

FLASH FLOODS

Flash floods are not a danger in Bryce, as they are in Zion and in some parts of Grand Canyon National Park. However, use good judgement and common sense when entering narrow canyons and creek beds.

LIGHTNING

Bryce Canyon can be hit by terrific storms and lightning. Signs at the lay-bys indicate that you should get into your car and stay in it with the windows closed until the storm has abated. Find shelter if you are out hiking during a storm.

INSECTS, BIRDS, REPTILES AND MAMMALS

Over 160 species of bird have been observed in the park. Many birds migrate in the winter, but jays, ravens, nuthatches, eagles and owls remain.

Mountain short-horned lizards may be seen sunning themselves on rocks. The Great Basin rattlesnake blends in well with the park's surroundings – be careful where you place your hands and feet. Leave these and other reptiles to their own meandering and they will return the same. Red ants follow crumbs of food and deliver a nasty lingering sting if they get too close. Try to avoid coming into contact with them.

Mule deer graze along the park roads in the evening, and elk and pronghorn antelopes are occasionally seen, having been re-introduced. Marmots, long-tailed weasels, squirrels and even the grey fox, usually looking for a handout, may visit your campsite. Black-tailed jack rabbits, striped skunks, gophers and coyote inhabit the surrounding hills. Mountain lions are extremely rare, and feed on mule deer. Please do not feed any of these animals.

SOME USEFUL WEBSITES

www.nps.gov/brca
www.bryce.canyon.national-park.com
www.brycecanyoncountry.com
www.utah.com/nationalparks/bryce.htm
www.brycecanyon.com
www.americanparknetwork.com/park info/bc
www.desertusa.com/bryce
www.nationalgeographic.com/destinations/Bryce_Canyon_National_Park
www.go-utah.com/Bryce-Canyon-National-Park
www.americansouthwest.net/utah/bryce_canyon
3dparks.wr.usgs.gov/bryce/index.html

CHAPTER 21

BRYCE CANYON NATIONAL PARK: CANYON AND RIM TRAILS

*Thousands of tired, nerve-shaken, over-civilised people
are beginning to find out that going to the mountains
is going home, that wilderness is a necessity,
and that mountain parks and reservations
are useful not only as fountains of timber
and irrigating rivers, but as fountains of life...*

John Muir

CANYON AND RIM TRAILS			
Trail	Distance (miles) one way	Distance (km) one way	Rating
Fairyland Loop	7.9	12.6	Moderate
Queen's Garden Trail	0.9	1.5	Moderate
Navajo Loop	1.3	2.1	Moderate
Rim Trail	5.5	8.8	Easy
Peekaboo Loop	5.5	8.8	Moderate
Bristlecone Loop	1.0	1.6	Easy
Riggs Spring Loop	8.8	14.1	Moderate

Fairyland Loop

Start	Fairyland Point (7770ft/2368m)
End	Fairyland Point (7770ft/2368m)
Distance, loop	7.9 miles (12.6km)
Time, one way	4hrs
Maps	Bryce Canyon, Bryce Point (United States Geological Survey 7.5'); Bryce Canyon National Park (TI)
Season	May through to October

Water	none
Rating	Moderate

Starting from Fairyland Point, North Campground or Sunrise Point, this 8 mile loop or 5.7 mile shuttle trip covers much of the significant area in the northern section of the park.

The Fairyland Loop can be accessed from Fairyland Point, North Campground or Sunrise Point. To begin from Fairyland Point, drive north of the visitor centre for 1 mile and turn east on the spur road, proceeding 1 mile on the road to Fairyland Point. This road doubles as a cross-country ski trail in the winter. To begin from North Campground, drive 100yds south from the visitor centre along Hwy 63 and turn east on the road to North Campground. Proceed past the check-in station and continue into the campground. If you wish to begin your walk at Sunrise Point, continue 0.4 miles south past the visitor centre to the Sunrise Point Road that branches east. Turn left and drive to the end of the road to the car park for Sunrise Point.

Directions

From Fairyland Loop Trailhead at Fairyland Point, proceed northeast along the track and descend gradually on the north side of Boat Mesa. The trail drops to the floor of Fairyland Canyon as views of the Sinking Ship open up. Boat Mesa looms in the southwest. The trail ascends as it crosses several draws. Turning west after some more ups and downs, the trail switchbacks into Campbell Canyon to reach the Tower Bridge Trail. This short, 200yd detour gives close-up views of Tower Bridge and makes a nice lunch stop.

Back on the trail, you begin your return ascent to the rim past the Chinese Wall as you cut through a break in the hoodoos. Your final ascent heads back up to the rim to meet the Rim Trail just south of North Campground. Turning right and joining the Rim Trail, in 5mins you pass North Campground, and after 2 miles a spur trail east leads you to the top of Boat Mesa. To close the loop, another 0.7 miles brings you back to Fairyland Point.

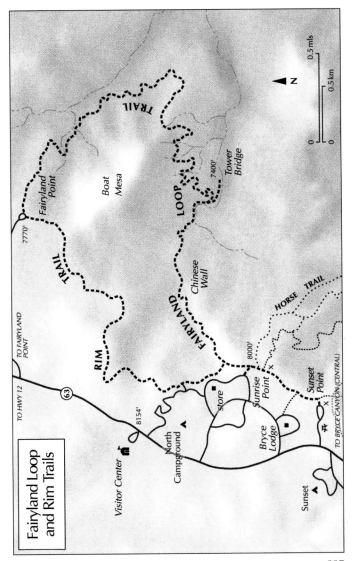

Fairyland Loop
and Rim Trails

TO HWY 12

TO FAIRLAND
POINT

Visitor Center

8154'

North
Campground

63

Store

Sunrise Point

Bryce
Lodge

Sunset

7770'

Fairyland
Point

RIM

TRAIL

Boat
Mesa

FAIRYLAND

LOOP

TRAIL

7400'

Tower
Bridge

Chinese
Wall

8000'

HORSE TRAIL

Sunset
Point

TO BRYCE/BRYCE CANYON (CENTRAL)

N

0.5 mls

0.5 km

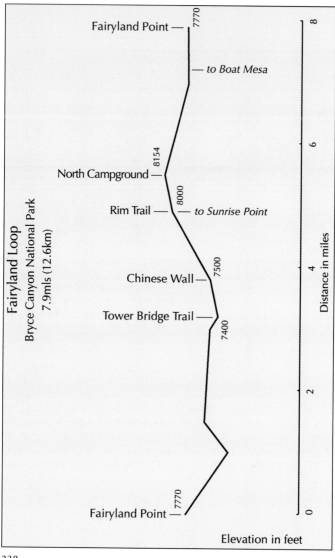

Fairyland Point — 7770

— to Boat Mesa

8154

North Campground — 8000

Rim Trail — — to Sunrise Point

7500

Chinese Wall —

Tower Bridge Trail — 7400

Fairyland Loop
Bryce Canyon National Park
7.9mls (12.6km)

7770

Fairyland Point —

Distance in miles

0   2   4   6   8

Elevation in feet

Queen's Garden Trail

Start	Sunrise Point (8000ft/2438m)
End	Sunrise Point (8000ft/2438m)
Distance, one way	0.9 miles (1.5km)
Time, one way	20mins
Maps	Bryce Canyon, Bryce Point (USGS 7.5'); Bryce Canyon National Park (TI)
Season	May through to October
Water	None
Rating	Moderate

The Queen's Garden Loop can be accessed from Sunrise Point or Sunset Point. To reach Sunrise Point, proceed 0.4 miles south of the visitor centre on Hwy 63 and turn east on the spur road to Sunrise Point. To reach Sunset Point, continue 1.2 miles south on the park road from the entrance station to the turn-off east to Sunset Point.

The Queen's Garden Trail, not a loop itself, best combines with the Navajo Loop or Peekaboo Loop. A good 6hr walk descends to the canyon bottom via Wall Street on the Navajo Loop, then circles the Peekaboo Loop and returns to the rim via the Queen's Garden Loop. (See the route profile for Queen's Garden Trail, Navajo and Peekaboo Loops for a mile-by-mile elevation profile of this walk, and the descriptions below of the Navajo Loop and Peekaboo Loop.)

Directions
To walk just the Queen's Garden Trail from Sunrise Point, walk a short way south to the Queen's Garden trailhead, the easiest of the trails that reaches the canyon floor. At first the trail descends below Sunrise Point heading east, then switchbacks 320ft into the canyon. Views of Sinking Ship, Boat Mesa and Aquarius Plateau open up to the northeast. When you meet the first junction, bear right. The trail continues to descend through a tunnel, passing numerous hoodoos. Turn east at the next trail junction to reach a viewpoint of the Queen Victoria formation. Retrace your steps back to the main trail. The most direct path to the rim turns north and returns the way you came.

To combine this walk with the Navajo Loop, turn right at the main trail and take the Queen's Garden Connecting Trail 1 mile to meet the Navajo Loop. You will pass through several tunnels before you join the Navajo Loop Trail. Turn right to ascend the Navajo Loop and, after reaching the rim, turn south at the Rim Trail and proceed 0.5 miles back to Sunrise Point.

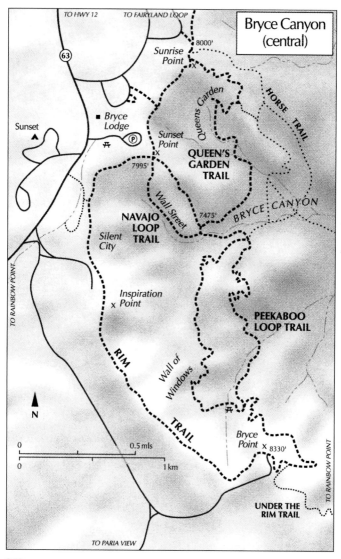

Bryce Canyon (central)

TO HWY 12   TO FAIRYLAND LOOP

8000'

63

Sunrise Point
x

Queens Garden

HORSE TRAIL

Bryce Lodge

Sunset

Sunset Point
x

QUEEN'S GARDEN TRAIL

7995'

Wall Street

BRYCE CANYON

7475'

NAVAJO LOOP TRAIL

Silent City

PEEKABOO LOOP TRAIL

Inspiration Point
x

RIM

Wall of Windows

TO RAINBOW POINT

N

Bryce Point
x   8330'

0   0.5 mls
0   1 km

TRAIL

UNDER THE RIM TRAIL

TO RAINBOW POINT

TO PARIA VIEW

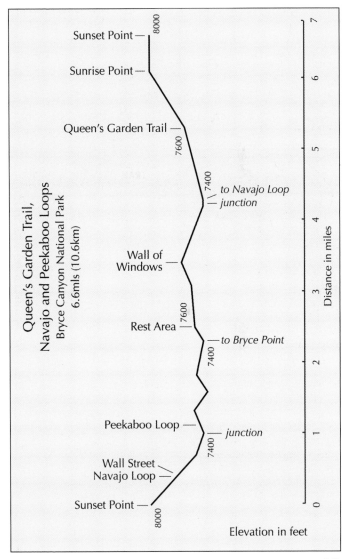

Queen's Garden Trail,
Navajo and Peekaboo Loops
Bryce Canyon National Park
6.6mls (10.6km)

Sunset Point — 8000

Sunrise Point —

Queen's Garden Trail — 7600

7400
to Navajo Loop junction

Wall of
Windows —

7600
Rest Area —
7400
to Bryce Point

Peekaboo Loop — *junction*
7400

Wall Street
Navajo Loop —

Sunset Point — 8000

Distance in miles

Elevation in feet

Navajo Loop

Start	Sunset Point (7995ft/2437m)
End	Sunset Point (7995ft/2437m)
Distance, loop	1.3 miles (2.1km)
Time, one way	45mins
Maps	Bryce Canyon, Bryce Point (USGS 7.5'); Bryce Canyon National Park (TI)
Season	May through to October
Water	None
Rating	Moderate

The Navajo Loop combined with the Queen's Garden Trail makes up the most popular of Bryce Canyon's walks. Best walked in combination, or better yet, with the Peekaboo Loop, the two or three trails together provide direct access into the central hoodoo area.

To reach Sunset Point, drive 1.5 miles south of the visitor centre on Hwy 63, then turn east and drive to the end of the spur road to the parking area.

Directions
From Sunset Point, drop off the rim onto the upper Navajo Loop and take the right fork towards Wall Street. Pass through the notch of hoodoos above Silent City with its 200ft high cliffs. Twenty-nine short switchbacks drop steeply down 520ft for 0.7 miles, as the trail criss-crosses through many tall hoodoos. These spires are reminiscent of New York's Wall Street towering skyscrapers. At the bottom, enter Wall Street itself through a narrow passage and break out into a sunlit, forested drainage on the other side of the passageway.

Turn right at the four-way junction to head for the Peekaboo Loop (see below). To remain on the Navajo Trail, turn left and climb northwest into a canyon to the Two Bridges. Above Two Bridges, the Navajo Loop continues upwards over switchbacks past the Sentinel and the obvious Thor's Hammer. Finally, you reach the rim as you return to your starting point at Sunset Point.

Rim Trail

Start	Fairyland Point (7770ft/2368m)
End	Bryce Point (8330ft/2539m)
Distance, one way	5.5 miles (8.8km)
Time, one way	2.5hrs
Maps	Bryce Canyon, Bryce Point (USGS 7.5'); Bryce Canyon National Park (TI)
Season	May through to October
Water	None
Rating	Easy

The popular Rim Trail, connecting Fairyland Point with Bryce Point, can be walked in sections or in its entirety. Access the trail from anywhere along its route: Fairyland Point, North Campground, Sunrise Point, Sunset Point, Inspiration Point or Bryce Point. Pavement allows wheelchair access between Sunset and Sunrise Points. If you don't want to retrace your steps, you'll need to arrange for a ride back to the start if a shuttle service is not operating.

From the Bryce Canyon visitor centre, drive north for 0.7 miles and turn east on to the Fairyland Loop road. Proceed to the parking area at the end of this road.

Directions
From Fairyland Loop, the trail proceeds southward along the rim and then winds in and out, away from the rim through a forested area. Northward views include Boat Mesa and Aquarius Plateau; to the east you can see Navajo Mountain. The trail continues to wind in and out along the rim, past the turn-off to Boat Mesa, then North Campground. Finally it reaches the junction to the southern end of Fairyland Loop. Continue right on the Rim Trail to reach Sunrise Point. You can see Boat Mesa and Sinking Sink on the horizon. Climbing a small hill to Sunrise Point, you meet the Queen's Garden Trail. Continue veering right along the Rim Trail.

In 0.5 miles you reach Sunset Point, just north, past the junction to the Navajo Loop. A spur trail leads through the forest to the lodge and to Sunset Campground. You climb a bit at first and then level off. Silent City predominates to the north and the Wall of Windows is visible to the southeast.

Now the trail, perhaps in its most beautiful section, climbs steadily to Inspiration Point. As you pass from point to point, the Wall of Windows becomes more prominent. Next the Bryce Canyon amphitheatre dominates the views. This is one of the best views of the park's largest amphitheatres. Silent City and the Wall of Windows are well seen from here to the northwest; Tropic, Utah can be seen to the southwest.

A narrow trail now meanders in various directions along the way to Bryce Point. This section of the trail is less used than its northern section. Undulating along the rim, splendid views of the Bryce amphitheatres line the horizon. Finally you meet the trail to the Peekaboo Loop and the trail's end at Bryce Point.

Peekaboo Loop

Start	Bryce Point (8280ft/2524m)
End	Bryce Point (8280ft/2524m)
Distance, loop	5.5 miles (8.8km)
Time, one way	3hrs
Maps	Bryce Point (USGS 7.5'); Bryce Canyon National Park (TI)
Season	May through to October
Water	None
Rating	Moderate

The actual Peekaboo Loop itself measures 3.5 miles long, but if you join the loop from Bryce Point you'll walk 5.5 miles. It is a great hike – do not be put off by the trail's relentless ups and downs and the smell of horses.

From the Bryce Canyon visitor centre, drive 1.6 miles south on Hwy 63 to the turn-off to Inspiration and Bryce points. Turn east and follow the signs to Bryce Point, the starting point for this loop.

Directions
From Bryce Point, head southeast, towards the Hat Shop, to the junction with the Under the Rim Trail. Turn north, then descend steeply for 1 mile on switchbacks through a tunnel to the junction with the Peekaboo Connector Trail. Turn west at

the junction and proceed around the Peekaboo Loop in a clockwise direction. Soon Bryce Point towers 400ft above you. Turn west at the next junction and you come shortly to a resting point for horses, a picnic area and pit toilets.

Continuing west, you rise up a series of switchbacks and pass through a small cavern. Soon you traverse the Wall of Windows, the highlight of the trail. Looking up you can see two large windows in the red walls. Descending to a draw, you come to the Navajo Connecting Trail. Turn east to stay on the loop and then, in a few minutes, turn south back on the Peekaboo Loop. The trail drops up and down, passing cliffs of hoodoos and looping under small arches with scattered pine and juniper trees. Next you meet the Bryce Point Connecting Trail; bear south for your climb back to the rim.

A longer, highly recommended day-hike starting at Sunset Point combines the Navajo Loop and Peekaboo Loop. Descend to the canyon bottom via Wall Street, then go around the Peekaboo Loop and finally ascend to the rim via the Queen's Garden Loop. (See Route Profiles: Queen's Garden Trail, Navajo Loop and Peekaboo Loop.)

Bristlecone Loop

Start	Rainbow Point (9015ft/2748m)
End	Rainbow Point (9015ft/2748m)
Distance, loop	1 mile (1.6km)
Time, one way	20mins
Maps	Rainbow Point (USGS 7.5'); Bryce Canyon National Park (TI)
Season	May through to October
Water	None
Rating	Easy

From the Bryce Canyon Visitor Centre, take Hwy 63 for 16.8 miles south to the end of the road at Rainbow Point.

Directions

From the trailhead near the parking area, the Bristlecone Loop winds southeast through a forest of fir and pine. You should be able to recognise bristlecone pines by the tuft of needles at the end of their limbs. These hearty trees, known to be some of the oldest living things on earth, survive in windy, desolate climates. Approaching the canyon rim, you loop back north at the viewpoint near a lovely

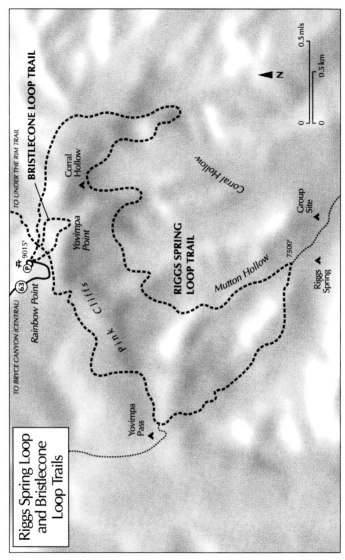

Riggs Spring Loop and Bristlecone Loop Trails

BRISTLECONE LOOP TRAIL

TO UNDER THE RIM TRAIL

Corral Hollow

Corral Hollow

RIGGS SPRING LOOP TRAIL

Group Site

Yovimpa Point

Mutton Hollow

7500'

Riggs Spring

TO BRYCE CANYON (CENTRAL)

63

Rainbow Point

9015'

P

Pink Cliffs

Yovimpa Pass

N

0   0.5mls
0   0.5km

bristlecone pine. Returning to Rainbow Point in an anti-clockwise direction, you pass the Under the Rim Trail.

Riggs Spring Loop

Start	Rainbow Point (9015ft/2748m)
End	Rainbow Point (9015ft/2748m)
Distance, loop	8.8 miles (14.1km)
Time, loop	4hrs
Maps	Podunk Creek, Rainbow Point (USGS 7.5'); Bryce Canyon National Park (TI)
Season	June through to October
Rating	Moderate

For backpackers, the Riggs Springs Trail offers a pleasant and shorter alternative to the longer Under the Rim Trail. The trail can be walked as a day-trip as well.

Drive 16.3 miles south of the visitor centre on Hwy 63 to the end of the road at Rainbow Point. If you are planning to camp overnight, you must first obtain a backcountry permit at the visitor centre and check on the availability of water sources.

This southern section of the park, seen by many fewer visitors than its northern counterpart, offers fewer spires and hoodoos to admire. The pleasant, cool forest that beckons during the hot summer day blocks some of the views along the trail. Rainbow Point itself, though, at the start of this walk, boasts some of the finest park views.

Directions
From Rainbow Point, follow the Bristlecone Loop going east to join the Under the Rim Trail and turn north at the junction. Descend to the next junction and turn south on to the Riggs Spring Loop. The trail now descends east and then south and then loops back north. After 3.5 miles you reach the Corral Hollow Campsite. Then you turn south and follow the Mutton Hollow Drainage for 0.8 miles to the Riggs Spring Campsite, a lovely spot, shaded by tall pine trees. The spring nearby gurgles behind a fence.

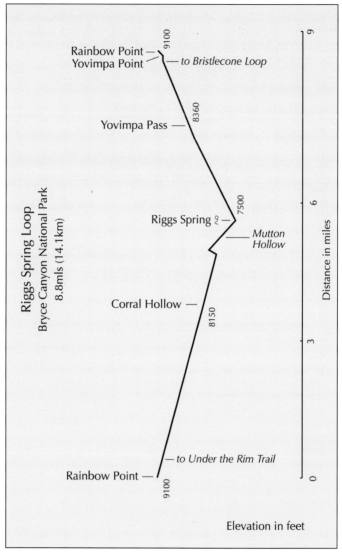

Riggs Spring Loop
Bryce Canyon National Park
8.8mls (14.1km)

Rainbow Point —
Yovimpa Point

9100

— *to Bristlecone Loop*

Yovimpa Pass —

8360

Riggs Spring ♀

7500

— *Mutton Hollow*

Corral Hollow —

8150

— *to Under the Rim Trail*

Rainbow Point —

9100

Distance in miles

9

6

3

0

Elevation in feet

Now, turning north, you ascend 900ft in 1.6 miles to the Yovimpa Pass Campsite. Next turn northeast, crossing above the Pink Cliffs back to Rainbow Point. Fine views of the Pink Cliffs and Mutton Hollow grab your attention along this traverse until you reach your starting point at Rainbow Point.

CHAPTER 22

BRYCE CANYON NATIONAL PARK: LONG-DISTANCE TRAIL AND CONNECTING TRAILS

Here you find the elemental freedom
to breathe deep of unpoisoned air,
to experiment with solitude and stillness,
to gaze through a hundred miles of untrammelled atmosphere,
across red-rock canyons, beyond blue mesas

Edward Abbey

LONG-DISTANCE TRAILS

LONG-DISTANCE TRAILS			
Trail	Distance (miles) one way	Distance (km) one way	Rating
Under the Rim Trail	22.8	36.5	Strenuous

Under the Rim Trail

Start	Bryce Point (8280ft/(2524m)
End	Rainbow Point (9015ft/2748m)
Distance, one way	22.8 miles (36.5km)
Time, one way	10–12hrs, 2 days
Maps	Bryce Point, Tropic Reservoir, Rainbow Point (USGS 7.5′); Bryce Canyon National Park (TI)
Season	June through to October
Rating	Moderate

The Under the Rim Trail and the Riggs Spring Loop (chapter 21) make up the only backpacking trails in Bryce Canyon National Park. The Under the Rim Trail, remaining below the rim for its length, travels through the less-visited southern half of the park. First, obtain a backcountry permit from the visitor centre. You'll need to check on water availability and be sure to bring water purification tablets with you.

Directions

Heading southeast from the Bryce Point car park, you soon reach the Peekaboo Connector Trail. Turn south on to the Under the Rim Trail. Switchbacking down to some level ground, you'll see hoodoos rise to the southeast. The Table Cliffs and glimpses of Tropic, Utah, highlight the views to the northeast. In 2 miles you reach the Hat Shop, where cap-rocks or 'hats' accent numerous pillars of rocks.

Now you descend into the Right Fork of Yellow Creek and pass its campsite. The trail turns southwest and heads to the main fork of Yellow Creek, passing the turn-off to the Yellow Creek Group campsite. Continuing northwest, you can see the Pink Cliffs. Next, pass the Yellow Creek campsite, with its outstanding views of the amphitheatre as a backdrop. Leaving the campsite you gain 400ft, with the Pink Cliffs providing stimulating views to encourage you on the ascent. Topping out on the saddle at 7700ft, you descend to near the Pink Cliffs and views of Rainbow Point open up. Now you descend steadily into Pasture Wash and climb again to another saddle.

At a four-way junction, the Sheep Creek campsite can be found a short way down a spur trail to the south. The Sheep Creek Connecting Trail ascends north to the park road. The Under the Rim Trail goes straight ahead towards Swamp Canyon. A bit further on, the Swamp Creek campsite and Swamp Canyon campsite are popular in summer with visitors descending from the rim for an overnight stay.

From the Sheep Creek Connecting Trail, ascend another small saddle and descend into Swamp Canyon. Soon you come upon the Swamp Canyon Connector Trail heading north to the park road. The Under the Rim Trail continues to head west into Swamp Canyon, soon passing the Right Fork Swamp Canyon campsite. Shortly you come to the Swamp Canyon Connector Trail veering up to the rim.

Now the trail leaves Swamp Canyon and soon you pass Swamp Camp, located on a wooded terrace above the trail. You reach the junction with the Whiteman Connector Trail; veer south at the junction. Descending into Willis Creek, Canyon Butte lines the skyline to the east. Soon you climb to a saddle and descend into the next basin, as the Natural Bridge marks the skyline to the west. At the bottom you pass Natural Bridge Camp and enter Agua Canyon. Getting out of Agua Canyon, you climb up a slope dotted with pine trees to the junction of the Agua Canyon Connecting Trail.

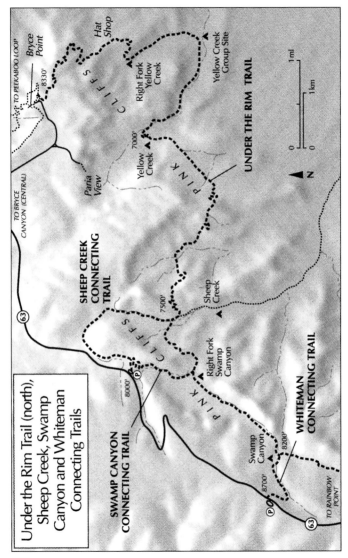

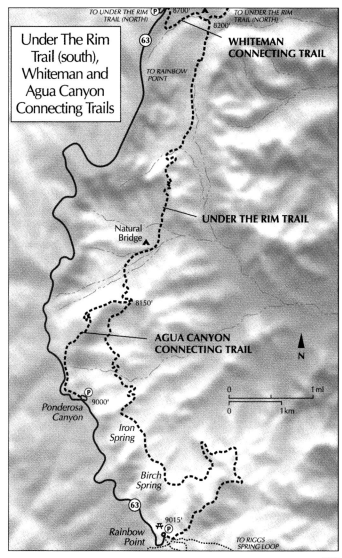

Under The Rim Trail (south), Whiteman and Agua Canyon Connecting Trails

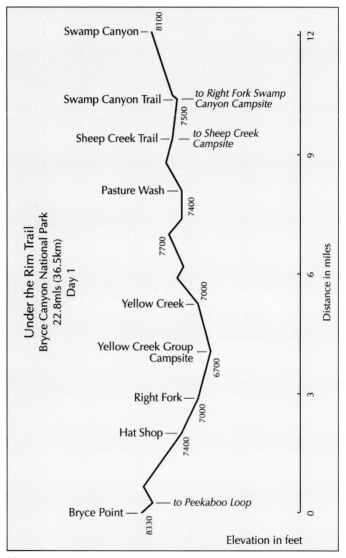

Under the Rim Trail
Bryce Canyon National Park
22.8mls (36.5km)
Day 1

Swamp Canyon — 8100

Swamp Canyon Trail — *to Right Fork Swamp Canyon Campsite* 7500

Sheep Creek Trail — *to Sheep Creek Campsite*

Pasture Wash — 7400

7700

Yellow Creek — 7000

Yellow Creek Group Campsite — 6700

Right Fork — 7000

Hat Shop — 7400

Bryce Point — *to Peekaboo Loop* 8330

Elevation in feet

Distance in miles

0   3   6   9   12

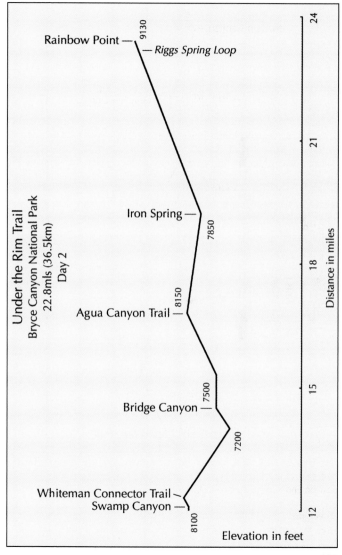

Under the Rim Trail
Bryce Canyon National Park
22.8mls (36.5km)
Day 2

Rainbow Point — 9130

— *Riggs Spring Loop*

Iron Spring — 7850

Agua Canyon Trail — 8150

Bridge Canyon — 7500

7200

Whiteman Connector Trail —
Swamp Canyon — 8100

Distance in miles

24   21   18   15   12

Elevation in feet

Descending from the junction into Ponderosa Canyon you pass several creeks and Iron Spring. Now the trail loops around to the north and east, beginning its final climb to Rainbow Point. Views spread all the way north to Bryce Point. Rounding a corner, the climb becomes steeper and then crosses a narrow ridge as it overlooks the Pink Cliffs. Finally, the Under the Rim Trail ends at Rainbow Point.

CONNECTING TRAILS

The Bryce National Park Connecting Trails link up the only automobile road in the park, Hwy 63, with the Under the Rim Trail. The four connecting trails, described here from north to south, Sheep Creek, Swamp Canyon, Whiteman and Agua Canyon, depart from the main road between Bryce Point and Rainbow Point. These trails can be used on day or overnight walks to meet the Under the Rim Trail. You may wish to loop back to another parking area. Views are often obscured by trees and there are fewer hoodoos than in the northern section. As a result, this part of the park is much less used than its northern section.

CONNECTING TRAILS			
Trail	Distance (miles) one way	Distance (km) one way	Rating
Sheep Creek Connecting Trail	2.0	3.2	Moderate
Swamp Canyon Connecting Trail	0.9	1.4	Moderate
Whiteman Connecting Trail	0.9	1.4	Moderate
Agua Canyon Connecting Trail	1.6	2.6	Moderate

Sheep Creek Connecting Trail

Take Hwy 63 for 5 miles south of the visitor centre and park in the lay-by on the east side of the road. This parking area is the roadhead for both the Swamp Canyon and Sheep Creek connecting trails.

Directions

From the parking area the path heads east, downhill, for a short way, and after 0.14 miles meets the connecting point of the two trails. To take the Sheep Creek

Towering rocks of Wall Street (Wall Street Trail, Bryce Canyon)

Natural bridge seen from the road above the Rim Trail (Bryce Canyon)

Connector, turn north at the junction through pine-studded slopes. The trail soon turns southeast in a draw and crosses a saddle spotted with juniper. Hoodoos line the views to the southeast. Now the trail turns south and descends below the rim through a break in the pink cliff walls. As you reach the bottom of the canyon, you meet the Under the Rim Trail. Continue south on the trail for 0.1 miles to meet the Sheep Creek Trail and, if you are going to Sheep Creek Campground, proceed straight ahead for 0.5 miles. Turn west on to the Under the Rim Trail to reach Swamp Camp.

Swamp Canyon Connecting Trail

From the parking area, drive 5 miles south of the visitor centre and park in the lay-by on the east side of the road. This parking area is the roadhead for both the Swamp Canyon and Sheep Creek connecting trails.

Directions
Begin by walking 0.14 miles northeast to the junction with the Sheep and Swamp connecting trails. Turn south on to the Swamp Connecting Trail. Descend steeply for 1 mile between limestone cliffs to reach the Under the Rim Trail. The South Canyon Butte lines the skyline to the south. A turn north heads you towards Bryce Point on the Under the Rim Trail and a turn south takes you to Rainbow Point.

Whiteman Connecting Trail

To reach the Whiteman Connecting Trail from the Bryce Canyon Visitor Centre, drive 9 miles south to the parking area on the east side of the road.

Directions
From the rim, follow the trail south through the juniper until you reach a wash. Turn northeast and remain along the wash as you descend to the Under the Rim Trail and the Swamp Canyon campsite.

Agua Connecting Trail

The Agua Connecting Trail departs from the Ponderosa Canyon Viewpoint, 13.7 miles south of the Bryce Canyon Visitor Centre.

Directions

Head north through forest, paralleling the road for 0.5 miles. Begin your descent, remaining in trees for another 0.5 miles. Soon the views open up to the gorgeous Pink Cliffs above; the canyon looms below you. The trail then switchbacks down a slippery slope into the canyon to meet the Under the Rim Trail.

BIBLIOGRAPHY
Suggested Reading

MAPS

Trails Illustrated/National Geographic Maps, PO Box 4357, Evergreen, Colorado 80437-4357, tel (800) 962-1643, international calls (303) 670-3457, www.nationalgeographic.com/maps.

United States Geological Survey (USGS), Box 25286, Denver, Colorado 80225, tel 303 202 4700, fax 303 202 4693, information 1-800-USA-MAPS, http://store.usgs.gov.

GENERAL

Baars, Donald **The Colorado Plateau** University of New Mexico

Chesher, Greer **Bryce Canyon: The Desert's Hoodoo Heart** from Bryce Canyon Natural History Association

De Courten, Frank **Shadow of Time, Geology of Bryce Canyon N.P.** from Bryce Canyon C

Euler, Robert **A Sketch of Grand Canyon Prehistory** Grand Canyon Association

Ghiglieri, Michael P and Myers, Thomas M **Over the Edge: Death in Grand Canyon** Puma Press 2001

Harmon, Will **Leave No Trace** American Hiking Society $6.95

Hughes, J Donald **In the House of Stone and Light** Grand Canyon Natural History Association

Hunt, Charles **Grand Canyon and the Colorado River** Grand Canyon Association

Grubbs, Bruce **Desert Hiking Tips** Falcon, PO Box 480 Guilford, CT 06437, $6.95

Lamb, Susan **Grand Canyon: the Vault of Heaven** Grand Canyon Association 2005

Lavender, David **Colorado River Country** University of New Mexico

Murphy, Dan **John Wesley Powell, Voyage of Discovery** KC Publications

Powell, John Wesley **Exploration of the Colorado River, 1869** Penguin Classics

Ranney, Wayne **Carving Grand Canyon: Evidence, Theories and Mystery** Grand Canyon Association 2005

Sadler, Christa **Life in Stone (Fossils and Geology)** Grand Canyon Association 2005

Witney, Stephen **A Field Guide to the Grand Canyon** by from the Grand Canyon Association

Grand Canyon Colour Picture Books, KC Publications, 3245 East Patrick, suite A, Las Vegas, Nevada, tel 1 800 626 9673

Introduction to Grand Canyon (Geology, Ecology and Prehistory trilogy)
   Grand Canyon Association

FAUNA
Peterson, Roger Tory **Birds of Grand Canyon** Peterson Guides
Alden, Peter **Mammals of Grand Canyon** Peterson Guides
Tekiela, Stan **Birds of Arizona** Adventure Publications Inc.

NATIVE CULTURE
Flora and Gregg **People of the Blue Water** University of Arizona
Courlander, Harold **The Fourth World of the Hopi** University of New Mexico
Locke, Raymond F **The Book of the Navajo** Mankind Publishing Company

APPENDIX A
Long-distance routes summary tables

Estimated times allow for carrying a 40 pound pack under good weather conditions. Times are affected by walker's fitness, the overall strength of the party, temperature, terrain and the direction travelled.

GRAND CANYON NATIONAL PARK
Boucher Trail to Hermit Trail Loop

Distance	*23 miles (36.8km)*
Days	*3–4*
Start	*Hermit Trailhead at Hermits' Rest*

30mins	Waldron Trail
30mins	Dripping Springs Trail
45mins	Boucher Trailhead
1hr	Yuma Point
1hr 15mins	Travertine Canyon
1hr	Whites Butte Saddle
1hr	Tonto Trail
15mins	Boucher Creek
45mins	Tonto Trail
1hr 15mins	Travertine Canyon
1hr 25mins	Hermit Creek
45mins	Tonto Trail to Hermit Trail
1hr 30mins	Cathedral Stairs
2hr 30mins	Santa Maria Spring
45mins	Waldron Trail
45mins	Hermits' Rest

Hermit Trail to Bright Angel Trail Loop

Distance	*22.9 miles (36.6km)*
Days	*3-4*
Start	*Hermit Trailhead at Hermits' Rest*

35mins	Waldron Trail
10mins	Dripping Springs Trail junction
30mins	Cathedral Stairs
30mins	Hermit Trail to Tonto Trail junction

30mins	Hermit Creek Trailhead
1hr	Hermit Rapids
1hr	Hermit Creek Trailhead
20mins	Hermit Trail to Tonto Trail junction
30mins	Monument Creek
45mins	Granite Rapids
50mins	Monument Creek
30mins	Cedar Spring
45mins	Salt Creek
1hr 45mins	Horn Creek
1hr 15mins	Indian Garden
45mins	Three Mile Resthouse
1hr 10mins	Mile-and-a-Half Resthouse
1hr 10mins	Bright Angel Trailhead at Kolb Studio

North to South Rim: Cross Canyon North Kaibab Trailhead to Bright Angel Trailhead

Distance:	*23.3 miles (37.2km)*
Days	*2–3*
Start	*North Kaibab Trailhead*

10mins	Coconino Overlook
45mins	Supai Tunnel
1hr	Roaring Springs
1hr 15mins	Cottonwood Camp
30mins	Ribbon Falls Turnoff
2hr	Clear Creek Trail
10mins	Phantom Ranch
5mins	Bright Angel Campground
5mins	Colorado River at Silver Suspension Bridge
1hr	River Resthouse
1hr 15mins	Indian Garden
45mins	Three Mile Resthouse
1hr 10mins	Mile-and-a-Half Resthouse
1hr 10mins	Bright Angel Trailhead at Kolb Studio

South Kaibab Trail to Bright Angel Trail

Distance	*16.3 miles (26.1km)*
Days	*2–4*
Start	*South Kaibab Trailhead at Yaki Point*

15mins	Ooh Ah Point
40mins	Cedar Ridge
25mins	O'Neill Butte
30mins	Skeleton Point
40mins	The Tipoff
45mins	Silver Suspension Bridge
10mins	Phantom Ranch
5mins	Bright Angel Campground
5mins	Colorado River at Silver Suspension Bridge
1hr	River Resthouse
1hr 15mins	Indian Garden
45mins	Three Mile Resthouse
1hr 10mins	Mile-and-a-Half Resthouse
1hr 10mins	Bright Angel Trailhead at Kolb Studio

Grandview Trail to South Kaibab Trail

Distance	*27.8 miles (44.4km)*
Days	*4–5*
Start	*Grandview Trailhead at Grandview Point*

1hr 30mins	Horseshoe Mesa
45mins	Cottonwood Creek
2hr	Grapevine Creek
3hr	Boulder Creek
1hr 30mins	Lonetree Creek
2hr	Cremation Creek (south arm)
20mins	Cremation Creek (southwest arm)
15mins	Cremation Creek (west arm)
1hr	The Tipoff
1hr	Skeleton Point
1hr	Cedar Ridge
1hr	South Kaibab Trailhead

Escalante Route: Tanner Trail to Grandview Trail

Distance	*33 miles (52.8km)*
Days	*5–7*
Start	*Tanner Trailhead at Lipan Point*

1hr	Seventy-five Mile Saddle
1hr	Escalante Butte

45mins	Cardenas Butte
15mins	Top of Redwall
4hr	Tanner Rapids
1hr	Unkar Delta
2hr	Escalante Creek
1hr	River at Escalante
30mins	Head of Seventy-five Mile Creek
30mins	Nevills Rapids
30mins	above Papago Creek
30mins	Papago Creek
1hr	Overlook
30mins	Colorado River
30mins	Red Canyon
30mins	Mineral Canyon
30mins	Shady Overhang
2hr	Hance Creek
45mins	Miner's (Page) Spring
1hr 15mins	Horseshoe Mesa
3hr	Grandview Trailhead

Kanab Canyon to Thunder River Route

Distance	*50.5 miles (80.8km)*
Days	*7–9*
Start	*Sowats Point*

1hr	South Arm Kwagunt Hollow at cottonwood trees
3hr	Jumpup Canyon
1hr	Indian Hollow
1hr 45mins	Kanab Creek
1hr 15mins	Pencil Spring
45mins	Showerbath Spring
45mins	Scotty's Hollow
1hr	Cave on north side of Kanab Creek
3hr	Whispering Falls
2hr 30mins	Kanab Creek
6hr	Fishtail Rapids
3hr 30mins	Deer Creek Falls
20mins	Deer Creek Narrows
5mins	Deer Creek Camping

30mins	Deer Creek Spring
1hr	Surprise Valley
1hr	Surprise Valley Rim above Thunder River
10mins	Thunder River Spring
20mins	Return to Surprise Valley above Thunder River
1hr 45mins	Surprise Valley Rim
2hr	Bill Hall Trailhead
1hr	Esplanade Camp
3hr	Indian Hollow

ZION NATIONAL PARK
Across Zion via Hop Valley and the West Rim

Distance	*37.6 miles (60.2km)*
Days	*4–5*
Start	*La Verkin Creek Trailhead at Lee Pass*

1hr	Shuntavi Butte
1hr	Corral
1hr 30mins	Kolob Arch Trail
10mins	Beatty Spring
5mins	Hop Valley and Willis Creek Trail junction
40mins	High Point
40mins	Hop Valley fence #1
30mins	Langston Canyon
1hr 15mins	Hop Valley fence #2
20mins	Connector Trail
2hr	to Wildcat Canyon Trailhead
5mins	to Northgate Spur Trail
1hr 15mins	Wildcat Spring
10mins	Wildcat Canyon Creek
30mins	West Rim Trail near Lava Point
10mins	to Sawmill Spring
2hr	Potato Hollow
1hr 15mins	West Rim Trail and Telephone Canyon Trail junction via West Rim Trail
1hr 15mins	Cabin Spring
1hr 30mins	bridge
20mins	Scout Lookout and Angels' Landing Trail junction
1hr 15mins	Grotto picnic area

The Zion Narrows

Distance	*15.5 miles (24.8km)*
Days	*2*
Start	*Chamberlain's Ranch*

1hr	Bulloch's Cabin
2hr 30mins	First Narrows
1hr	Waterfall
1hr	Deep Creek
45mins	Kolob Creek
15mins	Grotto
35mins	Goose Creek
45mins	Big Springs
2hr 45mins	Orderville Canyon
1hr 45mins	Riverside Trail
20mins	Temple of Sinawava

East Rim Trail via Cable and Deertrap mountains

Distance	*20.4 miles (32.6km)*
Days	*2*
Start	*East Entrance*

45mins	Cave Canyon
15mins	Rise
20mins	Jolley Gulch
1hr 10mins	High Point
10mins	Stave Spring
1min	Stave Spring Junction to Deertrap and Cable mountains
20mins	Y-junction
15mins	Knoll above Deertrap Mountain
45mins	Deertrap Mountain
35mins	Return to signed Y-junction
30mins	Cable Mountain
20mins	Return to signed Y-junction
15mins	Return to Stave Spring Junction
5mins	Spur to East Boundary
20mins	Above Echo Canyon
15mins	Echo Canyon Wash
10mins	Observation Point Trail

15mins	Hidden Canyon Trail
15mins	Weeping Rock picnic area

BRYCE CANYON NATIONAL PARK
Riggs Spring Loop
Distance   8.8 miles (14.1km)
Days   1–2
Start   Rainbow Point

1hr 15mins	Corral Hollow
1hr	Riggs Spring
45mins	Yovimpa Pass Campground
30mins	Yovimpa Point
5mins	Bristlecone Loop
5mins	Rainbow Point

Under the Rim Trail
Distance   22.8 miles (36.5km)
Days   2–3
Start   Bryce Point

5mins	Peekaboo Loop
1hr	Hat Shop
20mins	Right Fork Camping
30mins	Yellow Creek Group Site
30mins	Yellow Creek Camping
30mins	Saddle
1hr	Pasture Wash
20mins	Divide
30mins	Sheep Creek Trail
30mins	Swamp Canyon Connecting Trail
5mins	Right Fork Swamp Canyon Camp
40mins	Swamp Canyon Camp
10mins	Whiteman Connect Trail
1hr 10mins	Bridge Canyon Camp
40mins	Agua Canyon Connecting Trail
1hr	Iron Spring Camping
2hr	Rainbow Point

APPENDIX B
Useful addresses

United States Geological Survey (USGS), **USGS Info Services, Box 25286, Federal Center, Denver, Colorado 80225; tel 303 202 4700; tel 1-800-USA-MAPS; fax (303) 202-4693;** http://store.usgs.gov
National Park Service www.nps.gov
National weather service www.nws.noaa.gov
US Forest Service www.fs.fed.us
Emergency Road Services **USA 1 800-AAA_HELP, te 1 800 222 4357**
Utah Travel Council tel (800) 200 1160; www.utah.com
Utah State Parks tel (800) 322 3770; www.stateparks.utah.gov
Utah Road Conditions tel (801) 964 6000
Arizona Road Conditions tel (888) 411 7623
Car hire in the UK www.carhiredirect.com

HOTELS AND BOOKINGS
www.arizona.com
www.utah.com
Bed and Breakfast Inns of Utah; email: info@bbiu.org

GRAND CANYON NATIONAL PARK
Grand Canyon National Park, P.O. Box 129, Grand Canyon, Arizona 86023 (928) 638-7888; www.nps.gov/grca
Grand Canyon National Park Hotels, advance hotel reservations: Xanterra Parks and Resorts, 14001 East Iliff, Ste 600 Aurora, CO 80014; tel (928) 638 2631 same day or (888) 297 2757 for advance reservations
Grand Canyon Association, PO Box 399, Grand Canyon, Arizona 86023; tel toll free 1 (800) 858 2805; www.grandcanyon.org
Grand Canyon Field Institute, PO Box 399, Grand Canyon, Arizona 86023; tel (928) 638 2485, toll free tel (866) 471 4435; fax (928) 638-2484; e-mail gcfi@grandcanyon.org, www.grandcanyon.org/fieldinstitute
Backcountry Information Centre (BIC), Grand Canyon National Park, PO 129, Grand Canyon, Arizona 86023-0129 (928) 638-7875; fax (928) 638-2125
Campground reservations, www.reservations.nps.gov
Transcanyon Shuttle, PO Box 348, Grand Canyon, Arizona 86023; tel (520) 638-2820
24hr taxi service, tel (928) 638 2822 or (928) 638 2631 ext 6563

Open Road Tours runs two daily buses from Flagstaff to Grand Canyon Village on the South Rim. They also have a connection to Phoenix. For schedules and costs, tel (928) 226 8060 or (800) 766 7117.

The Grand Canyon Railway has a service from Williams to the Grand Canyon village, tel (800)-THE TRAIN for information.

Grand Canyon road conditions, **tel (928) 638 7888**

ZION NATIONAL PARK

Zion National Park, Springdale, Utah 84767-1099; tel 435 772 3256; fax 435 772 3426; e-mail ZION_park_information@nps.gov; www.nps.gov/zion

Zion Natural History Association, Zion National Park, Springdale, Utah 84767; tel (800) 635-3959

Zion National Park, Kolob Canyons Visitor Centre, Utah 84767; tel (435) 586-9548 CHECK

Campground reservations (Watchman Campground), tel (800) 365-2267; international calls (301) 722-1257

Campground reservations, www.reservations.nps.gov

The Zion Adventure Company, 36 Lion Blvd, Springdale, Utah 84767; tel 435 772 1001; www.zionadventures.com

BRYCE CANYON NATIONAL PARK

Bryce National Park, PO Box 640201, Bryce, Utah 84764-0201; tel 435 834 5322; fax 435 834 4102; brca_information@nps.gov; www.nps.gov/brca

Bryce Canyon Lodge, Bryce Canyon, Utah 84717 (April through to October); tel (888) 297 2757; www.brycecanyonlodge.com

Bryce Canyon Natural History Association, PO Box 640202, Bryce, UT 84764-0202; tel (800) 362 2642; fax (435) 834 4606; www.brycecanyon.org

Bryce Canyon Scenic Tours & Shuttles, PO Box 640025, Bryce; tel (800) 432 5383; e-mail taylor@color-country.net

Best Western Ruby's Inn, Hwy 63, Bryce, UT 84764; tel 1-866 878 9391 or (435) 834 5341

Garfield County Travel Council, 55 South Main Street, Panguitch, UT 84759; tel (800) 444 6689; tel 435 676 1160; www.brycecanyoncountry.com

APPENDIX C
Local facilities

A synopsis of facilities available at the three national parks and their surrounding communities is provided below. 'Full supplies' means that a wide range of food and camping supplies are available. 'Limited supplies' means that some camping and backpacking gear and food supplies are sold, but with a limited choice. 'Very limited supplies' means that only a few camping and backpacking items can be purchased and there may be only one small grocery store.

Abbreviations:
BCNP: Bryce Canyon National Park
GCN: Grand Canyon National Park, North Rim
GCS: Grand Canyon National Park, South Rim
ZNP: Zion National Park

Bryce Canyon National Park (BCNP): lodging, camping, very limited supplies, Bryce Canyon National Park Visitor Centre: laundrette, post office (in Bryce Lodge)

Cameron, Arizona (GCS): lodging, petrol, very limited supplies

Cedar City, Utah (BCNP, ZNP): lodging, petrol, full supplies, bank, post office, laundrette, airport, bus station

Desert View, Grand Canyon National Park (GCS): camping (seasonal), petrol (seasonal)

Flagstaff, Arizona (GCS): lodging, petrol, full supplies, bank, post office, laundrette, airport, train station, bus station

Fredonia, Arizona (GCN): petrol, North Kaibab Ranger Station, lodging (very limited)

Grand Canyon, North Rim (GCN): lodging, petrol, very limited supplies, camping, laundrette, showers, post office (in Bright Angel Lodge), visitor centre; backcountry reservations

Grand Canyon, South Rim (GCS): lodging, petrol, limited supplies, camping, bank, laundrette, showers, medical clinic, dog kennel, train station, airport, taxi, post office, bus service, backcountry reservations

Hatch, Utah (BCNP, ZNP): petrol, no supplies

Hurricane, Utah (ZNP): lodging, petrol, limited supplies, bank, post office, laundrette

Jacob Lake, Arizona (GCN): lodging, petrol, camping, North Rim Ranger Station

Kanab, Utah (BCNP, GCN, ZNP): lodging, petrol, limited supplies, bank, post office, laundrette

Las Vegas, Nevada (BCNP, GCN, GCS, ZNP): lodging, petrol, full supplies, bank, post office, laundrette, airport

Long Valley Junction, Utah (BCNP, ZNP): lodging, petrol

Mt Carmel Junction, Utah (BCNP, ZNP): lodging, petrol

Page, Arizona (GCN): lodging, petrol, full supplies, bank, post office, laundrette, airport

Panguitch, Utah (BCNP): lodging, petrol, limited supplies, bank, post office, laundrette

Phantom Ranch (GCN, GCS): lodging, camping, mail service

Phoenix, Arizona (GCS): lodging, petrol, full supplies, bank, post office, laundrette, airport

Rockville, Utah (ZNP): post office, lodging (very limited)

Springdale, Utah (ZNP): lodging, petrol, limited supplies, camping, bank, post office, laundrette, showers (at campground)

St George, Utah (ZNP): lodging, petrol, full supplies, bank, post office, laundrette, airport

Tropic, Utah (BCNP): lodging, petrol, limited supplies

Tusayan, Arizona (GCS): lodging, petrol, limited supplies, camping, post office, Grand Canyon airport

Williams, Arizona (GCS): lodging, petrol, limited supplies, bank, post office, train station (limited service), bus station

Zion National Park (ZNP): lodging, camping, Zion Canyon Visitor Centre, post office (in Zion Lodge)

APPENDIX D
Author's favourite walks

GRAND CANYON NATIONAL PARK
Day-walks, South Rim
Boucher Trail to Dripping Springs via Hermit Trail
Grandview Trail to Horseshoe Mesa
Hermit Trail to Santa Maria Spring or Cathedral Stairs
Rim Trail
Shoshone Point
South Kaibab Trail to Cedar Mesa, O'Neill Butte or Skeleton Point
Day-walks, North Rim
Bright Angel Point
Cape Final
Cape Royal
Ken Patrick Trail from Point Imperial
Overnight or Long-distance Trips
Boucher to Hermit Loop (South Rim)
Escalante Route, Tanner Trail to Grandview Trail (South Rim)
Grandview Trail to Horseshoe Mesa (South Rim)
Kanab Canyon to Thunder River (North Rim)

ZION NATIONAL PARK
Day-walks
Angel's Landing
East Rim Trail
Hop Valley Trail to Kolob Arch Trail
Northgate Peaks Trail
Observation Point
West Rim Trail
Up the Narrows to Orderville Canyon

Overnight or Long-distance Walks
Across Zion
East Rim Trail to Cable and Deertrap mountains
The Zion Narrows
West Rim Trail from Lava Point to Grotto picnic area

BRYCE CANYON NATIONAL PARK
Day-walks
Fairyland Loop
Navajo Loop to Peekaboo Loop to Queen's Garden Trail
Rim Trail

APPENDIX E
Index of tables and route profiles

ZION NATIONAL PARK ROUTES

BRYCE CANYON NATIONAL PARK ROUTES

APPENDIX F
Index of maps

APPENDIX G
Sample backcountry permit request form

Name . . . .

Home Phone . . . .

Method of Payment . . . .

Address . . . .

. . . .

Work Phone . . . . etc.

City . . . . .State (County) . . . .

Country . . . . .Organisation (if any) . . . .

Vehicle 1 (License Number) . . . . .No of people . . . .

Vehicle 2 (License Number) . . . . .No of stock? . . . .

Beginning Trailhead . . . . .Ending Trailhead . . . .

First Choice . . . . .Second Choice . . . . .Third Choice . . . .

Date . . . . .Date . . . . .Date . . . .

Use Area   Use Area   Use Area

or Campsite . . . . .or Campsite . . . . .or Campsite . . . .

Campsites must be listed   Campsites must be listed   Campsites must be listed

1 . . . .

2 . . . .

3 . . . .

4 . . . .

5 . . . .

6 . . . .

I am willing to accept variations to start date (between   and   ); campsites; trip length
(min   max)
278

NOTES

NOTES

NOTES

NOTES

NOTES

LISTING OF CICERONE GUIDES

BACKPACKING
The End to End Trail
Three Peaks, Ten Tors
Backpacker's Britain Vol 1 – Northern
    England
Backpacker's Britain Vol 2 – Wales
Backpacker's Britain Vol 3 –
    Northern Scotland
The Book of the Bivvy

**NORTHERN ENGLAND
LONG-DISTANCE TRAILS**
The Dales Way
The Reiver's Way
The Alternative Coast to Coast
A Northern Coast to Coast Walk
The Pennine Way
Hadrian's Wall Path
The Teesdale Way

FOR COLLECTORS OF SUMMITS
The Relative Hills of Britain
Mts England & Wales Vol 2 – England
Mts England & Wales Vol 1 – Wales

UK GENERAL
The National Trails

BRITISH CYCLE GUIDES
The Cumbria Cycle Way
Lands End to John O'Groats – Cycle
    Guide
Rural Rides No.1 – West Surrey
Rural Rides No.2 – East Surrey
South Lakeland Cycle Rides
Border Country Cycle Routes
Lancashire Cycle Way

CANOE GUIDES
Canoeist's Guide to the North-East

**LAKE DISTRICT AND
MORECAMBE BAY**
Coniston Copper Mines
Scrambles in the Lake District (North)
Scrambles in the Lake District (South)
Walks in Silverdale and
    Arnside AONB
Short Walks in Lakeland 1 – South
Short Walks in Lakeland 2 – North
Short Walks in Lakeland 3 – West
The Tarns of Lakeland Vol 1 – West
The Tarns of Lakeland Vol 2 – East
The Cumbria Way &
    Allerdale Ramble
Lake District Winter Climbs
Roads and Tracks of the Lake District
The Lake District Angler's Guide
Rocky Rambler's Wild Walks
An Atlas of the English Lakes
Tour of the Lake District
The Cumbria Coastal Way

NORTH-WEST ENGLAND
Walker's Guide to the
    Lancaster Canal
Family Walks in the
    Forest Of Bowland
Walks in Ribble Country

Historic Walks in Cheshire
Walking in Lancashire
Walks in Lancashire Witch Country
The Ribble Way

THE ISLE OF MAN
Walking on the Isle of Man
The Isle of Man Coastal Path

**PENNINES AND
NORTH-EAST ENGLAND**
Walks in the Yorkshire Dales
Walks on the North York Moors,
    books 1 and 2
Walking in the South Pennines
Walking in the North Pennines
Walking in the Wolds
Waterfall Walks – Teesdale and High
    Pennines
Walking in County Durham
Yorkshire Dales Angler's Guide
Walks in Dales Country
Historic Walks in North Yorkshire
South Pennine Walks
Walking in Northumberland
Cleveland Way and Yorkshire Wolds
    Way
The North York Moors

**DERBYSHIRE, PEAK DISTRICT,
EAST MIDLANDS**
High Peak Walks
White Peak Walks Northern Dales
White Peak Walks Southern Dales
Star Family Walks Peak District &
    South Yorkshire
Walking In Peakland
Historic Walks in Derbyshire

WALES AND WELSH BORDERS
Ascent of Snowdon
Welsh Winter Climbs
Hillwalking in Wales – Vol 1
Hillwalking in Wales – Vol 2
Scrambles in Snowdonia
Hillwalking in Snowdonia
The Ridges of Snowdonia
Hereford & the Wye Valley
Walking Offa's Dyke Path
Lleyn Peninsula Coastal Path
Anglesey Coast Walks
The Shropshire Way
Spirit Paths of Wales
Glyndwr's Way
The Pembrokeshire Coastal Path
Walking in Pembrokeshire
The Shropshire Hills – A Walker's
    Guide

MIDLANDS
The Cotswold Way
The Grand Union Canal Walk
Walking in Warwickshire
Walking in Worcestershire
Walking in Staffordshire
Heart of England Walks

SOUTHERN ENGLAND
Exmoor & the Quantocks
Walking in the Chilterns
Walking in Kent
Two Moors Way
Walking in Dorset
A Walker's Guide to the Isle of Wight
Walking in Somerset
The Thames Path
Channel Island Walks
Walking in Buckinghamshire
The Isles of Scilly
Walking in Hampshire
Walking in Bedfordshire
The Lea Valley Walk
Walking in Berkshire
The Definitive Guide to
    Walking in London
The Greater Ridgeway
Walking on Dartmoor
The South West Coast Path
Walking in Sussex
The North Downs Way
The South Downs Way

SCOTLAND
Scottish Glens 1 – Cairngorm Glens
Scottish Glens 2 – Atholl Glens
Scottish Glens 3 – Glens of Rannoch
Scottish Glens 4 – Glens of Trossach
Scottish Glens 5 – Glens of Argyll
Scottish Glens 6 – The Great Glen
Scottish Glens 7 – The Angus Glens
Scottish Glens 8 – Knoydart
    to Morvern
Scottish Glens 9 – The Glens
    of Ross-shire
The Island of Rhum
Torridon – A Walker's Guide
Walking the Galloway Hills
Border Pubs & Inns –
    A Walkers' Guide
Scrambles in Lochaber
Walking in the Hebrides
Central Highlands: 6 Long
    Distance Walks
Walking in the Isle of Arran
Walking in the Lowther Hills
North to the Cape
The Border Country –
    A Walker's Guide
Winter Climbs – Cairngorms
The Speyside Way
Winter Climbs – Ben Nevis &
    Glencoe
The Isle of Skye, A Walker's Guide
The West Highland Way
Scotland's Far North
Walking the Munros Vol 1 –
    Southern, Central
Walking the Munros Vol 2 –
    Northern & Cairngorms
Scotland's Far West
Walking in the Cairngorms

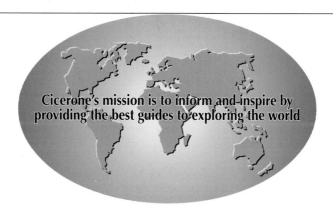

Cicerone's mission is to inform and inspire by
providing the best guides to exploring the world

Since its foundation over 30 years ago, Cicerone has specialised in
publishing guidebooks and has built a reputation for quality and reliability.
It now publishes nearly 300 guides to the major destinations for outdoor
enthusiasts, including Europe, UK and the rest of the world.

Written by leading and committed specialists, Cicerone guides are
recognised as the most authoritative. They are full of information, maps and
illustrations so that the user can plan and complete a successful and safe
trip or expedition – be it a long face climb, a walk over Lakeland fells, an
alpine traverse, a Himalayan trek or a ramble in the countryside.

With a thorough introduction to assist planning, clear diagrams, maps and
colour photographs to illustrate the terrain and route, and accurate and
detailed text, Cicerone guides are designed for ease of use and access to
the information.

If the facts on the ground change, or there is any aspect of a guide that you
think we can improve, we are always delighted to hear from you.

Cicerone Press
2 Police Square Milnthorpe Cumbria LA7 7PY
Tel:01539 562 069   Fax:01539 563 417
e-mail:info@cicerone.co.uk   web:www.cicerone.co.uk

CICERONE